AF328769

READING THE ODYSSEY

Reading the Odyssey

A GUIDE TO HOMER'S NARRATIVE

JONAS GRETHLEIN

TRANSLATED BY
SABRINA STOLFA

PRINCETON UNIVERSITY PRESS

PRINCETON & OXFORD

Published by Princeton University Press
41 William Street, Princeton, New Jersey 08540
99 Banbury Road, Oxford OX2 6JX

press.princeton.edu

All Rights Reserved

Library of Congress Cataloging-in-Publication Data

Names: Grethlein, Jonas, 1978– author. | Stolfa, Sabrina, translator.
Title: Reading the Odyssey: a guide to Homer's narrative / Jonas Grethlein; translated by Sabrina Stolfa.
Description: Princeton: Princeton University Press, 2024. | Includes bibliographical references and index.
Identifiers: LCCN 2023036240 (print) | LCCN 2023036241 (ebook) | ISBN 9780691182490 (hardback) | ISBN 9780691210995 (ebook)
Subjects: LCSH: Homer. Odyssey. | Homer—Literary style. | Narration (Rhetoric) | Rhetoric, Ancient. | BISAC: LITERARY CRITICISM / Ancient & Classical | POETRY / Ancient & Classical | LCGFT: Literary criticism.
Classification: LCC PA4167.A2 G7413 2024 (print) | LCC PA4167.A2 (ebook) | DDC 883/.01—dc23/eng/20231204
LC record available at https://lccn.loc.gov/2023036240
LC ebook record available at https://lccn.loc.gov/2023036241

British Library Cataloging-in-Publication Data is available

Editorial: Ben Tate and Josh Drake
Production Editorial: Theresa Liu
Jacket/Cover Design: Heather Hansen
Production: Danielle Amatucci
Publicity: William Pagdatoon and Charlotte Coyne
Copyeditor: Francis Eaves

Jacket image: migfoto / Adobe Stock

The translation of this work was funded by Geisteswissenschaften International–Translation Funding for Humanities and Social Sciences from Germany, a joint initiative of the Fritz Thyssen Foundation, the German Federal Foreign Office, the collecting society VG WORT and the Börsenverein des Deutschen Buchhandels (German Publishers & Booksellers Association).

This book has been composed in Classic Arno

Printed on acid-free paper. ∞

Printed in the United States of America

10 9 8 7 6 5 4 3 2 1

For Klara Elisabeth

CONTENTS

Map

Figures

READING THE ODYSSEY

FIG. 1. Max Beckmann (1884–1950), *Odysseus and Calypso*, 1943, oil on canvas, 115.5 × 150 cm, Hamburger Kunsthalle, Hamburg. Photo: Bridgeman Images.

1

Introduction

'I AM ODYSSEUS son of Laertes, known before all men / for the study of crafty designs, and my fame goes up to the heavens' (*Od.* 9.19–20).[1] These are the words with which Odysseus introduces himself to the Phaeacians. The assertion seems to have lost none of its validity— his fame indeed reverberates throughout modern literature. James Joyce's *Ulysses*, a key twentieth-century novel with its stream of consciousness narration, is merely one well-known example of the wide-ranging reception of Homer's *Odyssey*. Those who would rather not delve into the 33,333 verses of Nikos Kazantzakis's *Odyssey: A Modern Sequel* might like to try Franz Kafka's short story 'The Silence of the Sirens', or *The Penelopiad* by Margaret Atwood. Echoes of Odysseus can also be found in poetry, by poets as diverse as Paul Celan and Gabriele d'Annunzio, Ernst Jandl and Durs Grünbein. And on stage, Odysseus is not just a figure of ancient tragedy—he also appears in modern plays: by Jean Giradoux and Botho Strauß, for instance.

Additionally, Odysseus is a frequent motif in the visual arts. In a picture painted by Max Beckmann during his Amsterdam exile, Odysseus, embraced by Calypso, directs his gaze at the far horizon, arms folded behind his head (Fig. 1). While Picasso depicts him on the high seas surrounded by the Sirens (Fig. 2), Giorgio de Chirico's Odysseus rows across a sea that is a mere carpet in a living room (Fig. 3). Abstract

---

1. English translations of both the *Odyssey* and the *Iliad* in this volume are by Richmond Lattimore (with some slight modifications): see Lattimore (1975); Lattimore (1961 [1951]).

FIG. 2. Pablo Picasso (1881–1973), *Ulysse et les sirènes*, 1947, Ripolin paint and graphite on three eternit panels, 360 × 250 cm, Musée Picasso, Antibes. Photo: akg-images. © Succession Picasso/VG Bild-Kunst, Bonn 2023.

FIG. 3. Giorgio de Chirico (1888–1978), *Il ritorno di Ulisse*, 1968, oil on canvas, 59.5 × 80 cm, Casa Museo di Giorgio de Chirico, Rome. Photo: Luisa Ricciarini/ Bridgeman Images. © VG Bild-Kunst, Bonn 2023.

artists, too, were inspired by the *Odyssey*. A painting by Willem de Kooning, which is over two metres high and dominated by pastel shades, bears a title that includes a Homeric expression: *Rosy-Fingered Dawn at Louse Point*. Romare Bearden, in turn, merges the ancient myth with the Afro-American tradition. In his collages, the heroes of the *Odyssey* are represented as African tribal members and the savannah, along with other African landscapes, forms the background. Circe, for example, is a black sorceress who, adorned with heavy amulets, bends over a skull while a snake coils itself around her arm and a lion bares its teeth in the background (Fig. 4).

The title of one of the most famous films of the twentieth century, Stanley Kubrick's *Space Odyssey* (2001), refers to the Homeric epic, while

FIG. 4. Romare Bearden (1911–1988), *Circe*, 1977, collage on paper mounted to fibreboard, 38 × 24 cm, Chazen Museum of Art, University of Wisconsin-Madison, Colonel Rex W. and Maxine Schuster Radsch Endowment Fund purchase 2014.1. © Romare Bearden Foundation/VG Bild-Kunst, Bonn 2023.

the Coen Brothers' comedy *O Brother, Where Art Thou* (2000) is loosely based on the *Odyssey*. It depicts a Mississippi odyssey in the shape of convict Ulysses Everett McGill and his cronies' escape from prison. Many of their adventures, like the encounter with a one-eyed Bible salesman, treat the Homeric motifs in a satirical manner and Everett eventually returns to his wife, aptly named Penny, after numerous trials and tribulations. By contrast, the film *Ulysses' Gaze*, which won the Grand Jury Prize in Cannes in 1995, offers a serious treatment of the subject. Greek director Theo Angelopoulos presents a contemporary odyssey through the crisis-ridden Balkans where only melancholy testifies to a great past.

Odysseus reverberates not only through the arts—he also permeates intellectual history. Max Horkheimer and Theodor Adorno interpret the *Odyssey* as an illustration of the dialectic of the Enlightenment and ultimately, as the culmination of the Enlightenment in National Socialist barbarism. For them, Odysseus is an example showing how the attempt to overcome myth leads to new dependencies, and finally back to mythologies: 'no work bears more eloquent witness to the intertwinement of the Enlightenment and myth than that of Homer, the basic text of European civilization'.[2] The price which Odysseus pays for prevailing against primitive monsters is self-denial: 'the nimble-witted man survives only at the cost of his own dream, which he forfeits by disintegrating his own magic along with that of the powers outside him'.[3] And it is not only Odysseus who pays dearly for overcoming natural powers— he subjugates his companions and anticipates the oppression of the proletariat. While he listens to the Sirens' singing, or in other words, surrenders to culture, his companions are not permitted to do likewise. Instead, they have to row with all their might. Behind the supposed liberation, new dependencies lurk, and the Enlightenment reverts to myth.

While for critical theory, Odysseus stands for the bourgeois who, moreover, can quickly turn into a fascist, Peter Sloterdijk invokes him as the predecessor of a positive Enlightenment. For Sloterdijk, Odysseus is not only a proto-sophist; his cunning also represents the virtue that can

2. Horkheimer and Adorno (1969 [1947]): 37.
3. Ibid.: 45.

potentially shake modern Europeans awake before complacency causes them to slip into some self-inflicted, terminal ineptness until they are finally transformed into 'a nation of lotus eaters [. . .]. The great homecoming hero remains an indispensable, paradigmatic, absolutely exhilarating ally, the versatile teacher of how to not be helpless.'[4] Like Horkheimer and Adorno, Sloterdijk refers to Odysseus in his critique of civilization, but whereas the former see instrumental reason and the dawn of barbarism, Sloterdijk perceives *furbizia*, a kind of shrewdness that knows how to turn every deficiency into a challenge, every plight into a project.

The enduring presence of the *Odyssey* is evident not least from the fact that its title has become synonymous with the notion of prolonged wandering, ultimately with a favourable outcome. A flight from a despotic regime is referred to as an odyssey, for instance, as is the foreigner's arduous route to a railway station that is found only with great difficulty. Homer's epic is not usually thought of when the term is used on such occasions, which shows just how deeply it has entered our imaginations and everyday language. And yet, just as a forgotten metaphor can be revived, so the Homeric origin of the term 'odyssey' can be made to resonate afresh. This is seen in *The New Odyssey: The Story of the European Refugee Crisis* (2016), in which Patrick Kingsley analyses the refugee crisis using the fate of a Syrian man as an example. The text is preceded by an epigraph that quotes from the *Odyssey*: 'If any god has marked me out again for shipwreck, my tough heart can undergo it. What hardships have I not long since endured at sea, in battle! Let the trial come.' Many politicians and journalists also speak of the 'odyssey of the refugees', albeit without making any reference to Homer. Kingsley's quote draws attention to the origin of the term in order to emphasize the dignity, or even heroic status, of refugees, and to claim a place in Europe for them.

Even though the literary canon has been questioned, Odysseus remains an integral part of our shared imagination. He moves effortlessly through the various media of art, is at home in paintings and films as much as in literature and has found a new home in comics and computer games. He can be the main or a secondary character, a hero or charlatan,

---

4. Sloterdijk (2018): 177.

warrior or enlightener. As versatile and omnipresent as he is, Odysseus comes from an epic that originated in ancient Greece—the Homeric *Odyssey*. It was written in a language that was artificial even then, and is told in a style that is quite strange to us today. It is the aim of this book to make it accessible to today's audience in a new way, but without detracting from the strangeness of the Homeric epic. Reading the *Odyssey* is both an intellectual challenge and an aesthetic pleasure. Homer's narrative is not only brilliant—it also stimulates reflection, not least about narrative itself and its multilayered relationship to experience. Before embarking on an interpretation of the Homeric epic, however, some introduction to its special features will be required. The content and structure of the *Odyssey* and the history of its reception will be briefly recalled; the *quaestio Homerica*—the question of the genesis of the Homeric epics—will be examined and the liveliness of the epic narrative explored through important formal elements, such as formulaic language and typical scenes. All these aspects will serve to establish the perspective from which the *Odyssey* is interpreted in the chapters that follow.

Structure and Content

The *Odyssey* comprises over twelve thousand verses, which have been divided into twenty-four books since the Hellenistic editions. The three main parts are the Telemachy, Escape to the Phaeacians with the Apologoi, and the Mnesterophony, or Murder of the Suitors. The Telemachy occupies the first four books. At the outset, the gods decide that Odysseus, who is being kept prisoner by the nymph Calypso, should at last be allowed to return home. But the reader must read four books before finally meeting the hero of the epic. As the term 'Telemachy' suggests, it is Odysseus's son Telemachus who is at the centre of this initial narrative. When Odysseus had departed to join the Trojan War, he left behind his wife and their infant son. Now, twenty years later, the son has matured into a youth on the threshold of manhood, but finds himself in a difficult situation: his father's estate on the island of Ithaca has been taken over by a horde of a hundred and eight young men who are all courting his mother, Penelope. And not only do the suitors enjoy themselves at the expense of the house; they also threaten Telemachus's position. If Penelope were to remarry, he would lose his status as heir to any children from the second marriage. Penelope has so far succeeded in stalling the suitors by a ruse—she refuses to remarry until she has completed the shroud for her father-in-law, Laertes.

For several years, she has unravelled at night what she had woven during the day. But her maidservants betray the ruse to the suitors. Additionally, doubts have grown about Odysseus's survival and threaten to dash any hopes of his ultimate return—Penelope's new marriage seems inevitable. This is the situation when the goddess Athena, alternately hidden in the figures of Mentes and Mentor, approaches Telemachus and advises him to set off and seek news of his father. Is Odysseus still roaming in this tenth year since the fall of Troy, or has he died ignominiously at sea and been eaten by the fishes? Should Telemachus resist the suitors or permit his mother to be married to the best among them? After calling a people's assembly, which makes him the laughing stock of the suitors, Telemachus secretly boards a ship during the night and sails to Pylos in order to consult the aged Nestor. While Nestor is able to tell him about the return of many of the Greek warriors, he knows nothing of Odysseus's whereabouts. On Nestor's recommendation and accompanied by Nestor's son Peisistratus, Telemachus continues his journey to seek Menelaus, who had been the last of the warriors to return home. He meets him and his wife Helen in Sparta and listens to stories about the Trojan War and Menelaus's own valiant return. But all he learns of his father is that he had been seen with the nymph Calypso.

It is in the fifth book that the hero of the epic finally appears. A second meeting of the gods sends Hermes to Calypso to order her to let Odysseus go, and after seven years on the Ogygian island he finally sets out on a raft. He sails for seventeen days before Poseidon churns up the sea into a violent storm. For two days Odysseus is a plaything of the waves; it is not until the third day that he succeeds, with the last of his strength and more dead than alive, to reach the shore of the Phaeacian island of Scheria. On the beach he meets the king's daughter, Nausicaa, who falls in love with him in spite of his pitiful condition. With her help he reaches the king's palace, where Alcinous welcomes him. Without revealing his identity, Odysseus feasts, listens to bard Demodocus's songs and even competes with the Phaeacian nobility in an *agōn*. When he hears the bard sing about the Trojan War for the second time, however, Odysseus, as before, cannot hold back his tears, and now reveals his identity.

Most of this second part of the *Odyssey*, Escape to the Phaeacians—the story of Odysseus's stay on the Phaeacian island of Scheria—is taken up with the Apologoi, consisting of the hero's own account of his exploits and tribulations. In Books 9 to 12, he tells the Phaeacians of his adventures after the fall of Troy. He initially came to Ismarus in the land of the Cicones with twelve ships. The Greeks sacked the city but were surprised by other Cicones while celebrating their victory. They managed to flee but incurred great losses. A storm then drove the Greeks to the lotus eaters. Two men who tasted the lotus had to be forcibly returned to the ships. Almost the entire ninth book is taken up with their encounter with the cyclops Polyphemus, who imprisons Odysseus and his reconnaissance troop of twelve men in his cave. It is only after Polyphemus has devoured six companions that Odysseus succeeds in blinding him and escaping with the remaining men. Nevertheless, the episode proves disastrous—Polyphemus curses Odysseus and implores his father Poseidon to make his return home, if not doomed to failure, as difficult and painful as possible.

Initially, everything seems to work out well for Odysseus. He receives a hose that banishes unfavourable winds from Aeolus, Lord of the Winds. But, with Ithaca already in sight, Odysseus's envious companions open Aeolus's gift as he sleeps. The winds escape and drive the ship far off course. In a battle with the Laestrygonians, huge cannibals, Odysseus loses eleven ships and their crews. On the sole remaining ship, he reaches the island of Aeaea. There, Circe turns half of his companions into pigs. Only when Odysseus defeats her with the help of Hermes does she restore them to their human form. He becomes Circe's lover and, together with his companions, stays on Aeaea for a year. Then Circe sends him to the underworld, where he asks the seer Teiresias about his journey home and meets the ghosts of the dead, including Achilles and Agamemnon.

Odysseus returns to Circe and, following her instructions, continues his journey, first to sail past the Sirens, whose beguiling song he hears while lashed to the ship's mast, then to sail through a strait, with Scylla, a monster with six heads and three rows of teeth on one side of it, and Charybdis, who swallows the sea three times a day, on the other. The ship finally docks at Thrinacia, where the windless air holds up the voyage. Driven by hunger, the companions devour cattle dedicated to the sun god Helios, without Odysseus's knowledge and in spite of Circe's warning. Shortly after the ship can finally weigh anchor, it is caught in a terrible storm. Only Odysseus survives and, clinging to the mast, he has to pass Scylla and Charybdis again. After nine days, he arrives on Ogygia badly battered. There, Calypso takes him in and makes him her lover. He stays with her for seven years until the gods decide that he should be allowed to return home.

In the Apologoi, Odysseus tells of his wanderings up to the point where the plot begins in the fifth book. Homer thus allows his hero to tell a large part of his experiences himself; the spectacular adventures associated with the name Odysseus are therefore told from a first-person perspective. In the thirteenth book, the Homeric narrator takes over once more and recounts in this extensive third part, the entire second half of the work, how Odysseus reconquers his position on Ithaca, first with cunning, then by force. The Phaeacians, famous for their nautical skill, accompany him to his native island. Once there, he meets Athena, who gives him instructions and promises him her support. She transforms him into an old beggar so that he can prepare his return incognito. Odysseus first goes to his faithful swineherd Eumaeus, where he also sees Telemachus, who has just returned from his own voyage after having survived an attack by the suitors with Athena's help. In the first recognition scene, Odysseus reveals his identity to Telemachus and initiates him into his plans.

When Odysseus sets foot on his farm for the first time in twenty years in disguise, only his old dog, who lies neglected on a dung heap recognizes him, and, as if he had been waiting for him all that time, dies. The farm is full of suitors partying, loafing about, playing and dancing as if they owned the estate. They taunt the newly arrived beggar and only permit him to stay when he wins a combat with another beggar. When Odysseus is granted an audience with Penelope and tells her that her husband's return is imminent, she does not believe him. She sets up a challenge for the suitors—whoever can draw Odysseus's old bow and hit the target through twelve axes will become her husband.

None of the suitors succeeds. When the beggar is given the bow, he draws it effortlessly and hits the target. Then he aims again and shoots the second arrow into the throat of Antinous, one of the suitors' ringleaders. The suitors are shocked and seized by fear when the beggar is revealed as Odysseus. A bloodbath ensues. Together with two faithful shepherds who had been initiated into the plan beforehand, Odysseus and Telemachus slaughter all the suitors, who have been locked up in the hall. When the suitors succeed in obtaining weapons, Athena intervenes and helps Odysseus to complete his work. He forces the unfaithful servants to carry out the corpses and clean the bloodstained house, then has them executed. But even after Athena reverses his transformation and rejuvenates him, Penelope still does not recognize her husband. It is only when he tells her how he had himself built their marriage bed, which still stands immovably in the bedroom, that she falls into his arms. With Athena holding back the dawn chariot and thus delaying daybreak, Odysseus and Penelope reunite and tell each other of their experiences. The next day, Odysseus visits his father Laertes, who lives in seclusion in the country, and, together with him, Telemachus and his followers, meets the suitors' relatives, who are bent on revenge. The gods ultimately stop the fight and bring peace; Ithaca returns to order and the plot has come to an end.

Both the subject matter and narrative techniques of the *Odyssey* have had a lasting influence on storytelling in the Western tradition.[5] New Comedy, handed down primarily in Menander's fragments but also visible in Roman reception through Plautus and Terence, repeatedly returns to the motif of the separation and reunion of a couple. It follows the teleological plot structure of the *Odyssey*, which builds up tension

---

5. Lowe (2002) provides a thought-provoking analysis of the *Odyssey*'s plot and its reception history.

over the narrative trajectory, which then, at its *telos*, or culmination, is dispelled—after all their trials and tribulations, Odysseus and Penelope finally renew their marriage. It is no coincidence that the scenes of deception and recognition that are so popular in New Comedy resemble the second half of the *Odyssey*. And the *Odyssey* does not necessarily need to have served as a direct model; it may also have influenced Menander and other authors of New Comedy via tragedy: works such as Euripides's *Ion* and *Helen*, for example.

Apart from its influence on New Comedy, in the post-Christian era the impact of the *Odyssey* has been felt particularly in the novel. Any notion of a definitive Greek novel is misleading—it is difficult establish any common denominator to the five works by Chariton, Xenophon, Longus, Achilles Tatius and Heliodorus, not to mention other surviving novel fragments that indicate an even broader spectrum. Nevertheless, the continuity of motifs and narrative techniques found in both the *Odyssey* and New Comedy is unmistakable—most novels feature a couple who are torn apart, finally to be reunited. In many cases, this union is also linked to the return to a place of origin, which takes up the Odyssean motif of returning home, the so-called 'nostos'. The great economy of plot, and above all, the happy ending continue the narrative tradition of the *Odyssey* and New Comedy.

The *Aethiopica*, probably the most complex of the Greek novels to have survived to this day, narrates the love story of Theagenes, a descendant of Achilles, and the beautiful Ethiopian princess Charicleia, and includes a substantial examination of the *Odyssey*. Its author, Heliodorus, repeatedly quotes from the *Odyssey* and makes explicit comparisons between the central character Kalasiris and Odysseus. He even introduces an etymology of the name Homer into his characters' dialogue—Homer is said to owe his name to the hairy leg (*meros*) he was born with. Additionally, Heliodorus begins the story *in medias res* and blends in the backstory as a long internal narrative. Just as the second half of the *Odyssey* begins with the conclusion of the Apologoi, the end of Kalasiris's story marks the middle of the *Aethiopica*. Heliodorus's novel, as a culmination of ancient narrative art, is inconceivable without the *Odyssey* as a foundation.

The major theories of the novel only began with modernity and tend to view it as an expression of a specifically modern state of mind. Lukács, for instance, offers an analysis of the metaphysical homelessness which the contemporary self is subject to. Bakhtin does at least make reference to Menippean satire, named after its originator, Menippus of Gadara (third century BCE), as a source for the modern novel, but he generally contrasts the modern novel with the ancient epic.[6] Specialist studies, however, have demonstrated the profound influence which the ancient novel had on the development of the early modern novel.[7] The claim of the great humanist Julius Caesar Scaliger (1484–1558) reflects the spirit of the times: 'This particularly brilliant method of structuring is encountered in Helidorus's *Aethiopica*. I believe that any epicist must read this book with great care and keep it in mind as a perfect example.'[8] After the *Aethiopica* had been translated into European languages in the sixteenth and seventeenth centuries, many authors did follow Heliodorus's example and imitated the *in medias res* opening. While most of the Baroque writers are now forgotten and their often lengthy novels are only known to experts today, Heliodorus's influence can also be seen in Cervantes, especially in *Persiles*, which he considered to be his main work and far more important than *Don Quixote*.

Many works of modern and postmodern literature deliberately undermine the conventions of the classical plot; they play with those of its elements without plot relevance, or may deny the reader a rounded ending. And yet, the distinctive teleology found in the *Odyssey*, in New Comedy and the ancient novel are by no means extinct. It continues to be found in what literary scholars are frequently too quick to dismiss as popular literature. The road movie takes up the nostos motif, adventure novels use the idea of prolonged wanderings, and romantic novels incorporate the *Odyssey*'s love story. The fact that very few popular novels borrow directly from the *Odyssey* serves to underline the rich fruit which the epic has borne. The story of a man who roams the world,

---

6. Lukács (1971 [1916]); Bakhtin (1981); Doody (1996). Pavel (2003), who considers the importance of ancient Greece for the modern novel, is an exception.

7. See the literature in Sandy (1982): 95–124.

8. Scaliger (1964 [1561]): 144.

finally to return home to his wife, and its narrative techniques—suspense, recognition scenes and internal narratives—have all contributed to the fact that the *Odyssey* has influenced Western literary history more than any other work.

The Homeric Question

People were puzzled by Homer even in ancient times. Two Hellenistic epigrams name seven cities that claim to have been Homer's birthplace (AP 16.297–98) and during the Imperial period, several more candidates were added. There was also disagreement about Homer's lifetime; some ancient authors considered him an eyewitness to the Trojan War, while others placed him centuries later. Further epics were attributed to Homer in addition to the *Iliad* and the *Odyssey*, and at the same time there were philologists who claimed that the *Odyssey* and *Iliad* had different authors. The fantasies that abounded about Homer's life can still be admired today in ancient biographies. One finds, for instance, that Homer was the son of Phemius, who is a singer in the *Odyssey*, and that he died of depression after he failed to solve a riddle posed by a young fisherman. . . .[9]

For the most part, the Homeric epics were accessible to the Middle Ages only through scant Latin summaries, but they quickly gained in importance after the Renaissance, when translations into European languages appeared in the seventeenth and eighteenth centuries. The 'Homeric question' of the origin of the epics is generally thought to have started with Friedrich August Wolff and the publication of *Prolegomena ad Homerum* in 1795. Wolff developed the thesis that the Homeric poems had been handed down orally over several centuries, subject to constant change in the process, before they were finally written down, at which point they became fixed. Therefore, it is not a single poet named Homer, but rather a multitude of singers who are to be regarded as the authors of the *Iliad* and *Odyssey*. Wolff's originality should not be overestimated here. The Abbé d'Aubignac, Richard Bentley and

9. See Graziosi (2002).

Giambattista Vico had all doubted in their time that a single poet named Homer had written down these texts and lecture notes show that Wolff had developed his ideas from his lecturer Heyne in Göttingen. Nevertheless, it is Wolff's *Prolegomena* that uprooted the myth of the ingenious poet and gave a decisive impetus for modern Homer research.

In the nineteenth century and even at the beginning of the twentieth, philologists endeavoured to identify various stages of development in the texts of the Homeric epics. Where they perceived breaks in the text, they meticulously separated what they supposed were later additions in an effort to arrive at an original version. The *Redaktor* or 'editor' theory, which assumes that a poet had combined several poems into a single text eventually prevailed in research on the *Odyssey*. One of the most important analysts, Adolf Kirchhoff, tried to show that a poem about Odysseus's wanderings is the oldest core of the *Odyssey*. Accordingly, he thought that the revenge on the suitors was written as a continuation of this original text, and, like the Telemachy, was added later. Kirchhoff and other analysts used great ingenuity and ploughed through the narrative verse by verse in search of inconsistencies. Wherever they thought they had discovered any, they postulated more or less artfully blended poems.

In the first half of the twentieth century, this kind of analysis lost its primacy in Homer research. Two developments were decisive here—the increasing prominence of the unitarians and of the oralists. There had already been philologists, such as Gregor Wilhelm Nitzsch and Carl Rothe in the nineteenth century, who emphasized the unity of Homeric epics. Even if the epics did refer to earlier material, these scholars felt that both the *Odyssey* and the *Iliad* are unmistakably composed as a whole. But it was not until the twentieth century that the unitarians gained the upper hand. Their analysis discredited proponents of the editor theory, not least by highlighting that there was no agreement between them; indeed, there were almost as many models of origin as there were analysts. Many of the inconsistencies on which these proponents had based their theses proved to rest on questionable assumptions. While the unitarians mercilessly exposed the weaknesses and contradictions of these theses, their arguments also conceal a wider paradigm shift: preoccupation with the origin of epics was being replaced by an interest in the interpretation of the texts. Tensions which the earlier analysts had tried to explain in terms of genesis were interpretative challenges for the unitarians. The origin question was by no means solved, but people became more interested in the way the text was presented, in its effects and meanings.

It is appropriate to speak of a paradigm shift, since similar developments can also be observed in other fields of classical philology, albeit not necessarily concurrently. Until the middle of the twentieth century, for instance, scholars endeavoured to work out the stages of Herodotus's development in the *Histories*: he had first been a geographer and ethnographer and, after becoming a historian, had integrated his earlier studies into his historical work. Similarly to Homeric research, the idea of unity underlying such analyses was questioned. Historians of the nineteenth and early twentieth centuries may have been irritated by the breadth of material presented in the *Histories*, but their standards are by no means relevant to Herodotus, especially since he could not fall back on any prior concept of 'historiography', let alone genre conventions. While the analysts discovered discontinuities and explained them genetically, unitarians showed a clear compositional 'structure', with a succession of great empires as the mainstream of the narrative, from which ethnographic and geographical tributaries branch off whenever new peoples enter the plot.[10]

While in German-language Homeric philology the analysts ceded their ground to the unitarians, in Anglophone research they were almost entirely supplanted by the oralists. In 1928, at the age of twenty-six, Milman Parry submitted his dissertation, written in French, to the Sorbonne and laid the foundation for the thesis that the Homeric poems were not only based on oral poems, but had actually been composed orally. Together with his student Albert Lord, Parry went on to pursue field studies in the former Kingdom of Yugoslavia, where he used the

10. Jacoby (1913) and Fritz (1967) are examples of Herodotus analysis; Immerwahr (1966) and Cobet (1971) represent the unitarian position, which is already found in Regenbogen (1930).

example of an existing recitation culture to examine how epics are created and circulated without ever being fixed in written form. The epic formula, defined by Parry as 'a group of words regularly used under the same metrical conditions to express a specific and essential idea',[11] is fundamental to the oralists' thesis. According to Parry, formulaic language, which is particularly evident in recurring links between nouns and epithets—'the rosy-fingered dawn', 'the long-enduring Odysseus'—is an example of oral poetry in which singers use a traditional system of formulae to compose and memorize their songs. While both analysts and unitarians assume that the epics made use of oral poems but were in fact written down, Parry, Lord and their followers are convinced that they were composed entirely in oral recital.

The Homeric question does not stir up emotions today like it did fifty years ago, but it does remain controversial. Although analysis no longer plays a major role, it is still pursued by individual scholars, some of whom are well known.[12] Beyond that, German-speaking philologists tend towards unitarian positions, and their English-speaking colleagues towards oralist positions. The unitarians focus on the complex structure of the *Iliad* and the *Odyssey* and on recurring resonances within each epic, which, according to them, would be inconceivable without the use of writing. However, they wrestle with the question of how the epics might have been written down in archaic Greece. They must deal with difficult technical questions, such as in what medium such long texts are supposed to have been recorded. For example, there are no surviving papyri or parchment strips from archaic Greece. The naïve inscriptions on vases also contribute to doubts that several thousand verses could have been written down at that point, while the question of why an oral culture should write down poetry that was exclusively circulated through recitation is even more challenging.

Conversely, while oralists can rely on the oral tradition of archaic society, despite all attempts to find parallels from other epic traditions, it remains difficult for many philologists to imagine how such extensive

11. Parry (1971): 272.
12. See, for instance, West (2011); (2014).

and complex works could have been created in oral poetry. We cannot date the Homeric epics precisely, but linguistic and historical findings suggest that they were composed in the seventh, and perhaps as early as the eighth century BCE. What kind of institutional framework would have been able to ensure that they took a fixed form, to be reliably handed down for centuries? Oral traditions are only stable in exceptional cases; as a rule, they are adapted to the horizons of any given contemporary world. There is some evidence that singing guilds performed the Homeric epics at festivals such as the Panathenaia, but this is from a later time and should not be too much relied upon.

Although the Homeric question will probably remain a mystery and continue to cause headaches, we can conclude that like the *Iliad*, the *Odyssey*, contains formal elements of oral poetry, which distinguish it from later literature. However, these peculiarities do not make it impossible to interpret the Homeric epics, and the unresolved problem of genesis does not relieve us of the necessity of interpretation. It will therefore be useful to look at the most striking characteristics of oral poetry in early Greek epic and ask what role they play in interpretation.

Formulaic Language and Typical Scenes

Formulaic language conveys both the oral origins of the Homeric epics and, if we follow Parry and his followers, their oral composition. Fixed, recurring combinations of words form the building blocks from which the rhapsodists composed their songs. The formulaic combination of names with epithets, such as 'stony Ithaca' or 'wise Penelope' are those that initially stand out, but formulae can also take up an entire verse, or even several verses. Daybreak, for instance, is portrayed by the formula 'when rosy-fingered dawn appeared'. At banquets we often find the verse, 'When they had roasted the outer flesh and taken it from the spits, they divided the portions out and began the glorious feast.'[13]

---

13. Since the flood of publications on Homeric formulaic language subsided after the 1970s, the two survey articles by Edwards, (1986) and (1988) are still helpful. See also Russo (1997) and more recently, Bakker (2013): 157–69.

On another level, formulae continue in so-called 'typical scenes'.[14] In order to depict recurring actions, such as a sacrifice, assembly or bath, Homer makes use of fixed blocks of words, some of which consist of formulae. He reproduces the individual steps of an action in a specific sequence but varies the degree of detail. For example, the *Iliad* features four armouring scenes. The order in which the hero equips himself is identical in all of them—greaves, breastplate, sword, shield, helmet, spears and lance. But while Homer uses eleven verses to describe Paris's armouring, Agamemnon's occupies thirty-two. Detailed descriptions of the breastplate and shield prolong the scene and prepare for Agamemnon's *aristeia*, his distinction in battle. Similarly, the scene in which Achilles dons his armour in the nineteenth book is expanded, since it marks a turning point in the plot.

Many books and countless essays have been devoted to Homeric formulaic language and in many ways, they have changed Parry's somewhat rigid conception of formulae. As difficult as it may be to determine whether some phrases are formulae or not, it has become clear that the proportion of formulaic language in the epic is smaller than had been assumed by the pioneers of the orality thesis. While generic scenes such as the banquet do make extensive use of formulae, non-formulaic language predominates in many passages that are vital to the plot.[15] Parry's thesis that it was the constraints of metre that led to the formation of formulaic language has even been reversed. Gregory Nagy, for example, asserts that it was the formula which produced the metre, rather than the other way around.[16]

Above all, it has been recognized that formulae are not only a means of composition and aid to memory, but can in fact create meaning through repetition.[17] In Parry's eyes, many epithets were merely ornamental, metrically conditioned additions without any semantic value. When Achilles, sitting by the campfire, is described as 'swift-footed', this view seems confirmed. Isn't such a characterization contradictory? Not

14. See especially Arend (1933), and for a research overview, Edwards (1992).
15. Finkelberg (1990).
16. Nagy (1976).
17. Bakker (2013): 157–69 offers a balanced discussion. '

necessarily—after all, the epithet designates a characteristic of Achilles regardless of any specific situation. Thus the formula 'swift-footed Achilles' engenders its own meaning beyond the context. By resorting to a formula, Homer invokes an image of the hero which is firmly established in tradition. It's not just any Achilles who appears, but a specific character who is also referred to as swift-footed in other epics, and in this way the poet firmly embeds his work in the epic tradition.[18]

And even without referring to the epic tradition, formulaic language and typical scenes can be significant. An example from the *Iliad* serves to illustrate this point.[19] In Book 22, Andromache prepares a bath for her husband, but Hector is already dead. Achilles has just killed him at the gates of Troy after a long chase. Andromache, who is closest to Hector, is the last to hear of his death. In this scene, Homer plays with the two functions which the bath has in the *Iliad*: on the one hand, it refreshes the warrior returning from battle; on the other, it cleanses the corpse of the fallen. Hector's death turns the refreshing bath which Andromache has prepared into a bath for cleansing the dead. But not even this is granted to Hector while Achilles refuses to hand over his body.

Formulae and formulaic language underline the irony (*Il.* 22.442–46):

> She called out through the house to her lovely-haired
>   handmaidens
> to set a great cauldron on the fire, so that there would be
> hot water for Hector's bath as he came back from the fighting;
> poor, innocent, nor knew how, far from waters for bathing,
> Pallas Athene had cut him down at the hands of Achilles.

The formula 'when he came back home from the fighting' always denotes a hero doomed to die; in a prediction made by Zeus it even refers to the death of Hector (*Il.* 17.206–8):

> Still for the present I will invest you with great strength
> to make up for it that you will not come home out of the fighting,
> nor Andromache take from your hands the glorious arms of
>   Achilles.

18. Foley (1991).
19. For a more detailed discussion, see Grethlein (2007).

The example of 'come home from the fighting' shows that formulae do more than serve as building blocks that enable the composition of hexametric verses to aid memorization. They are also repeated to establish comparisons across set scenes and create specific meanings in this way. Through its usage elsewhere in the epic, this formula connotes a hero who will, in fact, die in battle rather than returning home. By using it in the twenty-second book, Homer cryptically and subtly underlines the futility of Andromache's action.

The phrase 'to set a great cauldron across the fire' is found in the eighteenth book of the *Iliad*, when Achilles instructs his companions to wash Patroclus's corpse (18.344). This repetition, likewise, not only serves as a compositional technique but is charged with meaning. Just like the formula 'come home from the fighting', the phrase intimates that Hector will no longer be able to enjoy a bath while alive, but will be ritually washed after his death, just as Patroclus was. Moreover, the repetition underlines the causal connection between their respective deaths—Achilles kills Hector in revenge for Hector killing his close friend Patroclus.

The formulaic half-verse 'setting tripod and cauldron on the fire' appears for the third and last time in the twenty-third book. The Greeks urge Achilles to take a bath, but he refuses. The renewed echo of the bath for Patroclus indicates that Achilles is now himself in the shadow of death. Just as Hector is bathed as a corpse, Achilles, as described in the *Odyssey* (24.43–45), will be ritually purified after his death. The formulaic repetition underscores the parallel between killer and victim: both suffer a premature death. Far from merely being a compositional device, the language reflects the dynamics of the plot. It crystallizes the chain of murders that underlies the action in the final third of the *Iliad*. Hector kills Patroclus and in turn is killed by Achilles, who, as he is aware from a prophecy, forfeits his own life in the process.

In the Homeric epic, whose formulaic language is shaped by poetry in recitation, not every repetition is as significant as in Hellenistic and Augustan poetry, which are firmly anchored in a book culture. Nevertheless, contrary to the original assumptions of the orality theorists, it has been shown that repetitions of formulaic language can be significant. Similar rules but different standards apply when compared to allusions that appear elsewhere in literature: the less frequent the repetition and the more specific the context, the more plausible it is to speak of an allusion. The phrase 'the rosy-fingered dawn appeared', repeated dozens of times in very different contexts, cannot be said to be an allusion. But when a half-verse such as 'setting tripod and cauldron on the fire' is used just three times in the *Iliad* and each time refers to the bath of a hero who has already died or is about to die, the repetition obviously carries significance. In interpreting the *Odyssey*, other instances will be encountered where formulaic language is used specifically to juxtapose individual scenes.

Homer's Language and Style

Even though we are examining the *Odyssey* in translation, it is useful to take a brief look at Homer's language and style beyond formulaic expressions. The Homeric epic was not only distinguished from everyday Greek by its hexametric verse form, but was also written in an artificial style that was not spoken anywhere at any point in time. Homer mixes different dialects—the basis is Ionic, but occasionally, Aeolic and Doric elements appear. In addition, different levels of language are amalgamated. Overall, Homeric language corresponds to the Greek of the eighth and seventh centuries BCE, but the epics also contain earlier forms and elements. In some cases, for instance, the metre presupposes the letter digamma, a 'w'-sound, which had already disappeared from Ionic by Homer's time. An example of this is *anax*, the word for lord or ruler, which for metrical reasons must often be read as 'wanax'. It has been known since the deciphering of the Linear B tablets that *wanax* was already documented in Mycenaean.

Homer's stylized language creates its own cosmos, which was already removed from the contemporaneous audience's everyday world. Old forms and words no longer in use lent the epic a patina and formally expressed the gulf that separated the heroes from the present. The following verses (*Il.* 20.285–87) present a succinct image of this:

> But Aeneas now in his hand caught
> up a stone, a huge thing which no two men could carry
> such as men are now, but by himself he lightly hefted it.

The impression which the Homeric language made on the Greeks can be gleaned from the fact that right up to the Imperial epoch, poets as well as prose writers incorporated Homeric words into their texts whenever they aspired to eminence or wanted to portray something as venerable.

Homer's language and style are not only monumental, but also extremely vibrant. Even in antiquity, audiences praised the *enargeia*, or vividness, of the *Iliad* and *Odyssey*—the narrative was so rich that they felt as though they were seeing the action at first hand. Similarly, modern Homer scholars often emphasize how intensely these epics appeal to the imagination. But they are faced with a paradox: the *Iliad* and *Odyssey* contain only a few, brief descriptions. Homer does not waste words on the spaces in which his heroes move. For example, on the basis of the descriptions provided, it would be impossible to draw a picture of Odysseus's court. A philologist put the question succinctly: 'So, how—to formulate the paradox—does Homer conjure up images without giving any descriptions?'[20]

Recent work in cognitive science provides some insights.[21] Psychologists and philosophers have rejected an assumption, widespread until the 1990s, which held that sensory impressions are condensed into a photographic or pictorial representations of what we consciously perceive. This pictorialist model has been replaced by an action-based model. Numerous experiments have shown that the environment is instead perceived selectively. People do not retain a picture of what they perceive within them, but focus their attention on aspects that are, or could become, relevant for their actions. If, for instance, we search for a tool to hang a picture on the wall and see a hammer, we may not perceive whether the shaft is brown or black, but rather, concentrate on those properties that determine the tool's suitability, such as whether

20. Radke-Uhlmann (2009): 12. There are more detailed descriptions of localities in the *Odyssey*, such as the island of Calypso and the palace of Alcinous, than in the *Iliad*; but even so, Radke-Uhlmann's question remains valid.

21. The cognitive approaches of scholars such as Noe, Gallagher and Damasio are here referred to as action-related, 'enactive' or 'embodied'. For a detailed account of these approaches in respect of the *Iliad*, see Grethlein and Huitink (2017).

the shaft is ergonomic or whether the head is the right size to drive the nail into the wall. If in spite of this we have the impression that we are fully aware of our surroundings, it is because we can potentially direct our attention beyond the immediately relevant aspects at any point.

The imagination seems to resemble perception. It too focuses on aspects related to the possibilities of interaction. For example, if we imagine stroking a cat, we do not necessarily visualize whether the cat has white paws or not. Yet it would be wrong to assume that the imagination is incomplete: it focuses on what is pertinent, such as whether the fur is soft or shaggy. If a roomful of people were asked to imagine a man running across a bridge and were then asked if the man wore glasses, most would reply that they didn't know. Like perception, the imagination does not work photographically, but in relation to action.

This is why descriptions that are very detailed can be felt to be tedious, rather than inspiring. A passage from Theodor Fontane's *On Tangled Paths* (*Irrungen, Wirrungen*) may serve to illustrate this:

> At the point where the Kurfürstendamm intersects the Kurfürstenstraße, diagonally across from the Zoological Gardens, there was still, in the mid-eighteen-seventies, a large market garden running back to the open fields behind; and in it stood a small, three-windowed house with its own little front garden, set back about a hundred paces from the road that went by and clearly visible from there despite being so small and secluded. However, the other building in the market garden, indeed without doubt its main feature, was concealed by this little house as if by the wings of a stage set, and only a red- and green-painted wooden turret with the remains of a clock face (no trace of an actual clock) under its pointed roof suggested that there was something hidden in the wings, a suggestion confirmed by a flock of pigeons fluttering up round the turret from time to time and, even more, by the occasional barking of a dog. The whereabouts of this dog eluded the viewer, although the front door on the far left stood open all day long, affording a glimpse of the yard.[22]

22. Fontane (2013): 7.

Fontane's description is exemplary in terms of its precision and richness of detail. If most readers nevertheless find it difficult to imagine the setting, it is because the narrative, which strives for photographic completeness, does not correspond to the way in which reality is perceived. It is not easy to determine, however, what kind of narrative style is 'cognitively realistic'. Literary scholars have only just started to draw on cognitive approaches in their studies. Yet some criteria are becoming apparent: texts that focus on actions, and which describe simple, purposeful physical movements, for instance, seem to be particularly vibrant. Vivid texts, moreover, describe objects and spaces insofar as they refer to potential interactions, and descriptions are provided when they are relevant to action. Generally speaking, descriptions that are embedded in action are more captivating than those which are detached from it. The reader's imagination seems to be stimulated when the narrative lasts for a similar length of time to the event being described.

Returning to Homer, a passage considered particularly 'vivid' in antiquity may be cited in this regard. A text from the early Imperial period, which is ascribed to an author named (Pseudo-)Demetrius, discusses vividness (*enargeia*) as an aspect of a simple style. The author mentions the example of a chariot race in the twenty-third book of the *Iliad*. He refers to the three verses in italics below, here reproduced with some additional lines for context. Eumelus's mares are at the head of the field:

> Out in front was the swift-stepping team of the son of Pheres,
> Eumelus, and after him the stallions of Diomedes,
> the Trojan horses, not far behind at all, but close on him,
> *for they seemed forever on the point of climbing his chariot*
> *and the wind of them was hot on the back and on the broad shoulders*
> *of Eumelus. They lowered their heads and flew close after him.*
> (*Il.* 23.376–81)

Ps.-Demetrius praises the depiction as 'vivid owing to the fact that no detail which usually occurs and then occurred is omitted' (4.210).[23] His focus on action rather than on the surroundings corresponds to the

---

23. Translation by William Rhys Roberts: see Roberts (2010 [1902]): 166–67.

above-mentioned criteria concerning vividness. Indeed, unlike Fontane, Homer does not provide any separate description of where the race takes place; he only refers to what is significant to the plot. A narrowing of the track becomes apparent when Antilochus uses it for a daring overtaking manoeuvre. The verses chosen by Ps.-Demetrius are also pertinent— instead of explicitly referring to the short distance between Diomedes and Eumelus, Homer uses simple action verbs; Diomedes's horses seem to mount the chariot in front of them. The passage captures their movements and makes the events almost tangible for the readers. Further, the narrator assumes the perspective of an eyewitness as he adds a tactile dimension: Eumelus feels the hot breath of the horses in his back.

Cognitive approaches to descriptive narrative are still in their infancy. Nevertheless, they can help to solve an apparent paradox in Homer research: the lack of detailed descriptions does not diminish the vividness that has been attributed to Homer since antiquity. By concentrating on the action in terms of simple and purposeful movements, and by limiting descriptions to aspects that are relevant to the action, Homer fulfils an important condition that seems to apply to enthralling narratives. Yet it is important to remember that not all aspects of the Homeric style contribute equally to the narrative's vividness. Homer also characterizes persons and objects with epithets that are not relevant to the plot and incorporates words the meaning of which was already obscure to ancient audiences. In this way, he creates a patina of venerability over the epic world. It is this venerable style coupled with vivid descriptions that has captivated ancient and modern audiences alike.

Narrative and Experience in the Epic

Having outlined the structure, content, *quaestio Homerica* and the formulaic and artistic language and style of the epic, we now have a background against which to view the *Odyssey*. The question that arises next is how to approach this text. At first glance, a thematic approach looks tempting: depending on temperament and inclination, the focus could be on narrative technique, Homeric society, the role of women or other aspects of the epic, in individual chapters. Any such approach, however, runs the risk of detracting from a crucial aspect of the work, or indeed of any narrative—its sequentiality. We read word by word, paragraph by paragraph and chapter by chapter. Literary scholars familiarize themselves with texts through multiple readings, or at least pretend to, and often interpret passages regardless of their place in the narrative flow. Such a de-temporalizing approach is legitimate, since it is often the only way to identify fundamental structures that are not apparent on first reading. Yet it also means that temporal dynamics that characterize the reading process can come to be ignored.[24]

When we read a narrative, we wonder about what has been concealed, are surprised by the unexpected, and above all are curious about how the plot will develop. We enter a flow of time that is categorically different from lived experience yet at the same time structurally analogous to it. The plot does not affect us directly; the reading experience is directed towards the experiences of the fictional characters—it's a second-hand experience. And yet, analogously to real life, the narrative either fulfils or disappoints expectations. Even though reading takes place within an 'as if' framework—being enthralled by Odysseus's travels does not mean that we entirely forget we are sitting on a garden bench holding a book in our hands—the reading experience can often be particularly intense. An artfully crafted plot can create a tension rarely experienced in daily life.

In order to do justice to this temporal dynamic or experiential character of the narrative, the *Odyssey*'s storyline will be essential to the interpretation that follows. This does not mean ignoring structural observations or aspects beyond a specific passage; such analysis should, anyway, be embedded in a sequential reading. Rather, interpretation is brought in line with the reading process—while reading, the plot is followed sequentially, and at the same time, the whole is kept in mind.

24. For a detailed discussion of the experiential character of reading, see Grethlein (2010c); also Grethlein (2015b): 276–79 on the difference between the phenomenological understanding of experience and 'experientiality', which Fludernik introduced into narrative research: Fludernik (1996).

There will be two points at which to investigate related areas and consider the *Odyssey* as a whole. The Polyphemus adventure affords an opportunity to consider the relationship of the Homeric epic to history. As will be seen, the *Odyssey* deals with the Greeks' experiences as they struck out into the wider world of the Mediterranean. The blinding of the cyclops also happens to be the first Homeric motif in vase painting. The illustrations which will be examined display a reflexivity that is not usually ascribed to archaic vases. Then, after this excursion into history and art history, the murder of the suitors will provide an occasion to examine ethics in the *Odyssey*. The justice of the gods and morality of the hero will here serve as the focal points.

To avoid the danger of retelling while exploring the *Odyssey*, this study will adopt a perspective which, it is hoped, will reveal the text anew to today's readers and show why the study of Homer continues to be worthwhile. A remark about the *Odyssey* in a text entitled *On the Sublime*, probably written in the first century CE and handed down under the name of Longinus, points in the right direction: the author remarks that the *Iliad*, composed at the height of Homer's creative powers, is dramatic and full of conflict, while 'most of the *Odyssey* is storytelling, as befits old age' (9.13). He goes on to declare that in the *Odyssey*, Homer is like the setting sun, which still has its radiance but no longer its previous intensity. While the comparison with the *Iliad* and comparatively negative judgement of the *Odyssey* may be disputed, the approach of the author of *On the Sublime* does draw attention to a central feature of the latter epic. The *Odyssey* is not only narrative in the sense that it fabulates. It also itself contains a multitude of narratives—bards appear on both Scheria and Ithaca; Helen and other characters recount the Trojan War; Odysseus himself describes his voyages at the court of the Phaeacians and on Ithaca deceives his interlocutors with tall tales.

Without neglecting other aspects such as Odysseus's ambivalent heroism, the role of the gods or the importance of the gaze, this book focuses on narration in the *Odyssey*.[25] It is particularly concerned with

25. See Goldhill (1991): 1–68; Segal (1994): 113–83; Olson (1995); Mackie (1997); Scodel (1998), who offer different perspectives and emphases on the narratives and songs contained in the *Odyssey*.

the forms and functions of narrative. The epic is not, of course, a philosophical treatise—Homer is not Aristotle—yet the many internal narratives in the *Odyssey* show how, why and to what end we tell stories. This gives the poem a meta-narrative dimension; it engages with the forms and functions that narrative can encompass. In other words, the *Odyssey* is a narrative about narrating.

In recent decades, the importance of storytelling has been examined from various perspectives. Psychologists describe how people establish their identity by narrating their lives, while the philosopher Paul Ricœur interprets narration as engagement with time. Historians and sociologists examine narratives that bind communities, or conversely, call them into question.[26] These debates on narrative theory not only enable new perspectives on the *Odyssey*, but in turn appear in a new light themselves, refracted through the prism of the poem. The narrative engagement with storytelling has a depth that remains unavailable to the distanced gaze of the theorist.

Above all, Homer is not a modern narrative theorist *avant la lettre*. The popular game of discovering supposedly (post)modern phenomena in the epic detracts from its hermeneutic richness as well as its strangeness. The *Odyssey* is far more complex than its position at the beginning of European literature would suggest, and, although its influence continues to be felt today, it resists all attempts at appropriation. Time and again, Homer frustrates our expectations and instead draws our attention to aspects that distinguish the Homeric epic, and perhaps ancient narratives in general, from the modern novel.

In a much-cited essay, Uvo Hölscher describes antiquity as our 'nearest *other*' (das nächste Fremde).[27] The appeal of Greco-Roman culture is that while it is the foundation of our own civilization on the one hand, it also provides a counterpoint to the present day. But today, the proximity of antiquity is perhaps no longer assumed in the same way as it was in 1962. In a world which sociologists describe as increasingly globalized and mobile, the spatially distant may be felt to be closer than the temporally

26. See, for instance, Bruner (1986); (1990); Ricœur (1984–88 [1983–85]); Anderson (1983); Smith (1999). For a broad overview of narrative, see Koschorke (2012).

27. Hölscher (1965): 81 (first given as a lecture in 1962).

past; present-day China may seem a nearer stranger than does ancient Greece.[28] If, as Hölscher claims for antiquity, the *Odyssey* allows the modern reader 'to think creatively of possibilities, to gain distance from the constraints of the taken-for-granted, the common consensus, the contemporary',[29] this is due not only to perceived distance, but also to the contemplation of the epic itself. It is the combination of reflexivity, strangeness and familiarity that makes reading the *Odyssey*, or the conversation with Homer, as rewarding as it is appealing.

28. Grethlein (2018).
29. Hölscher (1965): 81.

2

The Telemachy:
Tales of the Father

IT IS ENTIRELY possible, and even probable, that a version of the *Odyssey* which did not include the Telemachy initially circulated in archaic Greece.[1] The first four books of the *Odyssey* as it is known today are likely to have been added later. The plot of the Telemachy may even have been supplied by a separate Telemachus epic. Analysts avidly investigated which verses had come from Homer and which were supplied by subsequent editors, and this represented the most important strand of Homeric scholarship research until the beginning of twentieth century. Unsurprisingly, the Telemachy occupied the analysts more than the rest of the text. It presents a sub-plot, which at first glance seems incidental to the main plot: at Athena's request, Telemachus travels to Pylos and Sparta to ask veterans of the Trojan War about his father. The hero of the epic, Odysseus, does not appear until the fifth book. The scholarly disagreements and bitter polemics about where the philological dissecting knife should be applied testify to the problems that attend the attempt to trace the genesis of the *Odyssey* from the text as it is known today. But more importantly, the analytical approach has meant losing sight of the multiple narrative functions the Telemachy has at the beginning of the *Odyssey*.

---

1. For examples of an analytical study of the Telemachy, see Kirchhoff (1879); Page (1955): 52–81; 165–82. For a brief overview of older research, see Klingner (1964): 40–47.

Whatever its origins, the Telemachy is an integral part of the text that has come down to us today.

It will therefore be useful initially to explore the significance of the Telemachy within the overall structure of the *Odyssey*. This will invite discussion of a form of suspense that distinguishes ancient narratives from many modern novels. Another focus will be on the diverse stories that are embedded in these first four books, as they prompt reflection on narrative, and especially its effects on listeners and readers. Thirdly, the question of whether the Telemachy should be understood as a *Bildungsroman* (coming-of-age narrative), the view held by a majority of modern Homer scholars, will be addressed. The initial focus on suspense will be shown to be part of a characteristic of ancient narratives that is linked to the ancient understanding of personality.

The Significance of the Telemachy within the *Odyssey*

The first and second books of the *Odyssey* offer a striking image of Ithaca twenty years after Odysseus's departure for the Trojan War. His court has become a stomping ground for the *jeunesse dorée*, not only of Ithaca but also of the neighbouring islands. For several years, a hundred and eight suitors have vied for Penelope's favour. With Odysseus's father Laertes having retreated to the countryside, the suitors are endlessly enjoying themselves at the expense of the absent master of the house. They devour his resources, spend their days playing games and sports and shamelessly amuse themselves at the expense of the servants. Penelope has been able to protect herself from their attentions by insisting that she would only assent to a new marriage once she has completed weaving her father-in-law's shroud. Her trick of unravelling the fabric she wove during the day at night, however, is discovered by disloyal servants, who betray her to the suitors. Meanwhile, Telemachus is on the threshold of manhood and the time has come when Penelope must remarry, a condition Odysseus himself had stipulated twenty years previously as he departed for Troy.

By portraying the conditions on Ithaca, Homer creates a backdrop against which the return of Odysseus acquires a sense of urgency,[2] as well

2. Reinhardt (1960): 37–46.

as establishing a purpose for his wanderings. When the audience later learns of Odysseus's adventures, such as his encounters with Circe and Calypso, the journey to the underworld, the grotto of the cyclops and so forth, there is already a sense of where the journey will ultimately lead. The hero's longing to return home drives the plot, and the Telemachy provides a contour for the reader. It also lends a distinct geographical framework to the *Odyssey*; the action begins and ends on Ithaca.

While reading or listening to the Telemachy, the question arises of how Odysseus is going to regain the court that has been usurped by the crowd of suitors. Above all, the reader wonders if he will get there in time, before the suitors have killed Telemachus and forced Penelope to marry one of them. Time is pressing—the depiction of the situation on Ithaca creates suspense even before Odysseus has entered the plot.

This is a particular form of suspense that is characteristic of ancient storytelling. Since it invites more general reflections about narrative and time, it is worth exploring before considering the other functions of the Telemachy. Contemporary readers are probably familiar with the *Odyssey*'s ending, just as ancient listeners were—despite all the obstacles, Odysseus does succeed in returning to Ithaca in time and resumes his place next to Penelope. It is not only familiarity with the myth which vouchsafes this ending; it is also repeatedly anticipated in the *Odyssey* itself. Right at the beginning, Zeus assures Athena that he will ultimately grant Odysseus his homecoming, although it will not be an easy one, given Poseidon's resistance. In the people's assembly narrated in the second book, the aged soothsayer Halitherses, noticing a conspicuous bird migration, predicts that Odysseus will shortly appear and take terrible revenge. But his predictions are not taken seriously by the other characters. The suitor Eurymachus refutes Halitherses's words: 'I can give a much better interpretation than you can. / Many are the birds who under the sun's rays wander / the sky; not all of them mean anything' (2.180–82). He even insinuates that Halitherses is merely fishing for a gift from Telemachus. But the audience, aware of the plot and of conversations between the gods, understands the relevance of this prophecy as well as of other signs.

But how does suspense arise when the ending is already known? Isn't an unknown ending essential? While this may often be true, the *Odyssey* shows that the fact that the ending is known can actually help build suspense. The audience wonders how the plot is going to arrive at the anticipated outcome. Suspense arises from the *how*, rather than the *what*. If anything, while the predictions reduce tension related to the 'what', they increase it when it comes to the 'how'. In the *Odyssey*, anticipation, whether embedded in the plot or apparent only to the audience, remains nebulous, and this stimulates their imagination. After Halitherses's prophecy, for instance, one wonders how Odysseus will manage to escape from Ogygia, Calypso's island, and how he will manage to defeat the crowd of suitors once he is back in Ithaca.

Suspense in respect of the 'how' is a characteristic of ancient literature. Many genres that make use of the treasure trove of myth fall back on familiar subjects—tragedy is one such example. The audience of Euripides's *Orestes*, for instance, did not doubt that Orestes would ultimately escape. But this posed the question how Euripides would arrive at such an outcome, and this is a typical feature of ancient myth. Unlike Aeschylus, he does not set up a court to acquit the matricide. Orestes, condemned to death, takes Menelaus's daughter hostage after the king refuses to support him, and it is the intervention of the god Apollo which ultimately brings about the anticipated ending. The ever-widening gap between the development of the plot and the expected outcome kept the audience breathless in the Theatre of Dionysus.

Genres with non-mythical plots also make use of suspense that relates to the 'how'. The generic conventions of the Greek novel, for instance, serve a function akin to myth. The audience expects the radiant couple to overcome all obstacles after numerous adventures and tests, and to consummate their love at the end. In many cases, signs and oracles anticipate the outcome. In Heliodorus's *Aethiopica*, the novel about Charicleia and Theagenes which dates back to the third or fourth century CE, Pythia proclaims the following oracle:

'One who starts in grace [*charin*] and ends in glory [*kleos*],
    another goddess-born [*theas geneten*]:
Of these I bid you have regard, O Delphi!
Leaving my temple here and cleaving Ocean's swelling tides,

To the black land of the Sun will they travel,
Where they will reap the reward of those whose lives are passed
    in virtue:
A crown of black on brows of black.' (2.35.5)[3]

The plot, which leads the heroic couple to Ethiopia, is therefore out-lined in a roundabout way. In Greek, the names of the couple are al-luded to in *charis* (grace), *kleos* (glory/fame) and *theas genetes* (offspring of a goddess).

Ancient audiences seem to have valued knowing the ending, espe-cially when it was a favourable one. This is indicated by a grammarian's comment on a verse in the *Iliad*, in which the Greeks' victory over the Trojans is announced: 'In addition, he [Homer] appeases the listener by briefly hinting at Troy's ultimate capture. For who could bear to see the Greek ships burnt and Ajax flee unless the information that those responsible [the Trojans] would ultimately be defeated were made avail-able to the souls of the readers? (bT ad *Il.* 15.56). The same commentator offers a parallel from the *Odyssey*: 'The use of an anticipatory summary should be noted here. Odysseus anticipates the murder of the suitors [cf. *Od.* 16.267–307] and he [Homer] also tells how it will be done.' The idea that being able to anticipate a satisfactory ending enables the audi-ence to bear suffering and defeat with equanimity is also found in numer-ous other scholia. While such authorial frontloading reduces tension related to the 'what', it increases suspense in respect of the 'how'.

With its penchant for suspense in respect of the 'how', ancient litera-ture emphasizes a trait that is inherent to narrative. With the exception of anti-narrative experiments, stories open up a more or less closed uni-verse to the reader. As illustrated by the past tense as the narrative tense par excellence, stories are essentially told in retrospect. Even writers who adapt perspectives to the limited knowledge of the characters shape their narratives with an eye toward the ending. This is also evident in narrative economy. Anton Tchekhov—himself a brilliant dramatist—noted that,

---

3. Translation by J. R. Morgan: see 'Heliodorus: An Ethiopian Story', in Reardon (1989): 409.

if a pistol on a wall is mentioned in the first chapter, it will surely come into play in the second or third.[4] This is different from life, which consists of an open future with all its imponderables. In their cohesiveness, narratives offer a kind of certainty that does not exist in real life. The *Odyssey* and other narratives that let the audience glimpse the ending and experience suspense relating to the 'how' reinforce this closedness. They offer the reader a 'safe' experience: as in life, there are expectations about what will happen next, but as distinct from in life, the outcome is known. And in spite of this, suspense relating to the 'how' creates enthralment.

While suspense relating to the 'how' is a characteristic of ancient narrative, it is also found in contemporary narratives. The modernist novel has led us to associate suspense with an unknown ending, yet in popular narratives, all too easily dismissed as genre or light fiction, suspense relating to the 'how' is often paramount. It's not surprising when a novel set in a hospital ends with the attractive but insecure young doctor getting together with the kindhearted nurse. Ian Fleming, not unlike Euripides or Heliodorus, repeatedly puts the plot on a track that leads away from the anticipated ending:

> He (Bond) felt thoroughly dispirited and weak in resolve as well as in his body. He had to take too much in the past 24 hours and now this last stroke by the enemy seemed almost too final. This time, there could be no miracles. No one knew where he was and no one would miss him until well into the morning. The wreck of his car would be found before very long, but it would take hours to trace ownership to him.[5]

The phrase 'almost too final' surreptitiously plays to the reader's expectation that Bond will ultimately prevail once again—and the question of how he is going to manage to escape a seemingly hopeless situation becomes all the more pressing.

Medical and adventure novels are not highly rated by literary critics. Indeed, it is hard to get excited about clichés, two-dimensional characters

4. Tchekhov (1974 [1927]): 23.
5. Fleming (2006 [1953]): 123.

or language that is devoid of subtlety. Yet this parallel with ancient literature does provide a clue as to why far more people read Ian Fleming than read Henry James. Fleming's books do not merely offer ready entertainment; they also offer an encounter with time. Like the *Odyssey*, they reinforce the sense of coherence that the retrospective standpoint engenders: they give the reader a sense of being in control of events, rather than being at the mercy of them as in real life. Uncertainty about the future is replaced by a sense of confidence about the outcome. Yet at the same time, there is suspense—and it is primarily directed at *how* the events unfold. This is not to minimize the differences between Homer and Fleming, or between Achilles and James Bond—yet the comparison does allow popular fiction to appear in a new light.

When it comes to the Telemachy, it is not only the conditions on Ithaca that create suspense. These four books are devoted to a sub-plot. The audience is obliged to wait for the hero to appear and the delay increases tension in respect of Penelope's looming remarriage. Yet while Odysseus remains absent, his presence is felt throughout the Telemachy. Time and again, the characters invoke him when they either lament his death or long for his return. And Odysseus becomes the centre of attention in the third and fourth books, when Telemachus follows Athena's order to 'go out to ask about your father who is so long absent, / on the chance some mortal man can tell you, who has listened to Rumor / sent by Zeus' (1.281–83). Unlike Telemachus, the audience knows that Odysseus is being held by Calypso, yet still relates to Telemachus: we are just as eager to find out more about Odysseus's whereabouts and to finally meet him. It is through Telemachus that our perspective shifts to the world of the *Odyssey*; the son's search for the father draws the audience into the plot.

The stories Telemachus hears about Odysseus in Pylos and Sparta will be examined more closely later. At this point, it is worth mentioning briefly that Nestor, Menelaus and Helen all tell of Odysseus's deeds in the Trojan War. Nestor only alludes to Odysseus's trick of smuggling the Greek fighters into Troy in a wooden horse, while Menelaus takes pains to praise the shrewdness with which Odysseus ensured the success of their invasion. Helen, in turn, relates that Odysseus had ventured into

Troy incognito as a scout prior to the invasion. Telemachus, and with him the audience, learns of Odysseus the war hero who is as brave as he is cunning.[6] It is an image that serves as context for Odysseus's wanderings and sufferings, which are recounted from his own perspective in the Apologoi. The trickster who narrowly escapes monsters and forces of nature simultaneously appears as a warrior whose boldness ended a decade-long siege.

The homecoming stories—the *Nostoi*—told by the other Greek veterans in the Telemachy serve a function similar to the tales of the father. They refer to epics that probably circulated in archaic Greece around the same time as the *Odyssey*, and which were later captured in writing, although they are now only known to us in summary, through the writings of Neoplatonist Proclus from the seventh century CE. Embedded in the Telemachy, the short versions of the *Nostoi* create an overview that captures the audience's imagination. Like today's readers, the audiences of the ancient bards would have been aware of the plot of the *Odyssey* without necessarily remembering all the details. Moreover, different versions of the *Odyssey* are likely to have circulated before a Homeric canon of adventures, and finally the text that has come down to us, emerged. The fates of Nestor, Ajax, Agamemnon and Menelaus provide possible scenarios for Odysseus's adventures, so that audiences eagerly anticipate them.[7]

Indeed, these homecoming stories do include motifs that recur in the Apologoi. This is most clearly seen in Menelaus's account of his own return.[8] Like Odysseus, Menelaus travelled the Mediterranean world for many years. His statement that 'much did I suffer and wandered much' (4.81) refers back to the Proem, in which Odysseus is introduced as a man 'who was driven / far journeys' (1.1–2) and who suffered many pains 'in his spirit on the wide sea' (1.4). While Menelaus was stranded on the island of Pharos, Odysseus is held on Ogygia. The absence of winds which prevents Menelaus from leaving Pharos is

6. See Krischer (1988).

7. Klingner (1964): 77–79.

8. Rutherford (1985).

reminiscent of the situation experienced by Odysseus and his companions on Thrinacia. Eventually, Menelaus receives help from Eidothea, who reveals to him how he could induce her father, the old sea god Proteus, to enable his return. Eidothea thus plays a role similar to that of Circe, who supports Odysseus's return by sending him to Teiresias in the underworld.

Similarly, the other homecoming stories contain elements that are encountered again when Odysseus recounts his own adventures. Ajax suffers shipwreck; Agamemnon faces a hostile reception at home. Unlike them, however, Odysseus ultimately succeeds in his nostos (homecoming); like Menelaus, he returns. But before that happens, he experiences spectacular adventures, advances to even more remote regions and braves even greater dangers. Homer has Nestor and Menelaus recount the fates of the other Trojan fighters so that Odysseus can surpass them. And the glamour reflects on the narrator—just as Odysseus's adventures outshine the experiences of the other Greek warriors, Homer's epic outshines the other homecoming narratives.

The skill with which Homer sketches other stories as foils for the plot of the *Odyssey* is especially remarkable in the story of Atreus, which is also repeatedly alluded to after the Telemachy. The fate of Agamemnon, who is murdered by his wife Clytemnestra and her lover Aegisthus upon his return home and thereafter avenged by his son Orestes, is mentioned from different points of view. At the beginning of the *Odyssey*, Zeus makes a connection between Aegisthus, who pays for the sacrilege with his life, and the suitors, whom Odysseus will ultimately punish. In the further course of the Telemachy, Athena, variously disguised as Mentes and/or Mentor, Nestor or Menelaus, holds up Orestes's revenge as an example for Telemachus. During Odysseus's visit to the underworld as well as in the short underworld scene in the final book, Odysseus's fate is compared to that of Agamemnon. Particular emphasis is placed on the juxtaposition between the virtuous Penelope and the unfaithful Clytemnestra. The fact that the same story acquires different nuances when retold does not necessarily suggest that the *Odyssey* arose from different traditions, or even that it had multiple authors; rather, these variations arise from the manifold functions of the story: as a mirror for Odysseus and the suitors; as an example for Telemachus; as a foil for Penelope.[9]

This brief overview has demonstrated how important the Telemachy is to the structure of the *Odyssey*. The plot begins and ends on Ithaca and Odysseus's wanderings therefore take place within a given geographical frame. Further, the Telemachy forms the backdrop against which Odysseus's nostos gains focus. Like the tales of the conquest of Troy, the homecoming stories enable the audience to see Odysseus's suffering and wanderings in a new light. And finally, Odysseus's adventures surpass the experiences of other heroes, while the *Odyssey* surpasses the other epics. Moreover, the hero's delayed return alongside the escalating situation on Ithaca creates suspense. It is a type of suspense that has less to do with the ending than with the way it is achieved: a characteristic feature of ancient narratives. Like tragedy, or the novel, the epic mitigates the open-endedness that we experience in our lives, while still offering an experience of the tension between expectation and experience. Even if it were possible to remove the Telemachy from the *Odyssey*, the truncated Homeric poem would lose its force and depth.

The Fame of Odysseus

From the very beginning of the *Odyssey*, the audience's attention is directed at various narratives, since Odysseus first appears in the form of stories that are told about him, rather than directly. These stories take different forms. They are either told briefly and artlessly or recited with finesse at a banquet; at other times they are even the subject of a song. In each case, they portray scenes that not only create images of Odysseus, but also point to the effect of storytelling. Stories can enchant, yet the reactions they elicit can vary significantly from recipient to recipient. They can disturb, distract, or may even have a cathartic effect. But aside from the different ways in which they are received, the narratives

9. See D'Arms and Hulley (1946); Hölscher (1967a). Zeus: *Od.* 1.35–43; Athena as Mentes: 1.298–302, as Mentor: 3.232–35; Nestor: 3.193–200 and 3.254–316; Menelaus: 4.91–92; 4.512–49 (Proteus); 11.409–56; 24.95–97; 191–202. See also Odysseus at 13.383–85.

that are embedded in the Telemachy also emphasize the role of the narrator who shapes the material and thus pursues specific interests. A closer look at Athena's account and the song of Phemius in the first book, and Menelaus's lament as well as the Trojan anecdotes in the fourth book, will help to illuminate this point.

Mentes/Athena's Account

Telemachus first receives news of his father from Athena, who approaches him disguised as Mentes, an old friend of Odysseus. Mentes tells Telemachus that Odysseus is being held on a desert island by 'savage men'. But, as he goes on to prophesy, it won't be long before Odysseus returns, thanks to his ingenuity (1.196–205). Athena's information is only partially correct—Odysseus is indeed being held captive, but not by 'savage men'—it is Calypso who is holding him prisoner, as the narrator pronounces after the Proem, the introduction to the epic. The false statement emphasizes the human incognito Athena is using, while her mixture of fact and fiction anticipates a narrative principle that is developed more fully in the second part of the *Odyssey*—Odysseus's tall tales. The dramatic irony which arises from the disparity between the audience's and character's awareness is emphasized when the goddess says, 'the immortals / put it into my mind' (1.200–201).

Similarly to Menelaus (4.341–6; 17.132–7), Mentes imagines what Odysseus's revenge will be like when he recalls earlier events:

I wish he could come now to stand in the outer doorway
of his house, wearing a helmet and carrying shield and two spears,
the way he was the first time that ever I saw him
in our own house, drinking his wine and taking his pleasure,
coming in from Ephyre and from Ilos son of Mermerus.
Odysseus, you see, had gone there also in his swift ship
in search of a poison to kill men, so he might have it
to smear on his bronze-headed arrows, but Ilos would not
give him any, since he feared the gods who endure forever.
But my father did give it to him, so terribly did he love him.

I wish that such an Odysseus would come now among the suitors.
They all would find death was quick, and marriage a painful
    matter (1.255–66).

Despite its brevity, this vignette is multilayered. Helmet, shield and spears suggest a heroic appearance. But in Mentes's view, Odysseus appears as an archer,[10] and in the Homeric epic the bow is less heroic than other weapons, since it involves killing the enemy from a safe distance. Additionally, Odysseus is obviously seeking the poison against the will of the gods; he does not seem to shy away from using questionable means in battle. A scholiast notes that the poison later aids his revenge on the suitors (EQV ad 1.261). Even though poisoned arrows are not mentioned in the Mnesterophony (Murder of the Suitors), this initial anecdote about Odysseus foreshadows the eventual trial by bow and arrow, and execution of the first suitors. It prepares the audience for the fact that upon his return, Odysseus will have recourse not only to violence (*biē*) but also to cunning (*mētis*) and that in the process he will push at the limits of the heroic code of honour.

The Song of Phemius[11]

Telemachus's conversation with Athena alias Mentes is followed by a scene in which Odysseus is not mentioned directly. The song of a bard makes Penelope think of her husband and prompts Telemachus to talk about poetry. In the megaron, or great hall, a singer significantly called Phemius (Speaker) recites 'the homeward voyage of the Achaians' for the suitors; the 'bitter homecoming from Troy, / which Pallas Athena had inflicted on them' (1.326–27). Penelope, attended by two servants, leaves her room in tears and asks Phemius to sing of other actions of mortals and gods instead (1.337–38). The return of the Greeks makes her think of Odysseus and causes her great sorrow. But Telemachus intervenes at this point; he scolds his mother and tells her to go to her

10. See Dirlmeier (1966).

11. For a different interpretation of the scene, see Pucci (1987): 195–208, who contrasts Penelope, a 'sober reader', with Telemachus, an 'intoxicated reader'.

chamber and take care of her spinning work there. The role of this intervention in the development of Telemachus will be explored further later; the focus here is on what Phemius's song and the audience's reaction reveal about poetry and its effects.

The suitors, otherwise restless and boisterous, sit listening in silence (1.325–26). Similar to the Phaiacians later on (11.333; 13.1), they are entirely under the spell of the song as they listen to the account of Odysseus. A subtle irony becomes apparent in the first book: while the suitors hear with fascination how Athena had made the return journey difficult for the various Greek warriors, the goddess has just begun to prepare Odysseus's ultimate return—and revenge on them.

Two concepts lucidly describe the power of narrative.[12] Penelope refers to songs as 'enchantments' (*thelkteria*). In its literal sense, the Greek verb *thelgein* and the nouns derived from it denote the enchantment by which the gods change people's shape. *Thelgein* is used, for instance, when Circe transforms Odysseus's companions into pigs, wolves and lions (10.213; 291; 318). In its figurative sense it refers to the enchanting effect of songs and simple narration. Listeners who are drawn into the world of a narrator's story are indeed enchanted! They are as if bewitched, removed from their immediate environment. In other passages, too, Homer speaks of narrative enchantment. Eumaios, for instance, claims that Odysseus had 'enchanted' him with his stories and would do the same thing to Penelope (17.514; 521). In the song of the Sirens, which 'enchants' anyone who hears it (12.40; 44), the literal and figurative meanings merge. The Sirens' song doesn't just effect a temporary transformation—those who hear it forget their real intent altogether and are soon added to the skeletons which line the shores of the Sirens' island.

A second Greek word which encapsulates the power of narrative to transfix is *terpein*. Telemachus asks his mother, 'Why, my mother, do you begrudge this excellent singer / his pleasing [*terpein*] himself as the thought drives him' (1.346–47) The Homeric heroes revel not only in physical pleasures, such as a meal or sexual intercourse; *terpsis* also

12. On the terms *thelgein* and *terpein*, see Macleod (1983): 6–7; Halliwell (2011): 45–49.

refers to the sense of rapture evoked by song and tales. The singer Phemius is also referred to as the son of Terpias (22.330): even in the patronymic, the effect of the song is unmistakable. That *terpein* refers to a particularly profound form of commitment more than mere entertainment is made clear in the fact that it also applies to heroes' lamentations. In the underworld, Odysseus calls upon the shade of his mother: 'Mother, why will you not wait for me, when I am trying / to hold you, so that even in Hades' with our arms embracing / we can both take the satisfaction of dismal mourning [*tetarpomestha*]?' (11.210–12). Solace is also to the fore when Telemachus attests that Menelaus's testimony gives him 'such strange pleasure' (*ainos*) (4.597–98). *Ainos* is a term which Homer associates above all with fear. Narrative can captivate the heroes as only magic or horror would otherwise be able to do.

The *Odyssey* therefore emphasizes an aspect that has long been neglected by literary scholars. Even today, narratives can take hold of us, whether we are immersed in the world of a novel or weeping with emotion in the cinema. The tenets of critical theory and post-structuralism have meant that the enchantment which narratives produce has received little attention. It is only in recent years that literary scholars have responded to impulses from phenomenology and the cognitive sciences and have turned their attention to the experiential aspect of reading. Reception is not only intellectual, but also emotional, and even physical. Even though we do not lose the awareness that we are dealing with imaginative representation, we are eager to see a plot unfold, suffer with the characters and feel the resonance of their movements and actions. At a later juncture, there will be occasion to consider reading as an experience of 'as if', of the balance between absorption and reflection. What is of interest at this point is that Homer can stimulate debate in contemporary literary studies: Penelope's tears and the reactions of the heroes to song and story are an impressive ancient affirmation of the power of narrative.[13]

Penelope's reaction differs greatly from the attitude of the suitors. What has silenced them brings tears to her eyes. And while Phemius

---

13. On the experiential nature of reading, see for instance Caracciolo (2014); Cave (2016). See Grethlein (2015d); (2017) on the role that ancient texts can play in this debate.

recommences his recital after Telemachus's scolding, and the suitors once more turn 'to the dance and the delightful / song' (1.420–21), Penelope cries herself to sleep. The reason for her strong reaction is revealed in her own words—the homecoming of the Greek warriors reminds her that her own husband did not return. For Penelope, not only is the return of the Greeks a sad topic for a song, but the song is itself sad for her as well (1.327; 340–41). Her reaction shows that the effect of a story depends on the recipient's relationship to the protagonists.

Aristotle's *Poetics* offers a key to this.[14] According to him, successful tragedies (and epics) bring about catharsis by arousing compassion as well as fear in the audience. Leaving aside the difficult question of the meaning of 'catharsis' in Aristotle, what is important in the given context is the observation that both empathy and fear are involved. Alongside the perceived blamelessness of the sufferer, it is the balance of resonance, or proximity on the one hand, and distance on the other that are required for the audience to feel with the characters. If the audience feel alienated from characters, they do not experience empathy, and neither do they care about the action. If, however, they feel too close to a character, they suffer personally, rather than only suffering with that character. Accordingly, a little self-centred fear must accompany their empathy. At the same time, the listener must not feel either too close or too similar to a suffering character; otherwise their fear may exceed their empathy, which depends on maintaining a degree of distance.

An anecdote handed down by Herodotus illustrates this reception aesthetic (6.21). When, at the end of the 490s, Phrynichus brought his play *Capture of Miletus* to the stage of the Dionysus Theatre, 'the whole audience at the theatre burst into tears and fined Phynichus a thousand drachmas for reminding them of a calamity that was their very own; they also forbade any future projection of the play'.[15] Herodotus's anecdote is problematic since tragedies were not performed more than once until the second half of the fifth century. Historical or otherwise, however, it does read like a fitting exemplar of Aristotle's theory: the Athenians were

14. See Grethlein (2003): 41–47.
15. Rosenbloom (1993).

unable to sympathize with the characters because the play reminded them both of the failure of the Ionian uprising, which they had supported a few years previously, and of the continuing danger of a Persian invasion of their own country. Their fear and pain were intensified because the distance required for empathy to be experienced was lacking, so that the reception of tragedy was unsuccessful in this instance.

Penelope suffers similarly in the first book of the *Odyssey*. When she hears the homecoming stories, they are too close to her, and merely remind her of her missing husband. Rather than sparking empathy, the song makes Penelope herself suffer. The balance between empathy and fear is disturbed; her consternation takes the upper hand. It is a different story with the suitors; they are not close to Odysseus and even profit from his absence. Accordingly, they enjoy Phemius's song—the fates of the Greek fighters touch the suitors without affecting their own lives. Phemius's performance not only highlights the power which Homer ascribes to narrative, not least to his own; it also shows how an audience's reaction depends on the relationship of the listener to the characters. If a character's suffering affects the listener too closely, the aesthetic distance is removed and the vicissitudes of their own life surface, preventing any enjoyable reception of the narrated life.

Although Telemachus's response to Penelope is problematic, it does deepen and expand on this reflection on narrative. When he counters that it was Zeus rather than the singer who was responsible for the suffering, he confuses two aspects: the choice of song, which Penelope complains of, and who was responsible for the narrated suffering— while his attribution of responsibility to Zeus is itself questionable. At the beginning of the *Odyssey*, Zeus complains that people were too ready to blame the gods for their sufferings, when these were often a punishment for their own transgressions (1.32–34). Athena's anger at the Trojan fighters seems to be one such case. In the *Odyssey*, the reason for the hazardous return journeys is only alluded to (4.502; 5.108–9),[16] but another epic, the *Iliupersis*, or *The Destruction of Troy*, recounts in

16. Strauss Clay (1983): 133–85 offers an interpretation of the *Odyssey* in which Athena's anger is central.

detail the outrage perpetrated by Ajax the Lesser, who attempts to rape Cassandra in the temple of Athena. The responsibility for the Greeks' suffering, which Telemachus ascribes to Zeus, therefore evidently lies with the Greeks themselves.

Telemachus justifies Phemius's choice of theme further when he says, 'people, surely, always give more applause to that song / which is the latest to circulate among the listeners' (1.351–52).[17] It is not clear whether the newness here refers to the song itself, or to the narrated events—are the songs that broadcast the latest events popular, or is the preference for newly composed songs, whatever the content? In the case of Phemius's song, both seem to be the case. The *Nostoi* deal with recent years, and even if the songs of Phemius are not entirely new—Penelope complains of a 'sad / song which always afflicts the dear heart deep inside me' (1.341–42)—she is not likely to have heard it as often as the older songs.

Telemachus's comment may also be applied to the *Odyssey* itself. The *Odyssey* refers to more recent events than the *Nostoi*, let alone the *Iliad*. Odysseus recounts his adventures in the Apologoi himself, since they are still too fresh to have been sung about by the bards. The *Odyssey* presents events as having just occurred, and it is generally regarded as the more recent of the two Homeric epics. With the poetological maxim of the new, Telemachus seems to be preparing a brilliant stage for the *Odyssey*. Yet the subject of topicality can also be applied to Homer. Like the *Iliad*, the *Odyssey* is, after all, set in a distant heroic past from which no bridge leads to the present. Events which the Phaiakians are said to perceive as the latest news were already familiar to the audiences of the *Odyssey*. So, if the maxim concerns the newness of the poem, rather than the topicality of action, then time is inevitably against the *Odyssey*. The *Odyssey* may praise the new against the *Nostoi* and the *Iliad* within its own plot, but from the audience's standpoint, the value of the *Odyssey* is itself called into question where the novelty of the poem is concerned.

Perhaps even more remarkable, though less documented by Homer interpreters, is Telemachus's instruction on how Penelope should view the homecoming stories. He suggests that they can offer her consolation

17. See Biles (2003): 196–97.

because they show that others, too, have perished (1.353–55). One commentator refers to a 'Homeric cliché' in this case,[18] but however topical the consolatory effect of the suffering of others may be, its use in the context of the aesthetics of reception, as encapsulated by Phemius's performance, is incisive. The opposing reactions of Penelope and the suitors demonstrate how much the perspective of the audience contributes to the effects a narrative has, while Telemachus's instruction suggests that the same person might also react in different ways: instead of giving way to grief, Penelope might derive some comfort from the sufferings of the other Greek warriors. She is supposed to compare their fate to that of Odysseus, and this should not only remind her of her own suffering, but also help to put it into perspective.

Telemachus's words may even be intended to suggest that, by presenting the tribulations of Odysseus, the *Odyssey* can console audiences about their own misfortunes. At any rate, the poetological significance of the consolatory topos, as introduced by Telemachus, also appears in later texts. In a fragment from the comedy *Dionysiazousai*, Timocles, an author from the fourth century BCE., has a protagonist promote the *raison d'être* of tragedy (fr. 1 KA):

> Man is by nature burdened with toil, and life brings many afflictions in and of itself. However, the soul has found the following distraction from worry: the spirit, having forgotten its own sorrows by being occupied with the sorrows of others, returns with joy and, at the same time, instructed. So, consider first how tragedies profit everyone. For he who is poor, once he has learned that Telephus is even more miserable than he, endures his poverty more easily.

Greek historians also referred to the topos. For example, in his pragmatic proem, Polybius describes 'the memory of the upheavals to which others are subjected' as 'the most impressive and only means of learning how to bear the blows of fate in a noble way' (1.1.2).

18. De Jong (2001): 37, ad 345–59. For an interpretation which refutes that Telemachus presents Phemius's song to Penelope as comforting, see Lloyd (1987): 85–86. For a differentiated account of the various reactions to Phemius's song, see also Peponi (2012): 37–38.

The appearance of Phemius early on in the *Odyssey* demonstrates the powerful effect of narrative on the audience and at the same time, differentiates it in a remarkable way, to show that the audience is not simply exposed to it but can react to its contents in different ways. Homer emphasizes the rapturous effects of narration without denying the listeners their individuality and freedom. While the impact of narratives is extraordinary, it does not happen independently of the recipient.

Menelaus's Lament

Homer orchestrates the homecoming stories told in the Telemachy with great skill. He summarizes the song of Phemius in a single verse and thereafter has Nestor and Menelaus tell the fates of the Greek warriors in the third and fourth books. The stories are distributed with narrative economy—after Nestor recounts his and Diomedes's homecoming, Menelaus takes up the story of his own return at the point where he bids farewell to Nestor in Egypt. Having concluded, he omits Orestes's revenge on Aigisthus, which has already been told by Nestor, but he reports how Ajax the Lesser perished on the Gyrean rocks after boasting that he had saved himself from a storm against the against the will of the gods.

The narratives about Odysseus similarly follow a line of progression: in the song of Phemius, Odysseus is presented like a ghost. Even though he is not referred to by name, this disturbs some of the audience and he becomes the subject of conversation. Thereafter, Nestor mentions Odysseus explicitly, keeping his remarks general when he says that Odysseus and he had always been in agreement with each other. Odysseus's cunning, which Nestor only alludes to (3.120–22), is narrated in detail by Menelaus and Helen in Sparta. In the discussion that follows I will initially focus on how Menelaus laments the fate of his old comrade, and thereafter consider the narratives of Menelaus and Helen.

When Telemachus enters Sparta accompanied by Nestor's son Peisistratus, Menelaus is celebrating the weddings of two of his children. While his son Megapenthes is marrying the daughter of a Spartan, his daughter Hermione is sent to Phthia, where she is to be married to Achilles's son, Neoptolemus. The atmosphere is festive: a singer plays the phorminx, a type of lyre, and the many guests feast and dance—they are enjoying themselves. But there are darker notes beneath the cheerful ambience. By mentioning that Menelaus had already promised his daughter to Neoptolemus in Troy, Homer alludes to a war that the Homeric heroes remember only with great pain. The name of Menelaus's son resonates with this: Megapenthes means 'great sorrow'. In the Homeric epics, the son's name can reflect qualities of the father. Hector calls his son 'Scamandrius, but all of the others Astyanax [lord of the city]; / since Hector alone saved Ilion' (*Il.* 6.402–3). The name Telemachus can be understood in a similar way, since the father of the 'long-distance fighter' is himself an excellent archer, and also fights far away for twenty years.

Menelaus's grief, which is reflected in the name of his son, is evident from the very beginning of Telemachus's visit. Menelaus invites Telemachus and Peisistratus to dinner. Overwhelmed by the splendour of the palace, Telemachus whispers to Peisistratus,

> Son of Nestor, [. . .], only look at
> the gleaming of the bronze all through these echoing mansions,
> and the gleaming of gold and amber, of silver and of ivory.
> The court of Zeus on Olympus must be like this on the inside,
> such abundance of everything. Wonder takes me as I look on it
>   (4.71–75).

The brother of the leader of the Greeks at Troy possesses riches that make the property of Odysseus, who after all is himself the ruler of an island, seem paltry by comparison. And yet Menelaus laments when he hears Telemachus's remark. On his eight-year journey from Troy to Sparta, he had collected goods from Cyprus, Phoenicia, Ethiopia and Egypt, but in the meantime his brother Agamemnon had been murdered through the treachery of his wife, Clytemnestra. He would give two-thirds of his possessions to see the comrades who died before Troy alive. Above all, the fate of Odysseus, who suffered more than all the others, pains him—who knew if he was still alive? Laertes, Penelope and Telemachus were mourning him on Ithaca!

The lament over Odysseus brings tears to Telemachus's eyes. He covers his face with his robe, but Menelaus notices his agitation. Before

FIG. 5. Jean-Jacques Lagrenée (1739–1831), *Helen Recognizing Telemachus, Son of Odysseus*, 1795, oil on panel, 48 × 64 cm, Hermitage Museum, St. Petersburg. Photo: Leonard Kheifets. © The State Hermitage Museum.

Menelaus can ask his guest whether he is Odysseus's son, as he now suspects, Helen arrives 'looking like Artemis of the golden distaff' (4.122). She immediately recognizes Telemachus by his resemblance to Odysseus, which Menelaus also sees. Peisistratus introduces his companion and himself in all formality. Knowing he has Odysseus's son before him causes Menelaus to lament again. He does not articulate his grief over Odysseus's disappearance by reminiscing, but by outlining a counterfactual scenario. Had Odysseus returned he would have given him a city in Argos and resettled him along with his family and subjects. Menelaus and Odysseus would have enjoyed each other's company until their deaths. The hypothetical tale emphasizes his pain more than reminiscing would have done, since it makes the loss explicit: 'All this must be what the very god himself begrudged him, / who made only him an unhappy man, without a homecoming' (4.181–82).

Now everyone is crying—Menelaus, Helen, Peisistratus and Telemachus. Peisistratus asks them to stop talking about Odysseus, because 'for my part / I have no joy in tears after dinnertime' (4.193–94). Menelaus praises Peisistratus's sensibility, in which he takes after his father Nestor, and suggests that they return to their meal. The next day, he wishes to talk further with Telemachus. The situation is not dissimilar to the song of Phemius—while Menelaus's wistful scenario is not an epic song, both scenes introduce a subject that is disturbing to those present, so that they can no longer 'relish' it and ask for respite. Doesn't Telemachus's strong reaction to Menelaus's words contradict his earlier admonishment of Penelope? At first glance, it may seem that Telemachus does not live up to the demands he makes on others. However, his situation is not the same as that of his mother in the first book. The strategy suggested to Penelope—to use the suffering of others to relativize her own—does not apply here, since it is not the experience of strangers, but the reason for Telemachus's own suffering, that is the focus.

But the scene does shed new light on Penelope's consternation and Telemachus's admonition in the first book. It is Peisistratus, rather than Telemachus who asks Menelaus to speak no more of Odysseus. Homer introduces his request:

> Nor did Nestor's son, Peisistratus, have eyes altogether tearless,
> for he was thinking in his heart of stately Antilochus,
> one whom the glorious son of the shining Dawn had cut down.
> It was of him he thought as he addressed them in winged words.
> (4.186–89)

Peisistratus recalls Penelope's reaction. The suffering of another reminds him of his own—in this case, not of the disappearance of a husband, but the death of a brother. Like Penelope, he asks the speaker to stop, but while Penelope was harshly rebuked by Telemachus, Menelaus praises Peisistratus's sensibility. Apparently, the account of other people's experiences reawakens one's own suffering in an involuntary way, so that the idea that it may serve to put one's own pain in perspective, as imagined by Telemachus, is not entirely realistic.

Elsewhere in the Homeric epics, too, lamenting other people's misery evokes personal suffering. In the *Iliad*, Briseis speaks of the death of Patroclus, 'lamenting, and the women sorrowed around her / grieving openly for Patroclus, but for her own sorrows / each' (19.301–3). And as Achilles mourned, 'the elders lamented around him / remembering each those he had left behind in his own halls' (19.338–39). The lament that has both a shared and an individual aspect fulfils an important function at the end of the *Iliad*, when it leads Achilles to hand over the body of Priam's son to him. Priam succeeds in arousing Achilles's pity by comparing himself to the latter's father:

> So he spoke, and stirred in the other a passion of grieving
> for his own father. He took the old man's hand and pushed him
> gently away, and the two remembered, as Priam sat huddled
> at the feet of Achilles and wept close for manslaughtering Hector
> and Achilles wept now for his own father, now again
> for Patroclus. The sound of their mourning moved in the house.
>   (24.507–12)

The shared grief helps to release the tension of the epic plot and allows the *Iliad* to end on a calm note.[19]

The tears of Menelaus, Helen, Peisistratus and Telemachus show the powerful effect of narratives once more, even when it takes the form of a hypothetical sketch. It is not *terpsis*, however, but pain evoked by the memory of Odysseus. As the two Spartans and Telemachus lament Odysseus, Peisistratus's pain is directed at his own suffering, which the story of Odysseus has aroused in him. The distance which, according to Aristotle, is required for an audience to feel empathy proves to be very fragile. Even if the characters are strangers to the listener, their fates can recall similar experiences from their own lives. Homer therefore emphasizes the role of the recipient repeatedly. The perspective on the narrated action is crucial to whether it can be 'relished'. Similarly to Penelope's experience, Peisistratus's tears demonstrate the risk that the reality of the listener's life may break through and remove the required aesthetic distance.

19. See Grethlein (2006): 291–302.

Helen's Drug: Odysseus in Troy

Once Menelaus complies with Peisistratus's request and suggests that they all return to their meal, the evening takes an unexpected turn. Helen mixes a drug into the wine that causes forgetfulness of personal suffering and continues with the story. She tells how Odysseus, dressed in rags, once sneaked into Troy. She alone had recognized his disguise and had washed, anointed and clothed him. Thanks to her promise not to reveal his espionage to the Trojans until he was safely back in the Greek camp, Odysseus was able to kill many Trojans and gain important information. The Trojan women wept bitterly and only Helen rejoiced, since she regretted her flight from Sparta and wished to be reunited with Menelaus. Menelaus praises his wife's story but he then tells his own anecdote from the Trojan War. When the Greeks had smuggled themselves into Troy concealed in the wooden horse, Helen and Deiphobus approached the deceptive votive gift. She ran around the horse three times, imitating the voices of the Greek women in an effort to uncover the ambush. Odysseus, however, saved the Greeks by holding them back. One of them, Anticlus, had been intent on responding to Helen's entreaty so that Odysseus even had to cover his mouth with his hand by force.

Both stories narrate how Odysseus invades Troy. Menelaus's narrative follows Helen's and illustrates the same virtues in Odysseus: cunning, prudence, cold-bloodedness. But the stories are purposely juxtaposed; above all, they create contrasting images of Helen.[20] In her own anecdote, Helen recognizes Odysseus; in the second, Odysseus recognizes Helen. While Helen claims that she had sided with the Greeks, Menelaus sees her, perhaps under the influence of a daimon, as having been anxious 'to grant glory to the Trojans' (4.275). Helen's claim that she had longed to be back with Menelaus is belied by her relationship with Deiphobus, her third husband, whom she had married after Paris's death. Even though Menelaus attests to his wife that she has 'spoken aptly', his story is intended to correct her self-portrayal. He juxtaposes the

20. For a comparison of the two speeches, see Andersen (1977); Bergren (1981); Olson (1989b).

repentant Helen, who supported the Greek struggle from Troy, with the woman who for the second time married a Trojan, and who tried to bring destruction to the Greeks.

It has been rightly pointed out that these contradictions point to tensions existing in the royal house of Sparta.[21] However splendid the palace and wedding, the marriage between Helen and Menelaus does not seem harmonious, even after their return from Troy. For the present purpose, another observation is of greater interest, however. While the song of Phemius mainly serves to show how a narrative may be received, the anecdotes about Odysseus in Troy invite reflection on the narrator. The juxtaposition shows the extent to which a narrator's perspective and interests may shape a story—and may even distort history. Menelaus's contrasting position can either be seen to demonstrate that Helen uses her narrative talent to exonerate herself, or that Menelaus instrumentalizes his comrade's heroic deed to gain an advantage in a marriage that has become an ongoing crisis. Be that as it may, anyone who reads the couple's accounts attentively will approach other narrators in the *Odyssey* with caution, asking how their stories may be perspectivized and what strategic goals may guide them.

The narrator of the epic himself may be subject to the same distrust. Helen begins her narrative with a *recusatio*—'I could not tell you all the number nor could I name them, / all that make up the exploits of enduring Odysseus' (4.240–41), which echoes the invocation to the Muses in the ship's catalogue of the *Iliad*: 'I could not tell over the multitude of them nor name them, / not if I had ten tongues and ten mouths, not if I had / a voice never to be broken and a heart of bronze within me' (*Il.* 2.488–90).[22] Although, unlike Helen, the narrator of the *Iliad* invokes the Muses, both utterances are subject to the limits of their own narration. Further, Helen's imitation of the voices in front of the wooden horse reminds one of the Delian girls in the 'Homeric Hymn to Apollo' (1.162–64): 'They know how to impersonate all men's voices and all their / musical vocalizations, and each would imagine himself as /

21. See Schmiel (1972).
22. Ford (1992): 72–74.

sounding the words—so suited to them is their beautiful singing'.[23] When following these associations, the uncertainty regarding Helen's narrative art is quickly transferred to the epic narrator as well.

Helen's and Menelaus's speeches are not just designed as a pair that is relevant only to a given context; they also resonate with the plot that unfolds thereafter. They take up important elements in the *Odyssey* and allow them to appear in a new light in another event. Later on in the narrative, Odysseus's disguise as a beggar allows him to return to his court undetected. Like Helen, his nurse Eurycleia recognizes him, while she is washing him. Odysseus must forcibly stop Eurycleia from announcing her discovery, which is mirrored in the anecdote of Odysseus hushing Anticlus. This resonance underlines the similarity of the names, both of which contain the word *kleos* (fame)—appropriately, since both episodes are about Odysseus retaining his fame. At the same time, the interrogation Helen subjects Odysseus to mirrors the conversation between Odysseus and Penelope in the nineteenth book. Here as elsewhere, Helen serves as a foil for Penelope, who, though no less cunning, is faithful.

The Trojan anecdotes generally manifest a tension that is fundamental to the *Odyssey*: that between reality and appearance, truth and deception, between the inner and outer situation. It is not only Odysseus who pretends to be someone else; Helen, too, assumes a disguise, albeit phonically rather than visually. What looks like a colossal votive gift turns out to be an ambush; the wooden horse conceals a troop of Greek warriors. Time and again, discrepancies between appearance and reality are encountered in the *Odyssey*. Helen's attempt to lure the Greeks out of the horse by mimicking the voices of their wives is reminiscent of the Sirens, who strive to entice Odysseus to their shores. Their song is beautiful, but ruinous. His dog Argos, the only one to recognize Odysseus at first sight, is neglected despite being an excellent hunting dog. Odysseus's appearance suffers on his long voyage; nevertheless, he outshines the Phaiakians in their athletic contests. The beggar Iros, on the other hand, looks strong, yet proves weak in a duel with Odysseus.

23. Translation by Rodney Merrill: see Merrill (2011).

The tension between appearance and reality is also present in Helen's narrative. The drug she mixes with the wine causes feelings of sadness to be replaced by pleasure. One modern interpreter diagnoses Helen as a 'drug addict', this being 'the only way [. . .] to be able to go on living after so many experiences and so much guilt'.[24] Historical research has been concerned with whether the Egyptians mixed opium with wine, or whether another intoxicant, such as black henbane, was used. The allegorical interpretation of ancient Homeric exegeses, however, is of greater interest. Allegorical interpretations of the Homeric epics have been popular since ancient times; the interpretation of Helen's *pharmacon* as a symbol of the power of narrative and of the word, however, has only been documented since the Imperial era.

For the polymath Plutarch (c. 45–125 CE), author of an extensive series of biographies as well as numerous philosophical and scientific writings, Helen's drug symbolizes rhetoric which relies on gentle persuasion rather than on confrontation. Plutarch cites Plato's *Symposium* as an example for this (*Quaest. conv.* 614c). Some 250 years later, in the fourth century CE, the sophist Himerius declares the *pharmacon* to be an enigma (*ainigma*), which conceals 'sweet and all-wise speech, which, like a drug, is able to extinguish emotions that swell up from the depths of the heart' (*Or.* 16.1–2).[25] The Neoplatonic philosopher Macrobius, writing in the fifth century CE, refers to the Homeric Helen as part of his discussion about whether it is right to speak while eating. He is in favour, because the wonderful effect of her drug showed the power of language, which could contribute to *emendatio*, the improvement of the listener, even during a meal.

Allegorical interpretations were popular in past epochs right up to the Baroque period, but today they seem mostly alienating. Why should the real content of the Homeric epics be the cosmos? It may amuse us to read that Dionysus was identified with the spleen, but such an interpretation seems as implausible as equating Agamemnon, Achilles and

24. Kullmann (1992): 287.
25. Translation by Robert J. Penella: see Penella (2007): 77.

Helen respectively with ether, the sun and the earth.[26] The allegorical interpretation of Helen's drug, however, deserves at least to be considered. Helen uses the *pharmacon* not simply to cheer up the party, but to give those present the ability to be receptive to the narratives. Homer, therefore, closely associates the drug with storytelling. As it is introduced as a way of ensuring the listener's receptivity, Helen's *pharmacon* can be seen as a symbol of the enchanting power of stories.

The Byzantine commentator Eustathius (1493.10–15) asserts that the change of mood was achieved by altering the narrative theme: rather than focusing on Odysseus's disappearance, Helen and Menelaus turn to stories that present him as a successful trickster, and these tales distract the listeners from what causes them pain. According to this interpretation, Helen's *pharmacon* symbolizes the storyteller's ability to take their audience, if only temporarily, out of their own world and to transport them into another: narrative as the Homeric heroes' opium!

Another interpretation is also feasible. Helen and Menelaus are not narrating something random to please the listeners—their stories still relate to the man whose fate causes them grief. Helen's drug can therefore be interpreted as an allegory for the cathartic function of narration. Through narrative, we give shape to personal experience, and this can make it easier to come to terms with events that may have thwarted expectations or disappointed hopes. Odysseus's fate pains the people gathered in Sparta, but by talking about him they alleviate their pain. Storytelling can therefore serve the inner process of assimilation more than serving the purpose of distraction. When seen in this light, Helen's *pharmacon* expresses something of the potential healing power of storytelling.

Other passages in the *Odyssey* corroborate this interpretation of narrative function. We have already seen that Homeric heroes can 'relish' a lament. The clearest formulation of the cathartic function of narrative is probably seen in the swineherd Eumaeus, who entertains the as yet unrecognized Odysseus:

But we two, sitting here in the shelter, eating and drinking,
shall entertain each other remembering and retelling

26. See a papyrus fragment from Philodemus, *On Poems*, in Sbordone (1976): 222–25.

our sad sorrows. For afterwards a man who has suffered
much and wandered much has pleasure out of his sorrows.
   (15.398–401)

Terrible experiences not only take on a different shape in retrospect,
they are also assimilated when encountered in the form of a narrative.

The cathartic power of the *pharmacon* can hardly be emphasized
more strongly than it is by Homer in Book 4:

Whoever had drunk it down once it had been mixed in the
   wine bowl,
for the day that he drank it would have no tear roll down his face,
not if this mother died and his father died, not if men
murdered a brother or a beloved son in his presence
with the bronze, and he with his own eyes saw it. (4.222–26)

Helen's remedy allows the worst events, even if recently witnessed, to
be endured with equanimity. In accordance with this interpretation,
these verses can be seen to epitomize the cathartic power of narrative.
In a passage in the eighth book, which will be discussed in more detail
in the next chapter, Homer compares Odysseus's strong reaction to the
song of Demodocus of the pain of a woman who, having just become a
prisoner of war, is still clinging to her dying husband. While this parable
uses a terrible life event to demonstrate the effect that narrative can
have, in the fourth book it appears as a drug that allows the recipient to
process such experiences.

But Homer also limits the effects of narrative catharsis thereafter.
Telemachus replies to Menelaus's story of Troy,

Great Menelaus, son of Atreus, leader of the people:
so much the worse; for none of all this kept dismal destruction
from him, not even if he had a heart of iron within him.
But come, take us away to our beds, so that at last now
we can go to bed and enjoy the pleasure of sweet sleep. (4.291–95)

Telemachus's reply accords more with the interpretation of narrative as a
drug-like distraction. It takes the listener's mind off things for a while, but

the memory is all the more painful when it returns! Lasting relief does not seem possible. Telemachus calls for sleep, which will provide respite. Does this mean that sleep achieves what Helen's *pharmacon* cannot?

The various stories in the Telemachy reveal different facets of story-telling. Helen's and Menelaus's speeches draw attention to its pragmatic function. Narrators pursue specific interests and tailor their material in accordance with their intentions. The reactions of Penelope and Peisistratus demonstrate how fragile aesthetic distance is. Pleasure and respite can easily be diminished or lost when the narrative evokes personal suffering. This need not be referred to directly—the similarity of a narrated event to one's own situation suffices. On the other hand, Helen's *pharmacon*, interpreted as a symbol for narration, sets up a counterpoint to this. While a narrative may come to be overshadowed by an overwhelming personal experience, conversely, it may also act as a remedy that enables assimilation, or, at the very least, produce intoxication that can provide respite for a while.

The relationship of narrative to experience, a central theme of this book, is close, multifaceted and full of tension.[27] On the one hand, narrative derives its material from experience; on the other hand, experience only gains shape in narrative form. Narratives can be a means of assimilating experiences, but in some cases, experiences prevent such a process from taking place. At the same time, narrative can trigger experiences whose intensity is hardly inferior to those felt in real life. The stories told within the story of the *Odyssey* reveal the complex relationship between narrative and experience.

Is the Telemachy a *Bildungsroman*?

Telemachus's Development

As well as revealing different functions and effects of narrative, the first four books of the *Odyssey* raise the question whether the Telemachy effectively makes the *Odyssey* the first *Bildungsroman* (coming-of-age

27. On the interpenetration of narrative and experience, see Carr (1986); Waldenfels (2004): 50 ('Paradox of Narrative'); Koschorke (2012): 22 ('epistemological feedback').

narrative) in the history of Western literature. Most Homer interpreters see Telemachus as undergoing a process of development in the *Odyssey*:[28] at the outset he is described as a boy who spends his days dreaming of his father, and by the end he has matured into a man who assists Odysseus in purging the court of the suitors. His journey to Pylos and Sparta, which Athena prompts him to undertake, is viewed as decisive to his development—he learns about the heroic world with its conventions, hears of his father's deeds whilst there and gains a sense of orientation for his own life in the process. It is due to his experiences on the journey and the fact that it is an independent undertaking, embarked on without his mother's knowledge and against the will of the suitors, that he gains the necessary maturity to fight side by side with his father.

The leading Hellenist in the era of historicism, Ulrich von Wilamowitz-Moellendorff, resolutely opposed such an interpretation. In his characteristically apodeictic manner, he objects to the thesis that Homer wishes to show Telemachus mature into a man: 'Tracing the development of character is far removed from Hellenic poetry, and indeed from Hellenes in general.'[29] Who is right—Wilamowitz, with his contrasting assessment, or the *communis opinio*, according to which the Telemachy does serve to outline Telemachus's development? The attempt to find an answer leads us to a characteristic of ancient narratives, which has been previously alluded to when discussing how suspense works in epics. It can be argued that the treatment of suspense is, in fact, closely linked with the ancient view of personality. An initial task will be to subject the *Odyssey* to a closer examination in order to collect the findings.

Several details support the interpretation of the Telemachy as a coming-of-age narrative. Telemachus does indeed seem lost when Athena meets him, disguised as Mentes:

He sat among the suitors, his heart deep grieving within him,
imagining in his mind his great father, how he might come back

28. For example, Millar and Carmichael (1954); Clarke (1963); Murnaghan (1987): 33–38; Wöhrle (1999): 117–44.

29. Wilamowitz-Moellendorff (1927): 106.

and all throughout the house might cause the suitors to scatter,
and hold his rightful place and be lord of his own possessions.
  (1.114–17)

Without initiative or plans of his own, Telemachus fantasizes about how his father will restore order in Ithaca. Then there is his journey to the mainland—Athena tells him to go in search of his father's *kleos*, but on Mount Olympus, she had proclaimed the further aim 'that among people he [Telemachus] may win a good reputation' (1.95). Athena also cites this motif when Odysseus, after his arrival, asks her why she had not simply told him where he was (13.417–19). Telemachus's journey is unspectacular and free of heroic feats, yet through *kleos*, it achieves for him the recognition to which Homeric heroes aspire.[30] *Kleos* does not simply denote fame, but fame through the medium of epic song, and more generally, on account of being 'heard of'.[31] The heir of Odysseus makes his initial visit to the heroic world and becomes the subject of courtly conversation. Does this not fit in perfectly with a *Bildungsroman*?

The journey, likewise, provides scenes suggestive of a coming-of-age narrative. Telemachus falls silent before Nestor and asks Mentor how he should approach the venerable hero. In Sparta, the splendour of the palace overwhelms him—the new experiences obviously exceed his previous horizons. Menelaus then calls him *heros* for the first time, a form of address that seems to imply that he is a part of heroic male society. The idea that Telemachus adopts his father as a role model because of the stories told about the Trojan War is supported by the fact that, both in Pylos and in Sparta, he is compared to Odysseus. He is said to resemble him in face and stature (4.148–50) and to speak intelligently, as befits the son of Odysseus (3.124–25; 4.611). Nestor cites Orestes, a young man in a comparable situation, whose example could show Telemachus how he might prove himself worthy of his father: 'You too,

---

30. Clarke (1963): 136–37, Rose (1967), Fenik (1974): 21–28, Murnaghan (1987): 35 and Lateiner (1992): 141–42 think that Telemachus's journey mirrors Odysseus's adventures; Montiglio (2005): 10 stresses the difference between the son's purposeful journey and the father's meandering.

31. Olson (1995): 1–23.

dear friend, for I see you are tall and splendid / be brave too, so that men unborn may speak well of you' (3.199–200).

According to advocates of the thesis of the *Bildungsroman,* Telemachus's new maturity manifests itself when he meets Theoclymenos near Pylos in Book 15. The latter, a seer, has had to flee Argos, where he has slain a man, and he asks Telemachus for help. Without hesitating, Telemachus takes him on his ship to Ithaca (15.280–81). Through his journeying he has grown into the role of a householder who gives shelter to fugitives as he sees fit; the experiences of the voyage appear to have turned Telemachus into a man who is ready to take his place next to his father. All that remains is for Odysseus to return and the suitors would then 'find death was quick, and marriage a painful matter' (1.266; 4.346).

However, the first four books of the *Odyssey* don't fit the *Bildungsroman* interpretation quite as readily as this brief overview and the *communis opinio* would suggest. An unbiased reading encounters scenes and moments that call into question whether Telemachus undergoes any significant development during his voyage. He may dream of his father's return at the beginning of the *Odyssey,* but he is wide awake when Athena alias Mentes enters the court.[32] He is the first to notice the newcomer. While the suitors blithely continue their revelry, Telemachus welcomes, entertains and questions him, as befits a host. He prudently leads the guest to a corner, so that the suitors may not overhear their conversation. Telemachus therefore does not need to travel to Pylos or Sparta to learn heroic etiquette; he is familiar with the conventions of hospitality from the outset. In light of this scene, listening to Theoclymenos's request for help seems less a means of demonstrating newly attained maturity than another example of Telemachus's familiarity with the customs of his world.

But more importantly, Mentes's speech in the first book means that Telemachus experiences a decisive transformation *before* his journey, rather than during it.[33] Mentes assures him that Odysseus is still alive and will soon return to Ithaca. He instructs that Telemachus should visit

---

32. Olson (1995): 66–67.
33. See Allione (1963): 14–15.

Nestor and Menelaus and find out more about his father, taking Orestes, who earned early fame through courageous action, as his example. As Mentes flies away akin to a bird, Telemachus realises that his interlocutor had been a god. Encouraged, he is stirred to action, first at home, then in public. He rebukes Penelope for complaining about Phemius's song:

> Go therefore back in the house, and take up your own work,
> the loom and the distaff, and see to it that your handmaidens
> ply their work also; but the men must see to discussion,
> all men, but I most of all. For mine is the power in this
>   household. (1.356–59)

Not only does this show new determination, which causes Penelope astonishment; the wording is also significant. Homer has Telemachus use words similar to those of the Phaeacian king Alcinous when he says, 'the men shall see to his convoy / home, and I most of all; for mine is the power in this district' (11.352–53). And there is an even stronger parallel to the words used by Hector when he addresses his wife in the sixth book of the *Iliad*:

> Go therefore back to our house, and take up your own work,
> the loom and the distaff, and see to it that your handmaidens
> ply their work also; but the men must see to the fighting,
> all men who are the people of Ilion, but I beyond others.
>   (6.490–93)

It is not a specific allusion, but the parallels with Alcinous and Hector underline the fact that Telemachus appears as hero and landlord prior to his journey.

Moreover, in the first book, Telemachus is acting with a degree of cunning that would do credit to his father.[34] When Eurymachus asks who the stranger was, Telemachus conceals the fact that it must have been a god and states that no news is to be expected from his father, who must really have died. Not only does Telemachus hide the nature of the visit from the suitors, but he also conceals that he has received

---

34. See Austin (1969), who, however, overemphasizes Telemachus's cunning.

important news about his father. By voicing the belief that Odysseus must be dead, Telemachus ensures that the suitors do not suspect anything, so that he can pursue his plans in peace.

Telemachus's determination to act becomes even clearer in the second book, when he calls a people's assembly. In his speech he again takes note of the death of his father and deplores the doings of the suitors. He demands that they should leave his court immediately. Telemachus's intervention is unsuccessful—the suitor Antinous rejects the demand and blames Penelope for the situation. Telemachus is unable to assert himself, and yet with this speech, made before embarking on his journey to Pylos and Sparta, he takes up Odysseus's legacy, both in his own home and in public. The aged Aigyptios notes that the people's assembly had not been called since Odysseus's departure from Ithaca. That Telemachus is following in his father's footsteps is therefore made clear right from the beginning: 'he sat in his father's seat, and the elders made way before him' (2.14).

Telemachus's changed attitude at home as well as at the people's assembly contradicts the assumption that it is his journey to Pylos and Sparta, and the stories told by his hosts, which prompt his development from boy to man. Rather, Mentes's speech in the first book is decisive. It prompts Telemachus to action and causes him to insist that it should be he who determines what happens at Odysseus's court. Mentes's speech is not pedagogical in gist; it does not teach Telemachus any new norms or rules. He is already well aware that the suitors' freeloading is disgraceful and should be stopped if at all possible. What Mentes does is to arouse him from his lethargy. To speak of development in this context is not quite accurate: Telemachus does not mature, neither on Ithaca nor while sojourning. He is driven to action only once, and by a speech.

Nor can any transformation of Telemachus be deduced from the plot. When Telemachus re-enters the stage after the Apologoi, he plays a subordinate role.[35] Homer presents him as his father's helper but pays little attention to him beyond that. There is no suggestion that Telemachus

---

35. Allione (1963): 19–20; Clarke (1963): 136–37.

has changed—he neglects to lock the weapons chamber as instructed by his father and thus endangers the entire plan for revenge. He asks his father to spare Phemius and Medon, and he hangs the unfaithful maidservants. Telemachus's actions ultimately demonstrate little independence; his willingness to aid his father does not develop as the Telemachy progresses, but is the product of Athena's speech.

At the same time, the idea that the *Odyssey* shows character development should not be ignored. Homer shows Telemachus on the threshold of manhood. Instead of tracing his development in any detail, however, he provides only a snapshot. Uvo Hölscher analyses the crisis situation on Ithaca in order to capture Telemachus's peculiar temporality: 'In the Telemachy, all those moments where the character of Telemachus reveals itself happen with the youth poised between childhood and manhood.'[36] This does not run just through the Telemachy, but the entire *Odyssey*, and is made tangible in Telemachus's statement that 'before now [he] was only an infant'. The sentiment is found several times in the last third of the *Odyssey*, when Telemachus aids his father (18.229; 19.19; 20.310), but also at the beginning. Initially, there is Athena's admonition that 'you should not go on / clinging to your childhood. You are no longer of an age to do that' (1.296–97), which is quickly internalized by Telemachus when he addresses the suitors:

> Is it not enough, you suitors, that in time past you ruined
> my great and good possessions, when I was still in my
>   childhood?
> But now, when I am grown big and by listening to others
> can learn the truth, and the anger is steaming up inside me,
> I will endeavour to visit evil destructions upon you. (2.312–16)

Even before his journey he looks back on the time when he was still 'an infant'.

Telemachus's oscillating between childhood and manhood becomes poignant in the bow challenge. After the suitors have tried in vain to draw the bow, Telemachus dares to approach his father's weapon. Three times

---

36. Hölscher (1988): 54.

he tries in vain and then, 'pulling the bow for the fourth time, he would have strung it, / but Odysseus stopped him, though he was eager, making a signal / with his head' (21.128–30). Just as Telemachus almost manages to draw the bow, his heroic status remains a potentiality in the *Odyssey*: it is recognizable but not yet realized, caught in the transition from child to adult. Homer introduces Telemachus as being on the threshold between child to adult, without tracing his development in the plot.

A closer look therefore reveals that the *Odyssey* does not, in fact, outline Telemachus's development. And yet it is not surprising that the Telemachy is consistently interpreted as a coming-of-age narrative. Given Telemachus's age and the motif of journeying, Homer creates a framework which fits such a scheme. The *Bildungsroman*, shaped in Germany by Goethe's *Wilhelm Meisters Lehr- und Wanderjahre* (*Wilhelm Meister's Apprenticeship and Journeyman Years*) and Gottfried Keller's *Der grüne Heinrich* (*Green Henry*), is among the most prominent plot types in modern fiction. The development of a young person is at the centre of many important modernist novels, including Thomas Mann's *Der Zauberberg* (*The Magic Mountain*) and Marcel Proust's *À la recherche du temps perdu* (*In Search of Lost Time*), and it runs through the literature of the twentieth and twenty-first centuries right up to Christian Kracht's *Faserland* and Alessandro Baricco's *Emmaus*. It is also popular in film and can be found in screwball comedies such as *American Pie*, as well as in Rob Reiner's *Stand by Me* and Richard Linklater's *Boyhood*. The pattern of the coming-of-age novel is so familiar that it is difficult not to interpret the story of a young man who sets out in search of his father in that light.

The extent to which the character Telemachus evokes the *Bildungsroman* scheme is shown not least in François Fénelon's *Les aventures de Télémaque, fils d'Ulysse* ([1699]; *The Adventures of Telemachus, the Son of Ulysses*). Fénelon has Telemachus report on his later journeys to Egypt, Phoenicia, Cyprus and Crete, where he visits Idomeneus with Mentor, takes part in a campaign and falls in love with Antiope. Unlike Homer, Fénelon not only weaves extensive meditations on statesmanship into his narrative, but also narrates the mental processes of his hero in depth. Telemachus's maturation as a result of his experiences also serves as a model for the Dauphin, for whom Fénelon wrote his eighteen volumes while he was his tutor. *Les aventures de Télémaque* exploits a potential that is dormant in the *Odyssey*.

The confrontation of the hero's inner world with reality is a central aspect of the *Bildungsroman*, and readers of the *Odyssey* must supply this for themselves. In the classic *Bildungsroman*, the hero matures as a result of his experiences. The motif of a journey is therefore very popular—it inevitably confronts the protagonist with new worlds that serve to shape his personality. Even novels such as Flaubert's *L'éducation sentimentale* (*Sentimental Education*), which deny the protagonist any maturation, foreground the tension between the inner world and reality. Lukács's *Theory of the Novel* even postulates that the conflict between the protagonist's personal sphere and society is the essence of the genre.[37] The coming-of-age novel is characterized by the fact that the individual's reconciliation with the world comes about through the expansion of the psyche.

None of this is seen in Homer: during his visit to Pylos and Sparta, Telemachus expands his horizons, but his experiences are not reflected in his personality. He spends time with his Ithacan comrades on the ship, travels overland with his new friend Peisistratus and, above all, meets the greatest heroes of his time; but Homer does not mention the effect these experiences have on the young man. Rather, the journey bears the traits of a rite of passage: under the supervision of a *maître d'initiation*, a young man leaves the country with his peers, and after a certain period of time, he returns.[38] He achieves what he set out to do, but there is no sign of any inner change.

Narration and the Concept of Personality

The observation that Telemachus's experiences in Pylos and Sparta are not reflected in his personality should not be used to support the thesis that the Homeric hero lacks inwardness, however. In *The Discovery of the Mind: The Greek Origins of European Thought*, Bruno Snell claims that Homer did not yet have an integrated concept of a human being and

37. Lukács (1971 [1916]).
38. Moreau (1992).

merely knew separate capacities, such as *thymos* or *noos*: 'As a result there is in Homer no reflexion, no dialogue of the soul with itself.'[39] Hermann Fränkel notes in his equally influential study on the narrative and philosophy of early Greece that 'the man of the *Iliad* is entirely integrated in his world. He is not possessed of an inwardness that is at variance with an essentially different outside, but rather, experiences the whole as it contains and permeates him.'[40] Fränkel argues that the *Odyssey* is already subject to a new realism, but that subjectivity only arises with archaic lyric poetry.

The lexical method underlying such judgements is questionable.[41] Even though language undoubtedly reflects thought, it is hermeneutically unviable to infer a complete world of ideas from either the absence or the use of specific expressions. Homer may not have a word for 'soul' or 'consciousness' in the modern sense, but passages such as the beginning of the twentieth book demonstrate that Homeric heroes do have both an inner life and capacity for reflection: at night, Odysseus, still disguised as a beggar and unrecognized in his court, observes how the disloyal maidservants consort with the suitors. Homer describes the thoughts of Odysseus, who wonders whether he should put an end to the proceedings. His feelings are made vivid through a simile—his heart is growling like a dog whose cubs are threatened—and his thoughts are expressed in direct speech:

> 'Bear up, my heart. You have had worse to endure before this
> on that day when the irresistible Cyclops ate up
> my strong companions, but you endured it until intelligence
> got you out of the cave, though you expected to perish.' (20.18–21)

This passage refutes that there is no conception of an integrated personality in Homer. The reference to his heart reveals the complexity of Odysseus's inner life: torn between anger and reason, he sees himself in the light of his memories and plans.

---

39. Snell (1953 [1946]): 19.
40. Fränkel (1993): 89.
41. See, for instance, Schmitt (1990): 12–71; Gill (1996): 29–93.

The archaic understanding of the human being, therefore, cannot serve to elucidate whether or not the Telemachy is a *Bildungsroman*. Rather, the *Odyssey* adopts a different type of narration than is employed in the coming-of-age narrative, and I would argue that that type of narration is linked to the ancient view of personality. The two essential components of narrative, character and plot, are weighted differently in the ancient epic than in the modern *Bildungsroman*. While the latter tends to be especially concerned with its protagonists and their inner lives, the *Odyssey* focuses mainly on plot. In both texts, character and plot are closely interwoven, but the emphasis is different—a *Bildungsroman* shows how character is formed through the plot, while Telemachus is a character who is above all involved in the plot. Similarly, Odysseus is the hero of the epic, but it is not the processes of his consciousness that captivate the audience, so much as his adventures. Homer's attention is on the plot rather than on character.

The discussion of the phenomenon of suspense at the beginning of this chapter has shown that in the Telemachy, suspense is created with regard to the 'how' rather than the 'what', and that this is effective even when the audience knows how the *Odyssey* ends. Suspense is a fundamental form of plot design, achieved by the doubling of narrated time in narrative time—the recipient follows the temporal sequence of the plot in the temporal sequence of reading or listening. Each sign that, in a linear narrative, further unfolds the course of the plot excites the audience's expectations anew. Suspense requires neither introspection nor deviation from chronology; it arises from the sequentiality of events. The meaning of suspense in the *Odyssey*, as in ancient literature in general, indicates a type of narration that relies on plot rather than characters. It is therefore not a deficient image of the human being, but a particular narrative form that is responsible for a portrayal of Telemachus which does not correspond to the logic of the *Bildungsroman*.

Reliance on plot appears to be a characteristic of ancient narration in general. Plot is foregrounded not just in the epic, but also in the ancient novel.[42] Compared to characters in novels by George Eliot or

---

42. De Temmerman (2014) strives to demonstrate the complexity of characters in the ancient novel, but cf. Grethlein (2015a); (2015b).

Lion Feuchtwanger, even the protagonists of Achilles Tatius and Heliodorus are two-dimensional and idealized—types rather than individuals. Instead, a lot happens: the heroic couple is subject to shipwrecks, separation, enslavement and pursuit by lecherous suitors before they are reunited. The lack of interest in the inner life of the characters is manifest in an almost complete lack of a form of expression that is central to the modern novel: free indirect speech.[43] Here, the experiences of a character are communicated more or less from the grammatical perspective of the narrator: 'Anna crossed the street. Did she really have to take the train?' The second sentence represents a thought of the character, not from a first, but a third person perspective, while maintaining the past tense. In the modern novel, this blending of the perspectives of narrator and character is an important technique to achieve a subtle portrayal of subjective experiences. Of course, free indirect speech is not the only way to approximate the inner life of a character, but its absence in ancient narratives does show that subjective inner experience was not prioritized.

This is not to say that ancient literature is incapable of describing psychological processes poignantly and in depth. Tragedy offers many examples. The long soliloquy that sees Medea wrestling with herself about whether she should bear the ignominy inflicted on her by Jason or kill her own children to take revenge on him impressively demonstrates the ability of ancient authors to produce fine psychological sketches (Eur. *Med.* 1021–80). But many tragedies display more interest in external than in internal conflicts. Even reflections such as those of Medea are firmly bound up with a captivating plot. The audience is not only drawn into the disturbing world of Medea's thoughts, but also wonders how she is going to murder her children and then get away with it. Aristotle takes all this into account in his *Poetics* when he ranks the category of plot before the category of character.

It is important not to forget that plot-orientated narration is also common in contemporary fiction. Literary scholars tend to regard the nineteenth- and twentieth-century modernist novel as an ideal form.

43. See Laird (2008): 201–3 on the ancient novel; Bakker (2009): 119–22 on Greek literature in general.

But authors such as Stephen King and Ian Fleming undoubtedly have a wider readership than Henry James and Virginia Woolf. To return to the previously discussed example—the James Bond novels and films—the Bond character fascinates on the grounds not so much of his rich inner life, as his spectacular missions. *Goldfinger* and *From Russia with Love* create interest through suspense, and that suspense is focused on the 'how'. The audience wonders *how* Bond will manage to eliminate his adversaries this time—without wondering how his battles, perils and love affairs will affect his psyche. The typecast characterization found in Fleming's novels is a central feature of modern popular literature in general. It is also found in romances, medical and domestic novels, which similarly invite identification with more or less stereotypical protagonists and create suspense focused on the 'how' that leads to a foreseeable ending being achieved—whether this be the rescue of a home endangered by the building of a factory or the marriage of a confirmed bachelor to a bluestocking.

While modern popular literature is no stranger to plot-heavy narration, however, the tendency of ancient authors to prioritize plot over character seems to be rooted in a specific, ancient understanding of personality. This understanding is by no means deficient; rather, it is accentuated differently from the Cartesian subject. The difference is even evident in an ancient commentary on the Telemachy which modern interpreters like to use as a precursor for their own interpretation. The extensive work of the Neoplatonist Porphyry from the third century CE includes a discussion of various problems relating to Homer philology. One of these discussions deals with the question of why Athena sends Telemachus away on a journey just as the situation on Ithaca is coming to a head.[44] According to Porphyry, the real reason for Athena's mission is Telemachus's 'education' (*paideusis*). Only the journey is said to equip Telemachus with the necessary skills to assist his father in the Mnesterophony. As previously discussed, however, this thesis does not stand up to a closer analysis of the text. On his journey, Telemachus learns nothing that will be useful for him later; Athena's speech determines his course at the outset.

44. Porphyry, *Quaestionum homericarum ad Odysseam pertinentium reliquiae*, 1284.

Nevertheless, Porphyry's commentary does serve to illustrate the specificity of the ancient view of personality. His interpretation of the Telemachy as serving Telemachus's 'education' only anticipates the modern reading that it is a *Bildungsroman* at first glance. Porphyry argues that Telemachus, having been raised by a woman, and growing up amidst wanton suitors and wayward servants, cannot become a man. He must therefore be tested in a foreign land, where he can experience hardship and master challenging situations; this was the only way in which Telemachus could attain virtue (*arete*). This is where the difference from the modern interpretation of the Telemachy as a *Bildungsroman* lies: Porphyry's 'education' does not involve the *inner* maturation that is at the heart of modern coming-of-age narratives; rather, it entails *external* trials that lead to virtue. Such a concept of virtue is rather impersonal, and takes the place of a distinctive individuality formed in confrontation with the world.

Both the moral focus and lack of interest in subjective feeling distinguish Porphyry from modern interpreters, as shown in Christopher Gill's books and essays, which provide a nuanced discussion of the ancient understanding of personality.[45] Gill's interest in ancient literature and philosophy is not only historical; he proposes that it offers a counterpoint to modern contractions, which remains highly relevant today. Whereas in Cartesian thought personality is primarily described in terms of 'subjectivity' and from the perspective of the first person, ancient authors approached it from the outside, as an 'object', with ethical norms taking the place of subjective sensibilities. The focus of interest is general values rather than individuality, and the aim is to judge a character, more than to understand it. This view of personality is closely connected to the strong moral component seen in many genres of antiquity, including the novel, tragedy, historiography, biography and the epic.

The ancient 'objective-participatory' concept of personality creates a predisposition for plot-orientated narration. While an underlying focus on subjectivity leads to an intense preoccupation with characters and their inner lives, ethical concerns primarily come into play through

45. Gill (1990); (1996); (2006).

plot. Homer focuses more on Telemachus's role as a son than on his subjectivity. For this reason, Orestes is frequently evoked as a role model. This foil does not serve to shed light on Telemachus's particular feelings and thoughts; rather, it generalizes his obligation as a son. Telemachus is himself to serve as a role model for others in due course. It is not any individualizing reflection, but transferable action that is required for this. While Homer's use of Telemachus is by no means undifferentiated or archaic, it is clearly different from the treatment of character in a *Bildungsroman*. The figure of Telemachus could potentially be used to write a *Bildungsroman*, but the Telemachy itself is no such narrative.

As well as offering a multilayered reflection on narration, the Telemachy is a narrative that differs significantly from the modern novels that have shaped our understanding. Unlike the modernist novel, Homer focuses on plot rather than character. It is suspense rather than introspection which captivates the audience. While authors as wide-ranging as Jane Austen and Paul Auster offer an immersion in individual emotional worlds, the Homeric narrator primarily presents the audience with the question of *how* the plot will arrive at the anticipated ending, and in this the Homeric epic is strikingly similar to contemporary popular literature. The ancient tendency to prioritize plot over character, however, is not so much due to a desire to minimize complexity and entertain, as to a specific ancient understanding of personality. The view of the individual as a representative of general moral categories predisposes a plot-orientated narration. It is the interest in morality rather than in subjective feeling that makes the Homeric epic, the Greek novel and Plutarch's biographies seem strange today. Yet this strangeness also offers an opportunity to question modern ideas of narrative and personality.

3

From Listener to Narrator: Odysseus at the Phaeacian Court

ODYSSEUS FINALLY APPEARS in the fifth book and remains at the centre of the plot from then on. In a second meeting of the gods, Athena insists that Odysseus be allowed to return home to Ithaca as the gods had previously agreed. Zeus therefore sends Hermes to the island of Ogygia, where the 'lovely-haired' nymph Calypso keeps Odysseus prisoner far from human settlements. Odysseys himself has eyes neither for the beauty of the island, which astonishes even the messenger of the gods, nor for the charms of the nymph, who would marry him and make him immortal:

> By nights he would lie beside her, of necessity,
> in the hollow caverns, against his will, by one who was willing,
> but all the days he would sit upon the rocks, at the seaside,
> breaking his heart in tears and lamentation and sorrow
> as weeping tears he looked out over the barren water. (5.154–58)

In keeping with her name, Calypso has kept Odysseus hidden for seven years, but now she has to bow to Zeus's command and helps Odysseus build a raft.

After a seventeen-day voyage, Odysseus can see the mountains of Scheria, the island of the Phaeacians, but at that moment he is spotted by the sea god Poseidon. Still angry at Odysseus for having blinded his son Polyphemus, he churns up the waves. After two days and nights of being tossed in the storm, Odysseus is washed up on the shores of Scheria more dead than alive. He meets the king's daughter Nausicaa, who tells him the way to her father Alcinous's palace. Odysseus follows her instructions to beg the assistance of her mother, Queen Arete, once he arrives at the palace. His supplication is favourably met and Alcinous promises to take his guest home in a ship. When asked who he is, Odysseus tells of his journey from Ogygia to Scheria without actually giving his name.

On the following day, Alcinous orders a ship to be prepared for Odysseus's voyage home and takes him to the people's assembly, where he calls on the Phaeacian princes to bring gifts for the guest. At the banquet, the bard Demodocus sings of a quarrel between Odysseus and Achilles. Alcinous notices his guest's sorrowful demeanour and tactfully moves on to another heroic pastime, athletic games. The Phaeacians urge Odysseus to compete, but it is only when a young man named Euryalus taunts him that he demonstrates his prowess with two discus throws that eclipse the feats of the local athletes. A dance performance and a second song by Demodocus, this time about Aphrodite's clandestine affair with Ares, help to relieve the tensions that had arisen during the games.

Thrilled by the bard's performance, Odysseus asks Demodocus to recount the story of the Trojan horse. But when he hears that song, Odysseus is in tears again and can no longer evade his host's questions about his identity. He replies, 'I am Odysseus son of Laertes, known before all men / for the study of crafty designs, and my fame goes up to the heavens' (9.19–20). This marks the beginning of the Apologoi, in which Odysseus tells of his adventures after the capture of Troy. Late at night, when Odysseus breaks off his narrative just as he has got to his visit to the underworld, and announces that he wishes to rest, Alcinous and the Phaeacians are eager to hear more:

> It is not time yet
> to sleep in the palace. But go on telling your wonderful story.
> I myself could hold out until the bright dawn, if only
> you could bear to tell me, here in the palace, of your sufferings.
>   (11.373–76)

Odysseus continues, recounting the second part of his experiences, up to his arrival on Ogygia. On the following day, he receives rich gifts and is taken to Ithaca on a Phaeacian ship.

In Escape to the Phaeacians, the second part of the *Odyssey*, Odysseus appears first as a listener and subsequently as a narrator. Both roles show narrative as a fundamental part of being in the world and dealing with life. The Apologoi in particular can be interpreted as Odysseus's way of giving shape to harrowing experiences, thereby to come to terms with them. The songs of Demodocus will be the first point of focus—how do they fit into the eighth book, as well as the wider plot of the *Odyssey*, and how do Odysseus and the Phaeacians react to each one? Escape to the Phaeacians will be seen to continue and deepen the reflections on the power of narrative that are embedded in the Telemachy.

Something new happens in the Apologoi: the speaker takes up his own story. But before interpreting the Apologoi as the protagonist's way of processing his own experiences, Odysseus's role as narrator must be considered—can his account be trusted? Even ancient audiences questioned his credibility. Secondly, the structure of the Apologoi deserves attention—rather than being vignettes that have been arbitrarily strung together, the narrated adventures obey a specific compositional logic. The *Odyssey* may draw on earlier traditions for parts of the plot, but it artfully weaves them into a new whole.

The Songs of Demodocus

The singer Demodocus must be led into the hall by a guard: the Muse 'had loved [him] greatly, and gave him both good and evil. / She reft him of his eyes, but gave him the sweet singing / art' (8.63–65). Demodocus's blindness links him with the Homer of ancient lore—Homer himself is alleged to have been blind—although it is necessary to exercise caution in this respect. While there is no shortage of texts about the author of the *Iliad* and the *Odyssey*, they all date from a later period and therefore do not offer reliable information. As mentioned in the Introduction, it is even a matter of debate whether the two Homeric epics should be attributed to the genius of a single poet or to a longer oral tradition. Homer's own alleged blindness reflects the image which the Greeks had of the author and in fact, the notion that Homer himself had been blind may conceivably have arisen from the figure of Demodocus, who in antiquity was viewed as an alter ego of the poet. In any case, the singer's blindness not only differentiates him from his listeners, but also serves as a symbol of his impartiality, reflecting the idea that the Muse rather than his own perception was the inspiration for his songs.

Demodocus sings three songs. An anecdote about the gods is framed by two episodes of the Trojan war and the three songs are represented in different ways. Each is announced—'the quarrel of Odysseus and noble Achilles', 'the love of Ares and sweet-garlanded Aphrodite', 'the wooden horse which Epeius made with Athena helping'—but while the first and third songs occupy eight and twenty-one verses respectively, the second stretches to over a hundred. Here, Homer not only moves from indirect to direct speech, as he also does in the other two songs, but also renders the protagonists' words directly, so that the voices of Homer and Demodocus merge and become undistinguishable.

Despite the differences in form and content, the three songs revolve around a common theme: namely, cunning, which is an antithesis to physical violence.[1] The first song is performed in such a compressed form that it is quite obscure. At a feast, Odysseus and Achilles quarrel, which delights Agamemnon, who had previously heard the Pythia prophesy the disagreement. The lines 'for now the beginning of evil rolled on, descending / on Trojans, and on Danaans, through the designs of great Zeus' (8.81–82) may allude to the timing of the quarrel. A plausible interpretation is that the Pythia had told Agamemnon that Troy would fall when the best of his men quarrelled, and that Odysseus and Achilles' clash delights him for that reason.

The condensed rendering leads the *Odyssey's* audience to surmise that Demodocus is alluding to a story that was generally known, but there is no evidence of it in fragments of the epic cycle. Similarly, the Alexandrian

---

1. See de Jong (2001): 195–96, ad 8.73–82.

Homer critics do not seem to have known it.[2] The quarrel between Odysseus and Achilles must therefore be an ad hoc invention which makes use of motifs and formulae from the *Iliad*. The phrases 'Peleus' son Achilles', 'lord of men Agamemnon' and 'the will of Zeus' all appear in the Proem of the *Iliad*.[3] The quarrel is also reminiscent of the dispute between Achilles and Agamemnon, which follows the Proem, and to some extent of the dispute between Odysseus and Achilles in Book 19, when they argue about whether they should go straight into battle or have breakfast first. Homer draws his audience's attention to the *Iliad* without having Demodocus sing about Iliadic events directly.

Even though Homer does not mention the subject of the dispute, it obviously refers to the contest between 'the best of the Achaians'. Odysseus's confrontation with the protagonist of the *Iliad* means that he is being compared to another type of hero. Although himself a strong warrior, Odysseus is, above all, a sharp-witted trickster, while Achilles, although not lacking in rhetorical talent, is distinguished primarily by his physical strength. To put it simply, in their conflict, cunning and violence meet, and through the different protagonists of the *Odyssey* and the *Iliad*, different forms of the heroic epic are being juxtaposed.

In the second song of Demodocus, Ares embodies violence, Hephaestus cunning. The handsome god of war consorts with the wife of the limping craftsman, but the latter's technical skill triumphs over the physical advantages of his rival: Hephaestus fastens invisible bonds to his bed to catch Ares and Aphrodite *in flagrante* and expose them to the mockery of the gods: 'among the blessed immortals uncontrollable laughter / went up as they saw the handiwork of subtle Hephaestus' (8.326–27). Ares is only released when Poseidon promises that he will submit to his punishment.

Demodocus also praises shrewdness in the third song. The Greeks arrive at Troy concealed in a wooden horse, 'bearing death and doom

2. See Marg (1957): 20. Various interpretations of the first Demodocus song can be found in Rüter (1969): 247–54; Nagy (1979): 42–58; Finkelberg (1990); Strauss Clay (1983): 96–106, Taplin (1990).

3. Rüter (1969): 248–49. Burkert's argument regarding an allusion to the scene of the gods in the first book of the *Iliad* (1960) is less convincing.

for the Trojans' (8.513). Even though Odysseus 'endured the grimmest fighting that ever he had' (8.519) when he goes to the house of Deiphobus with Menelaus, it is nevertheless his clever deception that opens Troy's gates to the Greeks. Implicitly, the third song decides the contest which the first introduces—while Achilles's retreat from the ranks of the Greeks puts them in a tight spot, Odysseus's ruse finally enables them to conquer Troy. Just as with the gods, cunning triumphs over force, and intellect trumps strength.

The connection between the songs about the Trojan War and the plot of the *Odyssey* is obvious. They conjure up the heroic past of the man who is sitting in the audience unrecognized, without possessions and only narrowly escaping an unheroic death far away from family and friends. Demodocus takes up the same stories as Telemachus hears in Sparta, when Menelaus speaks of the wooden horse. At the court of Scheria, Odysseus's deeds in Troy prepare for the unveiling of his identity. Before he has introduced himself to the Phaeacians with tales of his post-Iliadic adventures, he arrives as the hero of the Trojan War in the bard's song.

It is less obvious how the second song, the anecdote about the gods, relates to the plot of the *Odyssey*.[4] Not only does the frivolous narrative suit the cheerful world of the Phaeacians,[5] however, and serve to cool tempers after the incident at the athletic games, but it also mirrors the confrontation between Odysseus and Euryalus. While the handsome Euryalus is explicitly compared to Ares (8.115; 176), Odysseus does not resemble an athlete (8.164), yet proves superior in contest. He lectures Euryalus on the value of appearances:

> There is a certain kind of man, less noted for beauty,
> but the god puts comeliness on his words, and they who look
>   toward him are filled with joy at the sight, and he speaks to
>   them without faltering
> in winning modesty, and shines among those who are gathered,
> and people look on him as on a god when he walks in the city.

4. See Burkert (1960); Braswell (1982); Olson (1989b); Schmidt (1998); Alden (1997); Rinon (2006).

5. Already in antiquity: Athens. 12.511 b/c; Scholion ad 8.267, 272; Eustathios ad 8.267, 335.

Another again in his appearance is like the immortals,
but upon his words there is no grace distilled, as in your case
the appearance is conspicuous, and not a god even
would make it otherwise, and yet the mind there is worthless.
   (8.169–77)

One detail in particular underlines the parallel between Odysseus and Hephaestus. After Odysseus has impressed the Phaeacians with his discus throws, he proclaims that he is a match for them in the other disciplines as well, and that it is only in running that he does not feel equal to them after his arduous voyage (8.230–33). His weakened legs remind us of the lame Hephaestus. Odysseus is also generally well versed in the craftsmanship of Hephaestus: Homer describes in detail how he expertly builds his raft on Ogygia (5.228–61), and Odysseus compares himself to a blacksmith as he drives the heated stake into the cyclops's eye (9.391). Both at the games at Scheria and in the bedroom of Hephaestus, the less handsome turns out to be superior. While Hephaestus uses his skill to outwit Ares, Odysseus contrasts his own eloquence with the Euryalus's handsome appearance.

The second song of Demodocus also relates to the wider plot of the *Odyssey*. In *Deipnosophistae* (5.19 Kaibel), Imperial writer Athenaeus notes that Ares's adultery refers to the situation on Ithaca, where suitors are courting Penelope.[6] Although Penelope does not ultimately betray Odysseus, the possibility is there, as repeated comparisons to Helen and Clytemnestra show. The gulf between gods and men is visible in the comparison between Penelope and Aphrodite—while Odysseus ultimately kills the suitors without mercy for their blatant pursuit of his wife, the gods quickly settle their conflict over the adultery that has taken place. The moral, that there is 'no virtue in bad dealings. See, the slow one has overtaken the swift' (8.329), is put into perspective by Hermes's comment that 'there could be thrice this number of endless fastenings, / and all you gods could be looking on and all the goddesses, / and still I would sleep by the side of Aphrodite the golden'

---

6. See Thornton (1970): 44–45. Alden (1997) even claims that the anecdote of the gods serves to justify the murder of the suitors.

(8.340–42).[7] The ease with which the gods negotiate infidelity makes the audience feel the painful heaviness of the human world all the more keenly.

The words with which Odysseus praises Demodocus's art and requests a third song demonstrate how the audience reacts to the three songs:

> Demodocus, above all mortals beside I prize you.
> Surely the Muse, Zeus's daughter or else Apollo has taught you,
> for all too right following the tale [*kata kosmon*] you sing the Achaians'
> venture, all they did and had done to them, all the sufferings
> of these Achaians, as if you had been there yourself or heard it
> from one who was. Come to another part of the story, sing us
> the form of the wooden horse, which Epeius made with Athene helping,
> the stratagem great Odysseus filled once with men and brought it
> to the upper city, and it was these men who sacked Ilion.
> If you can rightly tell me the course of all these things as they happened [*kata moiran*],
> I will speak of you before all mankind, and tell them
> how freely the goddess gave you the magical gift of singing.
>   (8.487–98)

Odysseus praises not only the accuracy, but also the form and appropriateness of the song.[8] His comment interweaves epistemological, aesthetic and ethical perspectives, which all appear in the word *kosmos*.[9] When Odysseus tells Demodocus that he has performed 'the Achaians' venture [. . .] all too right following the tale', *kosmos* initially denotes the chronological order in which the song narrates the events. The mimetic dimension is underlined by the fact that Odysseus also speaks of the *kosmos* of the wooden horse. The juxtaposition of the *kosmos* of the

---

7. Olson (1989b): 138–39.

8. Macleod (1983): 4–5; Walsh (1984): 8–9; Pratt (1983): 44. Ledbetter (2003): 15–19 emphasizes the role of accurate representation.

9. Halliwell (2011): 85 n. 97 gives an overview of the different interpretations of *kosmos* in *Od.* 8.489.

depiction with the *kosmos* of the depicted illustrates that Demodocus faithfully reproduces reality.

The meaning of *kosmos*, however, also goes beyond the notion of sequentiality. It can refer to ornamentation, and more comprehensively denotes the form of representation. Solon, Parmenides and Democritus speak of the 'ornament of words' (*kosmos tōn epeōn*), and Pindar has the chorus 'build the colourful, sounding ornament of words'.[10] The ordering praised by Odysseus is therefore not limited to mimesis, or the faithful reproduction of events; it also encompasses the beauty of representation, here highlighted by the contrast with 'sufferings'.[11]

Another component of *kosmos* comes into play in the eighth book, when Odysseus rebukes Euryalus for having 'stirred up anger deep in the breast within me / by this disorderly speaking [*ou kata kosmon*]' (8.178–79). Odysseus is less incensed by his undistinguished manner than by the unseemly insinuation that he, the guest, knew nothing about sport. The ethical aspect inherent in *kosmos* is emphasized when Odysseus urges Demodocus to sing rightly about the wooden horse, in 'the course of all these things as they happened [*kata moiran*]'. The singer is supposed to assign everyone the place they deserve based on their deeds. Odysseus's judgement of Demodocus's song is therefore not only epistemological and aesthetic, but also ethical.

The comparison of Demodocus to an eyewitness can be seen to refer not only to his faithful rendition, but also to the liveliness of his performance, which allows the audience to visualize the events described.[12] Significantly, while Odysseus compares the speaker to one who has 'been there himself', in ancient literary criticism, the eyewitness also serves as an image for a captivated audience. The term *enargeia*, popular in Hellenistic and Imperial rhetoric, denotes the ability to narrate so vividly that the listeners become, as it were, spectators. In the songs of Demodocus, Odysseus finds the same quality as that which distinguished the Homeric epics in the eyes of ancient literary critics.

10. Solon fr. 1 W, 2; Parmenides B 8, 52; Democr. B 21; Pindar fr. 194.2–3 Snell-Maehler.
11. Halliwell (2011): 85.
12. Macleod (1983): 6; de Jong (2001): 215.

We intuitively tend to separate form from content. An artistic representation can easily lead to doubts as to the truthfulness of depicted events. Even Thucydides criticized poets for 'embellishing events to make them appear greater' ('epi to meizon kosmountes', 1.21.1). In the Homeric epics, however, form and content are often closely linked. To affirm that he believes Odysseus's account of his adventures, Alcinous says,

> You have
> a grace [(*morphē*] upon your words, and there is sound sense
>   within them,
> and expertly [*epistamenos*], as a singer would do, you have told
>   the story
> of the dismal sorrows befallen yourself and all of the Argives.
>   (11.366–69)

The beautiful form of the recital seems to vouch for the truth of the content; the 'sound sense' denotes both rhetorical skill and first-hand knowledge of the events reported. Epistemological and aesthetic value also coincide in the Sirens' claim that he who listened to them was 'well-pleased, knowing more than ever he did' (12.188).

The Homeric heroes, however, are quite capable of distinguishing between the beauty and the truth of a representation. In Book 14, for example, Eumaeus emphasizes how moved he was by the story of his guest, yet he did not believe that the latter was telling the truth when he claimed that Odysseus was still alive (14.361–68). The beauty of the telling—Eumaeus later compares it to a bard's song (17.518–21)—does not guarantee its veracity. At the same time, his indignation shows that aesthetic and epistemological quality were expected to go hand in hand: 'Why should such a man as you are / lie recklessly to me?' (14.364–65). In the song of Demodocus, by contrast, beauty and truth do coincide, as has been shown.

When it comes to the effect of his songs on the audience, reactions to the first and third renditions are divided. The Phaeacians 'rejoice', Odysseus weeps. While Odysseus still covers his face and wipes away the tears during the first song, he 'melts' during the third, so that 'from

under his eyes the tears ran down, drenching / his cheeks' (8.522–23).
An allegory depicts Odysseus's agitation:

> As a woman weeps, lying over the body
> of her dear husband, who fell fighting for her city and people
> as he tried to beat off the pitiless day from city and children;
> she sees him dying and gasping for breath, and winding her body
> about him she cries high and shrill, while the men behind her,
> hitting her with their spear butts on the back and the shoulders,
> force her up and lead her away into slavery, to have
> hard work and sorrow, and her cheeks are wracked with pitiful
>   weeping.
> Such were the pitiful tears Odysseus shed from under
> his brows. (8.523–32)

The depicted scene closely follows the subject of Demodocus's song and
seems to continue the story of Troy's fall, since it describes the taking
of prisoners of war, which follows the conquest of a city. How should it
therefore be interpreted? Does his comparison to a prisoner of war
imply that Odysseus weeps because he now feels compassion for his
own victims? Or is he lamenting purely for his own sake—in Schopen-
hauerian terms, is he shaken by the gulf that separates him from his
former heroic self?[13]

Regardless of how one reads Odysseus's reaction to the tale, the com-
parison highlights his emotion. His reaction is likened to an experience
that can hardly be surpassed in terms of sadness: a woman watches her
husband die. The comparison gains complexity through a double inver-
sion. Not only is Odysseus compared to a woman, but, himself a perpe-
trator, he is also being aligned with the victim: the poignancy of the
aesthetic experience is vividly portrayed here. Less obvious but never-
theless notable is the comparison of Odysseus, who *hears* a story, to a
woman who *sees* her husband die. It is at this point that the transforma-
tion from listener to narrator, later referred to as *energeia*, emerges. In

---

13. On the thesis that Odysseus feels pity for his victims, see, for instance, Macleod (1983):
11; Rutherford (1986): 155–56; Garvie (1994): ad 521–35; Segal (1994): 121–23.

this passage, as also in other places, the Homeric epic demonstrates the irresistible attraction which narratives can have. Audiences are far from being the ideal of a sober, intellectual recipient that many literary scholars still assume them to be. Odysseus's reaction illustrates that stories can not only stir up emotions, but may even have a physical impact.

It may seem surprising that an *encomium*, a poem of praise, should bring tears to Odysseus's eyes. Should he not be rejoicing, since the fall of Troy means the success of the Greeks, and the wooden horse signifies his personal achievement? If the allegory implies that Odysseus identifies with his victims, then the contradiction is resolved. Yet even without this interpretation, the heroes' memory of Troy is undoubtedly painful. Nestor, for example, when asked by Telemachus about his father's deeds in Troy, says, 'Dear friend, [. . .] you remind me of sorrows which in that country / we endured, we sons of the Achaians valiant forever' (3.103–4).

The Phaeacians' quiet enjoyment of the arts serves to draw attention to Odysseus's mortification. At first glance, the juxtaposition reminds us of the contrast between Penelope and the suitors in the first book. Just as the stories of the homecoming touch Penelope's but not the suitors' hearts, Demodocus's song affects Odysseus differently from the Phaeacians. But this time, rather than calling to mind the listener's own passive suffering, the song is about events in which the listener had been involved. Odysseus is directly affected, since the subject of the song is his own story.

And there is another difference between Penelope and Odysseus. While Penelope asks Phemius to choose a different subject, Odysseus asks for the very song that subsequently overwhelms him: 'If you can tell me the course of all these things as they happened, / I will speak of you before all mankind and tell them / how freely the goddess gave you the magical gift of singing' (8.496–98).[14] As painfully as the Trojan war touches Odysseus, he feels the need to hear about it in song. In the recital, the misfortune of the Achaians, how much they have done and endured, becomes a *kosmos*, a well-ordered ornament. This highlights

---

14. See Goldhill (1991): 51–54; Halliwell (2011): 79–92.

an important function of narrative: once they are given shape, past experiences lose something of their intensity. Narrative allows us to come to terms with suffering, yet this is not a painless process, nor is it capable of closing the wound entirely.

The general reaction to the anecdote about the gods appears in stark contrast to the songs of Troy, and it is unanimous: 'So the famous singer sang his song, and Odysseus / enjoyed it in his heart as he listened, as did the others / there, Phaeacians, men of the long oar, famed for seafaring' (8.367–69). The revelling of the listeners extends the dynamics of the aesthetic experience as previously captured in the Telemachy. Demodocus's second song deals with a precarious subject. While the Trojan War is past and the final song is an *encomium*, Aphrodite's adultery hints at an acute danger, one which Odysseus is unable to counteract. Being far from Ithaca, he does not even know if Penelope is intending to take a new husband. Or perhaps another man is already sleeping in his bed?

Despite the parallel between narrative and reality, Odysseus, along with the Phaeacians, enjoys the rendition. It might be surmised that the reason is that the adultery is set in the world of the gods, sufficiently distant from Odysseus's own sphere of experience. As Aristotle notes, empathy can only emerge if the protagonist is neither too similar nor too close to the audience. By singing about divine actors, Demodocus's second song introduces the necessary aesthetic distance, which had been absent while Odysseus was listening to his own story.

The songs of Demodocus and the listeners' reactions develop reflections on narrative that first appear in the Telemachy. They reveal the intensity of the aesthetic experience: listeners feel transported to the scene of the action and as if they are seeing the narrated events with their own eyes. The intensity of the reception experience is heightened for Odysseus because it is his own experiences that are being narrated. While the Phaeacians revel in the songs about the Trojan War, for Odysseus the aesthetic distance is diminished, and the events are too close to the mark for him. At the same time, his desire to hear about the Trojan War and his praise of Demodocus indicate that narrative also serves to give shape to traumatic experiences and can help to overcome them.

The Structure of the Apologoi

In Escape to the Phaeacians, Odysseus, who is initially in the role of listener, becomes the narrator of his own story. Having heard his own deeds recounted, he tells the Phaeacians about his adventures after the Trojan War in Books 9 to 12. A simile in Book 21 captures his dual role of hero and narrator well:

> but now resourceful Odysseus,
> once he had taken up the great bow and looked it all over,
> as when a man, who well understands the lyre and singing,
> easily, holding it on either side, pulls the strongly twisted
> cord of sheep's gut, so as to slip it over a new peg,
> so, without any strain, Odysseus strung the great bow.
> Then plucking it in his right hand he tested the bowstring,
> and it gave him back an excellent sound like the voice of a
>   swallow. (21.404–11)

After Odysseus's sustained period of subterfuge on Ithaca, Homer compares him to a singer just before he shoots the first suitor and reappears as a hero. At this crucial point, the comparison of bow and lyre captures Odysseus's double identity as hero and singer-like narrator.

Odysseus's role as narrator is announced in the eighth book when he requests that Demodocus should sing about the trick with the wooden horse: 'If you can tell me the course of all these things as they happened, / I will speak of you before all mankind, and tell them / how freely the goddess gave you the magical gift of singing' (8.496–98). In a strange reversal, Odysseus here adopts the singer's task of broadcasting renown, which in this case is concerned with the fame of the singer himself. Soon thereafter, he proclaims his own fame. The discussion that follows will provide a brief summary of Odysseus's account before focusing on its structure. The miraculous beings whom Odysseus encounters give rise to the question of whether he is telling the truth—a pertinent question if the Apologoi are to be interpreted as the medium through which Odysseus processes his experiences.

The beginning of the Apologoi features his encounter with the Cicones, a people living in Thrace. After the Greeks have sacked Ismarus, the Cicones bring reinforcements and manage to decimate their opponents—each of the twelve Greek ships loses six men. A completely different danger looms from the Lotus Eaters. Those who taste the lotus become addicted and forget to return home. Odysseus has to put two of his men in fetters to force them to return. He then reaches Goat Island and ventures into Polyphemus's cave on the opposite shore with his twelve best men. The cyclops imprisons the intruders and devours six of them before Odysseus manages to blind him and escape with his surviving companions. On Aeolus's island, Odysseus and his men are able to recover from their ordeals. The Lord of the Skies even gives Odysseus a hose containing the winds to aid his return home. But when Ithaca is already in sight, Odysseus falls asleep and his companions, envious and suspicious of the gift, open the hose. The escaping winds drive the ships back to Aeolia, where they are refused further assistance.

Odysseus then loses eleven ships in his encounter with the Laistrygonians and, with his only remaining ship, reaches the island of Circe. She turns half of his companions into wild animals before Odysseus is able to defeat her with Hermes's help. He regains his companions, who have become younger and more handsome. He doesn't continue his journey until a year has passed, when, at Circe's behest, he travels to the underworld. There, he meets various friends he had known and has his fortune told by Teiresias. Resuming his journey, he is able to listen to the Sirens' song without succumbing to it, thanks to Circe's instructions. He also succeeds in manoeuvring the ship past Scylla, but loses six more men in the process. A lull in the wind then traps them on Thrinacia, where nymphs graze the cattle of the sun god. While Odysseus is asleep, his companions, who are tormented by hunger, eat the cattle against the express prohibition of Circe and Teiresias. The punishment is not long in coming—shortly after the Greeks have set sail, a violent storm arises. Only Odysseus can save himself, by clinging to the keel and mast of the broken ship. He is almost engulfed by Charybdis but does finally reach Ogygia.

FIG. 6. Roman fresco from the Esquiline, *Ulysses in Hades*. Photo: bpk/Scala.

The recurring formula 'we sailed on further along, glad to have escaped death, but grieving still at heart' (9.62; 105; 565; 10.77; 133) may give the impression that Homer is stringing the individual adventures together in a simple catalogue, but even a cursory glance reveals parallels and correspondences that stand out and suggest a more elaborate composition. Perhaps the most obvious example is that Calypso and Circe are both goddesses who make Odysseus their lover and obstruct his return home. Both are 'lichen-beautiful' and each is described as a 'dread goddess who talks with mortals'. Odysseus himself comments on the parallel:

> For in truth Calypso, shining among divinities, kept me
> with her in her hollow caverns, desiring me for her husband,
> and so likewise Aiaian Circe the guileful detained me
> beside her in her halls, desiring me for her husband. (9.29–32)

The similarity is sufficiently striking for earlier Homeric scholarship to have been convinced that one figure was derived from the other, albeit without being in agreement about who was the original and who the copy.[15]

15. For an overview, see Scully (1987): 406 n. 6.

Through such parallels, a distinct structure can be discerned in the Apologoi on closer inspection.[16] At the beginning, a two-day storm separates Odysseus's encounter with the Cicones, who still belong to the Iliadic world, from a cosmos populated by giants and mythical creatures, and a second storm, again lasting two days, marks the change to the world of the Phaeacians, who represent his transition to life back on Ithaca. The visit to the underworld, which takes up the entire eleventh book, is at the centre and serves as a resting point, as it were. It divides Odysseus's adventures into two symmetrical internal parts, as illustrated by Figure 7. Both parts are framed by encounters with beings who want to either seduce or force Odysseus to stay and endanger his nostos: the lotus eaters and Circe in the first half; the Sirens and Calypso in the second. Adversaries who want to devour Odysseus—Polyphemus, the Laistrygonians, Scylla and Charybdis—form an inner ring. At the centre are Aeolia and Thrinacia, two adventures where Odysseus and his companions are punished for the latter's 'evil counsel' (10.46; 12.339) of flouting a prohibition while Odysseus is asleep.

In the dialectic between eating and being eaten, food is a theme that occurs in almost all the adventures, as though refracted in a kaleidoscope.[17] The monsters that threaten to devour Odysseus and his companions are juxtaposed with passages in which the Greeks themselves are eating—often with disastrous consequences. The Cicones succeed in avenging the capture of Ismarus because the Greeks are celebrating with a banquet rather than continuing their journey straight away. Consumption of the lotus causes amnesia and endangers the nostos. Transformed into pigs by Circe, Odysseus's companions turn to eating acorns. Calypso, on the other hand, wants to give Odysseus ambrosia, so that he will become immortal and her husband. Finally, the slaughter of cattle on Thrinacia is an outrage that costs Odysseus's remaining companions their lives. Food also connects the Apologoi both with their own

16. The following structure essentially follows Niles (1978). For alternative structures of the Apologoi, see Germain (1954): 332–33; Whitman (1958): 288; Redfield (1983): 235–37; Scully (1987); Cook (1995): 65–92.

17. See Cook (1995): 56–59; Bakker (2013).

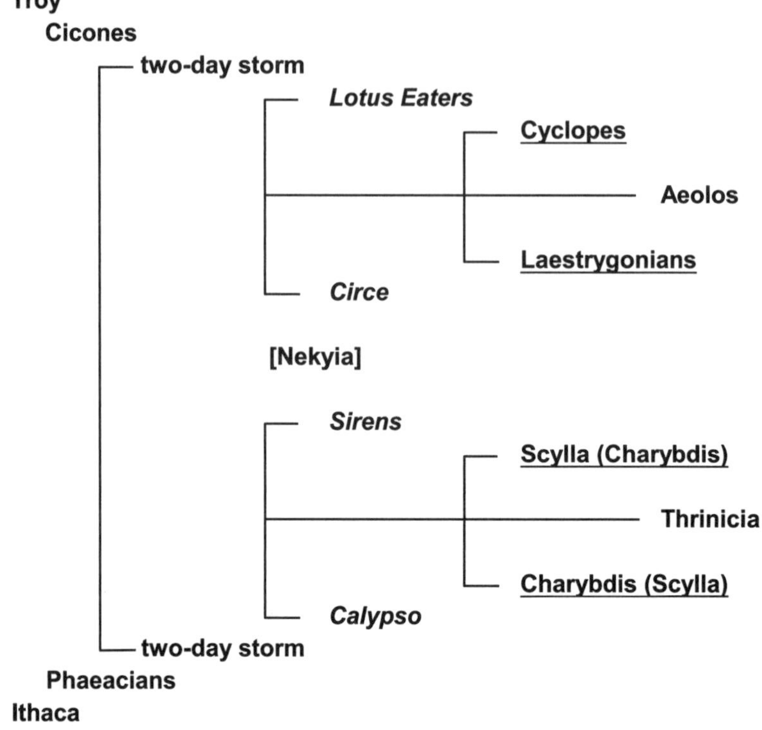

FIG. 7. Structure of the Apologoi, according to Most (1989): 22.

setting—Odysseus narrates his adventures at a feast—and with the wider plot: on Ithaca, the suitors are consuming Odysseus's possessions.

The *Odyssey* reflects the central role of food in Greek anthropology.[18] Strictly regulated, food intake assigns people their place in the cosmos. People find their place between gods and animals above all by offering sacrifices. By killing animals, they assert their power over nature while simultaneously subordinating themselves to the gods in the ritualization of slaughter. When Polyphemus and the Laistrygonians consume raw human flesh, they shatter a foundation of Greek civilization. Although Odysseus's companions offer a sacrifice on Thrinacia, the slaughter of Helios's cattle means that they help themselves to food

18. See Vernant (1979): 37–132 on the definition of human beings through food, especially in Hesiod.

while disregarding the power of the gods. Conversely, Odysseus refers to a joyful banquet accompanied by song as the 'best of occasions' (9.11). The banquets in Sparta, Pylos and Scheria represent harmony and order.

Viewing the Apologoi as a whole, an interim climax becomes noticeable between the first and second halves—both the exotic element and the threat increase. In the first part, Odysseus chiefly encounters adversaries who practise non-civilized ways of coexisting.[19] The cyclopes negate fundamental values and institutions of Greek civilization: they do not cultivate the land, refuse to serve the gods and know neither assemblies nor laws. Aeolus lives in a family unit without a ban on incest; his sons and daughters are married to each other. The Laistrygonians are a pastoral people who create paths and live in a city with a palace. However, they turn out to be cannibals.

In the second part, Odysseus encounters fabulous creatures: the Sirens, who sing irresistibly amidst faded bones; Scylla, a monster with twelve feet and six heads, all barking like puppies; and across from her, Charybdis, who sucks the sea into herself three times a day, only to spit it out again. The rise of the exotic element is first seen in the Sirens and lotus eaters. At the beginning of each half of the Apologoi, Odysseus is asked to stay. But while the lotus eaters have since antiquity inspired the imagination of researchers, who have located them in various places in Libya, Illyria, Sicily and the far west, the Sirens obviously belong to a dream world. They only threaten those who listen to their song: anyone whose ears are not covered by wax is at their mercy. Two companions succumb to the culinary temptation of the lotus, while Odysseus encounters the Sirens' song alone.

The trials of the first part of the Apologoi have little in common with the Iliadic battlefield, but while Odysseus seeks out Polyphemus and the Laistrygonians, he is forced to face Scylla and Charybdis. Increasingly, Odysseus has to bear what happens to him, rather than being the initiator of the action. It is true that he has to endure terrible things in the first half as well, such as when Polyphemus devours two companions before

19. Cook (1995): 67.

his eyes, and that conversely, he does not lose courage even when going into the underworld. Nevertheless, there is an overall shift of emphasis from active to passive heroism.[20] Instead of seeking out adventures so that he can prove his bravery, Odysseus is forced into the role of victim, and proves himself as a hero who endures various attacks on his life.

This development becomes clear in a comparison between the cyclops and Scylla, which is explicitly made in the *Odyssey*.[21] Before they sail into the strait between Scylla and Charybdis, Odysseus reassures his men that 'this is no greater evil now than it was when the Cyclops / had us cooped in his hollow cave by force and violence' (12.209–10). Scylla, who like Polyphemus resides in a cave, is also referred to as a 'monster' (*pelōr*, 9.428; 12.87). She devours as many companions as does Polyphemus—in both cases it is six—yet she is more terrible by far. While Odysseus can overpower the cyclops by depriving him of his sight, Scylla eludes his gaze and therefore his control. Nowhere is the futility of Iliadic heroism more evident than when Odysseus prepares himself and waits in vain for Scylla to show herself:[22] whereas in the Polyphemus adventure, the human mind triumphs over a monster, it has now become a matter of sheer survival.

That Odysseus has changed from hunter to hunted is made tangible in a detailed comparison of Scylla with an angler:

> And as a fisherman with a very long rod, on a jutting
> rock, will cast his treacherous bait for the little fishes, and sinks
>   the horn of
> a field-ranging ox into the water,
> then hauls them up and throws them on the dry land, gasping
> and struggling, so they gasped and struggled as they were
>   hoisted up the cliff. (12.251–55)

The story reverses the relationship between man and nature. Fishing no longer represents dominion over, but rather being at the mercy of, nature. For Odysseus, the sight of his wriggling companions is 'the most

20. See Cook (1999) on Odysseus as an active and passive hero. Cook does not note the development outlined here, however.

21. Hopman (2012a): 3–13.

22. Reinhardt (1960): 59–60.

pitiful scene that these eyes have looked on in my / sufferings as I explored the routes over the water' (12.258–59). As Karl Reinhardt puts it, 'there are horrors that can only be suffered'.[23]

The increase of tension in the Apologoi is reinforced by the fact that the audience does not experience the adventures in the same order as Odysseus. Regardless of any question of priority, the episode with Circe is more spectacular than that with Calypso. Although Odysseus spends only a year with the former and seven years with the latter, the encounter with Circe is more richly depicted—how she turns half of his companions into pigs and feeds them acorns; how Hermes reveals the properties of the herb moly to Odysseus, to enable him to protect himself against Circe's magic; how Circe touches Odysseus in vain with her magic wand, then invites him to her bed and finally gives his companions back their human form. Although Odysseus meets Circe before Calypso, the audience learns of his stay on Aiaie after hearing of his sojourn on Ogygia. The narration of the adventures in the Apologoi means that the more colourful story follows the paler one.

Even though the Apologoi may bring together adventures that originally circulated separately, they are combined into a whole which acquires momentum from increasing danger, as well as from alternating episodes that feature life-threatening adversaries with those that offer respite. Not only do monsters and cannibals try to devour Odysseus, but the substances he and his companions eat, be they the lotus or the cattle of the sun god, also endanger their nostos. Initially, Odysseus is still seeking out adventure, but ultimately, he proves himself a hero by virtue of enduring in the face of terrible attacks. Before going on to explore the functions of the narrative structure outlined above, however, an urgent question needs to be addressed.

The Apologoi—Is It All a Lie?

Divine lovers with magical powers, one-eyed giants and monsters with six heads only appear in the adventures told by Odysseus himself. Neither the Telemachy nor the second half of the *Odyssey* feature any

23. Reinhardt (1960): 60.

comparable creatures, which raises the question of whether Odysseus's account should be taken at face value. This is not about the historicity of the *Odyssey*, which today's Homeric scholars, if they ask the question at all, deny, but about whether Odysseus tells the Phaeacians the truth within the fictional world of the *Odyssey*. Athena considers Odysseus to be the best liar among his compatriots (13.291–98), and on Ithaca he shines as he narrates invented adventures. Can his account in the Apologoi, therefore, be trusted?

This question was already asked in antiquity. In antiquity, critics, who unlike contemporary scholars were almost all convinced of the historicity of the Trojan War and its heroes, were predominantly concerned with Homer's credibility. When they did not seek to emphasize the supra-historical significance of the epics by allegorizing them, they tried to extract their historical core by rationalizing them.[24] Yet some ancient authors do cast doubt on the reliability of Odysseus as a narrator. In the fifth century, Pindar, who attacks Odysseus in several odes, remarks,

> Myself, I hold that what is said
> about Odysseus has turned out to exceed the things he suffered,
> thanks to Homer and his sweet speech,
> since on his lies, and soaring craftsmanship,
> there rests some quality of awe. Poetic skill
> deceives, leading astray with stories. (*Nem.* 7.20–23)[25]

The theme of suffering suggests that this discourse is not about the dispute between Ajax and Achilles over the latter's weapons, which the verses that follow outline, but about the adventures recounted in the Apologoi. The possessive form 'his' leaves open whether Pindar meant it was Homer or Odysseus who acquires a touch of the sublime on account of 'his lies through soaring craftsmanship', but the vagueness

---

24. A critique of the Apologoi is found in Polybius 34.2; Dio Chrysostom 11.34; Longinus, *De sublimitate* 9.13–14; Strabo 1.27, 9–19, 36–37.

25. Translation by Andrew M. Miller (with translator' s lineation): see Miller (2019). For verse 7.22 (fourth line of cited translation), I follow the conjecture *te* also adopted by Snell-Maehler, which, unlike Schmid's *ge*, prevents three datives from following each other in an unharmonious relationship (translation here adapted accordingly).

suggests that Pindar accuses both of dishonesty, since it is Homer who has Odysseus narrate implausible events.[26]

The claim that Odysseus is lying at the court of the Phaeacians is found unambiguously in *A True Story*, by Imperial author Lucian of Samosata, a fictional travelogue which recounts experiences that are obviously implausible, such as a trip to the moon, and supports them with common truth topoi.[27] In the introduction, Lucian expects that the audience will delight not only in 'the novelty of its subject, the humour of its plan and because I tell all kinds of lies in a plausible and specious way', but also because 'everything in my story is a more or less comical parody of one or another of the poets, historians and philosophers of old, who have written much that smacks of miracles and fables'. Lucian names Homer's Odysseus as the 'guide and instructor in this sort of charlatanry', who 'told Alcinous and his court about winds in bondage, one-eyed men, cannibals and savages; also about animals with many heads, and transformations of his comrades wrought with drugs; this stuff, and much more like it, being what our friend humbugged the illiterate Phaeacians with' (1.3).[28]

The idea of the Apologoi as invented stories fits perfectly into Lucian's dizzying play with literary tradition between fact and fiction. However, there is nothing in Homer that justifies such an interpretation of Odysseus's travelogue. While the Cretan stories are lies that help Odysseus to hide his identity on Ithaca, this is obvious to the audience, and there are no signals that his account should not be trusted when he addresses the Phaeacians. Individual adventures are even confirmed by being referred to in the main narrative. The Proem mentions the sacrilege on Thrinacia (1.7–9); Polyphemus is commented on by both the narrator and Zeus (1.68–71; 2.19–20; see also 20.18–21), and Odysseus's encounter with Circe is confirmed by a knot he had learned from her (8.447–48).

---

26. See Most (1985): 150–51.

27. See Kim (2010): 151–56. Besides Pindar and Lucian, see also Juvenal 15.13–26. In modern research, Ahl (1989) and Alden (1992) doubt the credibility of Odysseus. In contrast, see especially Parry (1994); Richardson (1996).

28. Translation by A. M. Harmon (slightly adapted): see Harmon (1913): 249–50.

Homer undoubtedly does portray Odysseus as a skilful orator who knows how to adapt his words to his audience. When he includes the catalogue of women as he tells of his journey to the underworld, for example, this is directed primarily at Arete, queen of the Phaeacians, who subsequently praises him and asks that further gifts should be bestowed on him. And in the twenty-third book, when Odysseus tells Penelope about his nostos, he mentions Circe and Calypso without including any of the amorous dimensions of his sojourns. But if omitting his love affairs can be attributed to Odysseus's calculations (rather than to the narrator summarizing his discourse), this demonstrates Odysseus's rhetorical skill rather than that he invents adventures. Finally, while Odysseus changes his story in the tall tales he relates while in disguise, he tells Penelope the same as he had previously told the Phaeacians.

Nevertheless, Homer does raise the possibility that Odysseus may also be dissembling while in Scheria. Alcinous praises his storytelling, saying,

> Odysseus, we as we look upon you do not imagine
> that you are a deceptive or thievish man, the sort that the black earth
> breeds in great numbers, people who wander widely, making up
> lying stories, from which no one could learn anything.[29]
> (11.363–66)

Alcinous provides a description of what Odysseus could potentially be and anticipates the role he later acts out on Ithaca when he recounts his tall tales: 'a deceptive or thievish man'. Although Alcinous cannot verify Odysseus's account, his surmise parallels the audience's conclusion about the integration of the Apologoi in the *Odyssey*, that he does not invent his adventures, and that they are therefore told sincerely. The idea that Odysseus might be fooling the Phaeacians as he later does the Ithacans appears only for a moment, and in negated form.

29. See Peradotto (1990): 92.

The Function of the Apologoi

The Apologoi have also challenged interpreters of the *Odyssey* beyond the question of authentic narration. In antiquity, the epic was read allegorically from the sixth century BCE onwards;[30] Neoplatonists interpreted the adventures as allegories for temptations which the philosopher must resist. For Christian readers, Odysseus was a Christ-like figure—the stake to which he is tied as he listens to the Sirens corresponded to the cross, while his sufferings mirrored Jesus's martyrdom.[31] Modern readers have interpreted the Apologoi psychologically, or as a type of ritual. They compare Odysseus's voyage to a rite of passage that leads him away from everyday life and finally back to society on a new level. In this interpretation, the challenges and trials which Odysseus undergoes challenge his identity and by defying them, he consolidates his ego and is finally able to return.[32]

While all these approaches interpret the Apologoi symbolically in one way or another, Glenn Most has sought a more pragmatic approach and asks what function Odysseus's narration has in the overall plot. According to Most, Odysseus becomes a narrator to ensure his return home. In the Apologoi, hospitality plays a paramount role, and being a stranger may lead to the protagonist being devoured or prevented from continuing his journey. Odysseus therefore recounts manifold violations of hospitality to remind the Phaeacians that it was their duty as hosts to feed rather than to kill him, and to aid his return journey rather than delaying it.[33]

Indeed, Nausicaa initially warns Odysseus of the Phaeacians' xenophobia. But upon his arrival at the palace, Odysseus receives a promise from Alcinous that he

---

30. Lamberton (1986).

31. See, for instance, Clemens Alexandrinus, Protr. 12.118.4; Hippolyt, El. 7.13.2.3; Maximus Turinus, Hom. 49. See Rahner (1984): 300–28 for further evidence.

32. See, for instance, Austin (1975): 130–78; Segal (1994).

33. Most (1989).

shall think of conveyance, and how our guest without annoyance
   or hardship
may come again, convoyed by us, to his own country,
in happiness and speed, even though it lies very far off,
and on the way between suffer no pain nor evil
until he sets foot on his own country. (7.192–96)

The Phaeacian princes approve the plan and 'encouraged / convoy for the stranger' (7.226–27), while Alcinous repeats his promise once more (7.317–18). Repeatedly affirmed, Phaeacian aid is something Odysseus is therefore assured of early on, which obviates the need for him to tailor his narrative in an effort to secure it.

At the people's assembly the following morning, Alcinous announces to the Phaeacians that Odysseus

urges conveyance, and entreats us for its assurance.
So let us, as we have done before, hasten to convey him,
for neither has any other man who has come to my house
stayed here grieving a long time for the matter of convoy.
Come then, let us drag a black ship down to the bright sea,
one sailing now for the first time, and have for it a selection
from the district, fifty-two young men, who have been the finest
   before. (8.30–36)

Odysseus's departure is postponed by one day because his own narrative takes that long, and Alcinous's speech refutes the idea that there is any danger of the Phaeacians holding Odysseus against his wishes. The Apologoi serve to portray him as vying for neither a friendly reception nor for a swift return home.

Hospitality is an important theme in the Apologoi, and Odysseus does remind the Phaeacians of this theme while he is their guest. However, it would be a mistake to infer the narrator's intention from this. Even though Odysseus's narrative includes violations of the laws of hospitality, he does not relate these to secure his favourable treatment; in fact, his reception on Scheria contrasts sharply with his earlier experiences. Nevertheless, Most deserves merit for drawing attention to the pragmatic dimension of Odysseus's narrative. The Apologoi not only serve to depict adventures which the narrator has previously kept back, but also have a specific function in the action. They are both story and speech act: the rendering is itself an action. Even if Odysseus aims to impress the Phaeacians, the pragmatic dimension lies in Odysseus processing his own experiences rather than in an attempt to manipulate his audience for his own benefit. He first requests that Demodocus perform songs that lend his adventures *kosmos*, or renown, and then turns narrator himself, giving shape to his experiences and overcoming what had previously overwhelmed him. In this way, he becomes free and ready for his return to Ithaca.[34]

The beginning of Odysseus's narrative seems to contradict this thesis, since when asked by Alcinous why he was weeping over the song of the wooden horse, Odysseus replies, 'but now your wish was inclined to ask me about my mournful sufferings, / so that I must mourn and grieve even more' (9.12–13). However, as a modern interpreter of Homer notes, 'Odysseus may complain beforehand that telling his story demands painful recollection, but that does not preclude the process from bringing him pleasure ultimately.'[35] Similarly, as previously noted, Eumaeus's words show that lamenting can relieve and even delight the Homeric hero: 'But we two, sitting here in the shelter, eating and drinking, / shall entertain each other remembering and re-telling / our sad sorrows' (15.398–400). The twenty-third book makes clear that Odysseus also derives *terpsis* from recounting his own adventures when he and Penelope share their experiences of the past decade: 'When Penelope and Odysseus had enjoyed their lovemaking, / they took their pleasure in talking [*terpesthēn mythoisi*], each one telling his story' (23.300–301).

---

34. There are some interpretations that focus on the narrative of the Apologoi, but they interpret it differently than suggested here. Segal (1994): 14–25 views the adventures themselves as 'a voyage of the soul, from life to death and back to life' (20) and the story told to the Phaeacians as indicating that Odysseus was ready to return. Cook (1999): 162 interprets the Apologoi as a 'mimetic reconstruction of Odysseus' full heroic identity'. Crotty (1994): 160–80 sees Odysseus's acceptance of his own mortality in them.

35. Mackie (1997): 88.

A closer look at the structure of the Apologoi helps to explore the extent to which Odysseus comes to terms with his experiences by recounting them. The story he tells the Phaeacians illustrates the way we process reality by narrating it. Being confined to a first-person account, the Apologoi are subject to certain limitations.[36] That said, at certain points, Homer has Odysseus report details he cannot actually know himself. Although he had not seen what Circe had done with his scouting party, his account is considerably more detailed than that of the escaped messenger, which is given in direct speech (10.210–43; 251–60). Strictly speaking, Odysseus also cannot know what his companions say while he is asleep on board the ship, or at Thrinacia (10.34–45; 12.339–51). But such inaccuracies, which are for the most part detected by philologists examining minutiae, need not be given any undue weight.

On the whole, Homer does stick to the limits of a first-person narrative, as the references to the gods show. Whereas the Homeric narrator mentions individual gods, Odysseus usually refers vaguely to a god, gods or a daimon.[37] The effort to stick to Odysseus's perspective is particularly clear in a conversation between Zeus and Helios, who both condemn the consumption of the cattle on Thrinacia and bring about the final shipwreck. Before the audience can wonder how Odysseus knows about this, he adds that he owes this information to Calypso, who had previously received it from Hermes (12.374–90).

In spite of the first-person narration, the Apologoi do not actually offer a direct account of Odysseus's adventures. Although he recounts his own experiences, he is temporally separated from them, and the retrospective view gives him a control he did not have while undergoing them. Odysseus uses this control in various ways. For instance, when he embarks on an episode involving new peoples, he introduces them first. In doing so, he draws both on experiences that were still in the future for him at the time, and on general knowledge. Before the experiencing Odysseus has sent out scouts, the narrating Odysseus informs us that the island is inhabited by Lotophagi 'who live on a flowering food' (9.84).

---

36. On the Apologoi as a first-person narrative, see especially Suerbaum (1968).

37. See *Od.* 9.52, 67, 142, 158, 339, 381; 10.141, 157; 12.169, 295, 313, 337, 371–72, 445, 448.

When the Greeks land on Goat Island on a moonless night, he describes it in detail at the outset (9.116–48). Here as elsewhere, the narrating character gives a detailed account of peoples and places that the experiencing character had yet to meet, often in painful encounters.

The control which the retrospective view engenders becomes even more tangible when the narrating Odysseus anticipates future experiences of the experiencing Odysseus. For instance, after the conquest of Ismarus, he 'was for the light foot and escaping, / and urged it, but they [his companions] were greatly foolish and would not listen' (9.43–44). The disastrous results are implicit in the phrase 'greatly foolish'. In the narration of the episode of the cyclops, the future consequences are made explicit: this time it is Odysseus who does not listen to his companions and insists on waiting in the cave. He reflects that 'it would have been better their way, / not [to wait] until I could see him, see if he would give me presents. / My friends were to find the sight of him in no way lovely' (9.228–30). When the ships sail from the island of Aeolia, they are aided by Aeolus, who 'set the West Wind free to blow me and carry / the ships and the men aboard them on their way; but it was not / so to be, for we were ruined by our own folly' (10.25–27). As with other anticipated events, the details remain vague enough for the audience's curiosity to be aroused, creating suspense relating to the 'how': by what folly do Odysseus and his companions deprive themselves of their swift return home, and what does being 'ruined' mean? However vague the anticipatory references are, they show that the narrating Odysseus's perspective is broader than that of the experiencing Odysseus, and demonstrate his narrative skill. He is able to look back on trials that at the time he had yet to overcome, and on sufferings he was yet to endure.

The gap between the narrating and experiencing characters is bridged where anticipatory references are embedded in the plot. In the second part of the Apologoi, after the Nekyia (the visit to the underworld), prophecies serve to reduce the uncertainty about the future. After Teiresias has told Odysseus's future, Circe gives him detailed instructions for his journey. Informing Odysseus of the dangers ahead underscores his capacity to endure, which comes increasingly to the fore in the second part of the Apologoi. As Reinhardt puts it, 'prediction changes danger into inevitable fate'.[38] However, while the prophecies narrow the gap between the narrating and the experiencing Odysseus, they don't close it entirely. Circe anticipates the dangers, but she does not say exactly what will happen. Like Teiresias, she sketches alternative scenarios, such as when she talks about the cattle of the sun god, using the same words as Teiresias:

> Then, if you keep your mind on homecoming and leave these
>   unharmed,
> you might all make your way to Ithaca, after much suffering;
> but if you do harm them, then I testify to the destruction
> of your ship and your companions. (11.110–13 = 12.137–40)

If predictions narrow the gap between the narrating and experiencing character, it can be closed if the former tacitly allows the latter to participate in his greater perspective. Odysseus may use this trick in at least one place. He wants to see if the cyclops will give him a gift (9.229) and turns a deaf ear to his companions' warnings. Trapped in the cyclops's cave, the wine of Maron proves to be an important aid. It intoxicates Polyphemus, so that the Greeks are able to ram a glowing staff into his eye and escape the cave the next morning. The narrating Odysseus claims that he had deliberately brought the wine along, 'for my proud heart had an idea that presently / I would encounter a man who was endowed with great strength, / and wild, with no true knowledge of laws or any good customs' (9.213–15).

Two interpretations are possible here. Either Odysseus shows the same foresight as, for instance, on Ismarus, when he wants to leave immediately after its capture, and when he is the only one to moor his ship outside the harbour of the Laistrygonians; or the narrating Odysseus is endowing the experiencing Odysseus with a premonition that he did not actually have. Is his premonition of meeting a wild, lawless man compatible with his desire to see Polyphemus in the hope that he will receive gifts from him? This does not necessarily involve a contradiction, since Odysseus can be both curious and prepared for a fiend at the

---

38. Reinhardt (1960): 87.

same time. Nevertheless, a blending of the narrating and experiencing Odysseus is worth considering, since the foreboding anticipates the retrospectively informed description of the cyclops as lawless (9.112–15; 189).[39] It could also be viewed as a strategy of the narrating Odysseus to improve his role in an adventure from which, although victorious, he emerges with the death of six companions on his conscience.

One might be tempted to speculate that Odysseus's foresight in other episodes is also due to a shift from the narrating to the experiencing character. But as has been seen, the interpretation of Odysseus as an unreliable narrator is not justified. There are no breaks or tensions that point to misrepresentation beyond a degree of rhetoric self-stylization. At the same time, the narrating Odysseus repeatedly sets himself apart from his former self through his descriptions and anticipatory remarks; as the narrator of the Apologoi, he freely uses his retrospective perspective. This engenders control over events that presented mortal danger at the time. The once-still-uncertain future has become the past, which Odysseus can survey and recount as a past future. He narrates the experiences of his voyage knowing their ultimately favourable outcome, and banishes their horrors. Eumaeus captures this idea when he proclaims that, 'for afterwards a man who has suffered / much and wandered much has pleasure out of his sorrows' (15.400–401).

The contingencies which the experiencing Odysseus must endure are replaced by the structure which the narrating Odysseus gives events in retrospect. Both the schematization and repetition play a major role in this. Odysseus presents his adventures as variations on the scheme 'introduction of the adversary—confrontation—escape'; he first describes the beings concerned, then narrates the encounter, and finally the escape. As different as the individual adventures are, they can be grouped, as we have seen. The women who invite Odysseus to linger are juxtaposed with monsters who seek to devour him, and between the individual episodes a dense web of correlations emerges. While the schematization does not make the adventures identical, it does make them comparable, and gives terror a shape, so that it is no longer overwhelming. As part of

39. See, for instance, de Jong (1992): 2–3.

a series, the forces that once threatened to overwhelm Odysseus are tamed.

Additionally, Odysseus links the individual episodes into a causally motivated plot. The blinding of Polyphemus angers the latter's father, Poseidon, who hears Polyphemus's petition and decrees that Odysseus, if his nostos be destined, should 'come late, in bad case, with the loss of all his companions' (9.534). Poseidon's resentment is therefore the root cause of Odysseus's extended wanderings (see 11.101–3). Even towards the end, by which time he has become the plaything of preternatural beings, Odysseus attributes causality as he narrates events. The shipwreck off Thrinacia is the result of his companions having slaughtered the cattle of the sun god. When he describes how he had tried to prevent the landing on Thrinacia, and, unsuccessful in this, had emphasized the prohibition to his companions, he doesn't only highlight his own innocence. He also shows that the narrative is driven by an urge to understand: Odysseus sees the death of his remaining companions as a consequence of transgression, regardless of whether it was wilful, negligent or involuntary. The causal link means that the individual experiences become comprehensible and can be processed.

The discussion above of the Telemachy and the songs of Demodocus has shown that the reception of narrative may not only be enjoyable, but may also provide an opportunity to engage with the structure of experience. Narratives give listeners and readers the chance to participate in the experiences of characters from a safe distance, as it were. They are subject to the same tension between expectation and experience as they are in their own lives, but within an 'as if' framework: however much they may sympathize with the characters, the narrated actions and sufferings do not directly affect them. Moreover, the known ending gives audiences of the *Odyssey* a reassurance that does not exist in real life. An important reason why people tell their own stories emerges from the Apologoi. Odysseus becomes the narrator of his own experiences and in the process, he deals with them: the retrospective perspective gives him control over events in which he had no longer been an actor, only a victim. As narrator, he gives his experiences shape and makes them tangible and comprehensible.

One might be tempted to think that Homer merely mentions Odysseus's adventures at Aeolia and saves the complete account for the court of the Phaeacians, because by the time he arrives on Scheria he is able to narrate his adventures in their entirety. But the choice of Scheria as the place where Odysseus recites the Apologoi follows a deeper logic than simple narrative sequence. Scheria is Odysseus's last stop before Ithaca. He can only return home once he has mastered his experiences, and this happens through narrative; he must come to terms with them before being able to resume his roles of ruler, son, husband and father.

The Apologoi therefore fulfil a significant function, one which psychologists and philosophers ascribe to narrative. As an attempt to order events and give them meaningful contexts, narrative is a fundamental way of dealing with reality. In retrospection, contingency is given a definite shape. Time, which eludes our control while experiencing it, becomes malleable as narrated time. The plausibility of Paul Ricœur's thesis, that time becomes 'human time to the extent that it is organized after the manner of narrative; narrative, in turn, is meaningful to the extent that it portrays the features of temporal existence',[40] rests in no small degree on this. One might say that engagement with time is a key function of narrative.

Narrative engagement with experience is also central to individual identity.[41] To a large extent, identity is contingent on the type of story that informs the life lived to date. Even without actually telling stories, lives are lived along narrative lines. The kinds of stories told to others or even just to oneself establish who we are. In the process, narratives create not only individual but also collective identities. Clans and cities, tribes and nations acquire their self-image through narratives, especially those that provide a picture of the past as a basis for the present.

---

40. Ricœur (1984–88 [1983–85]), 1: 3. For a critique and an attempt to define the narrative reconfiguration of time, see Grethlein (2010c).

41. For a philosophical perspective, see, for instance, Ricœur (1984–88 [1983–85]); for a psychological perspective, Bruner (1986); (1990); on narrative and identity, Brockmeier and Carbaugh (2001).

Narrative, however, not only follows experience, it can also precede it.[42] Personal actions and perceptions follow cognitive schemata or scripts that are based on experiences, individual as well as socially mediated, that have taken root in our consciousness. Such a schema is seen when, before passing Scylla and Charybdis, Odysseus reassures his companions that 'this is no greater evil now than it was when the Cyclops / had us cooped in his hollow cave by force and violence'[43] (12.209–10). Odysseus, not yet having the sovereignty he will have as narrator, compares the impending danger to an earlier experience. The interlacing of experience and expectation therefore acquires another level of complexity. The discussion of the Telemachy has previously established that, on the one hand, narrative relates to experience, and on the other hand, experience acquires shape through narrative. But experience itself is also narratively pre-structured. The interlocking of the two, which has been seen in the Telemachy, is particularly tangible in the Apologoi. Homer not only narrates the spectacular voyages within the frame of a magical cosmos; he also shows how Odysseus manages them—as narrator.

42. Waldenfels has repeatedly emphasized this intertwining of experience and narrative. See, for instance, Waldenfels (2002); (2004).

43. In a similar vein, Odysseus appeals to his own heart to remain calm at the sight of his court, as previously cited (20.18–20).

4

Polyphemus: Narrative, Art and History

THE PREVIOUS two chapters explored the flow of the Homeric narrative, considering first the Telemachy, then the Apologoi. This chapter focuses on one particular episode of the Apologoi—the Polyphemus adventure—before moving on in the next chapter to consider Odysseus's return to Ithaca. The encounter with a one-eyed fiend is a common fairy-tale motif which Homer appropriated and made into a 'centerpiece' of the *Odyssey*, or into the 'most Odyssean of all the adventures'.[1] Almost the entire ninth book is taken up by the hero's encounter with Polyphemus. The importance of this adventure is underlined when Odysseus later recalls the one-eyed adversary on two separate occasions. Passing Scylla and Charybdis, he tries to reassure his companions that there was no greater evil in store for them 'than it was when the Cyclops / had us cooped in his hollow cave by force and violence' (12.209–10). Upon his return home, he suppresses his anger at the sight of the promiscuous maidens on Ithaca: 'Bear up, my heart. You have had worse to endure before this / on that day when the irresistible Cyclops ate up / my strong companions' (20.18–20). For Odysseus, the Polyphemus

1. Quotes from: Bakker (2013): 53; Strauss Clay (1983): 112. Grimm (1887 [1857]) was the first to discover the fairy-tale motif in the Polyphemus story. See also Hackmann (1904); Page (1955): 1–20; Glenn (1971). O'Sullivan (1987) counters the assumption that the Polyphemus story can be understood as an adaptation of a fairy-tale motif. Burkert (1979): 30–34 sees the myth of the 'lord of animals' as the basis.

adventure therefore seems to be a standard against which to measure other experiences.

The cyclops episode also deserves special attention because it illuminates the *Odyssey*'s historical background. Homer shapes the fairy-tale motif in such a way that it reflects the experience of early Greek colonization. While previous chapters have discussed the internal narratives of the *Odyssey* in the light of the multifaceted relationship between personal experience and narrative, this chapter highlights the reciprocal relationship between historical experience and the Homeric narrative, using Polyphemus as an example. Like other forms of literary fiction, the epic is a response to experience rather than a simple description of it, and it impacts on the world of experience in turn. Additionally, Polyphemus's gaze is the first reliably attested Odyssean motif in vase painting—a series of illustrations from the seventh and sixth centuries shows Odysseus and his companions ramming an elongated object into the cyclops's eye. The ninth book therefore lends itself both to a detour into ancient history and to a discussion of the reception of the *Odyssey* in the visual arts.

Before turning to history and art history, however, it will be useful to take a closer look at the Polyphemus adventure itself: Odysseus's confrontation with Polyphemus is subject to the tension between heroic self-assertion and existential threat, and Odysseus can only save himself by resorting to trickery. Additionally, the struggle between Odysseus and Polyphemus, or the contest between mental superiority and physical strength, is reflected in a deep violation of the concept of the host gift. By the time Odysseus finally wins the fight, he has paid a high price for his victory.

Odysseus and Polyphemus: Cunning versus Violence

Odysseus's twelve ships dock at Goat Island at night and in complete darkness. On the following day, the Greeks see smoke and hear sheep and goats bleating on the island. It is not only curiosity which prompts Odysseus to take a ship to 'go and find out about these people, and learn what they are, / whether they are savage and violent, and without justice, / or hospitable to strangers and with minds that are godly'

(9.174–76); the desire for honour and recognition also play a role.[2] When Odysseus's companions lead the cattle out of Polyphemus's cave and onto the shore they want to leave, but Odysseus objects, as he wants to wait 'until I could see him' and to find out 'if he would give me presents' (9.229). Full of self-confidence, Odysseus introduces himself, albeit without revealing his identity, and he asks Polyphemus for a gift:

> We are Achaians coming from Troy, beaten off our true course
> by the winds from every direction across the great gulf of the open
> sea, making for home, by the wrong way, on the wrong courses.
> So we have come. So it has pleased Zeus to arrange it.
> We claim we are of the following of the son of Atreus,
> Agamemnon, whose fame now is the greatest thing under heaven,
> such a city was that he sacked and destroyed so many
> people. (9.259–66)

Polyphemus is not impressed to find himself confronted with warriors returning from Troy and has no respect for the laws of hospitality. Instead of entertaining the Greeks, he devours them, eating two on the first evening, two more for breakfast on the following morning, and a further two for dinner:

> [He] sprang up and reached for my companions,
> caught up two together and slapped them, like killing puppies,
> against the ground, and the brains ran all over the floor, soaking
> the ground. Then he cut them up limb by limb and got supper
>   ready,
> and like a lion reared in the hills, without leaving anything,
> ate them, entrails, flesh and the marrowy bones alike. (9.288–93

The host gift which Polyphemus gives to Odysseus is the promise to eat him last (9.369–70). Odysseus counters this perversion of a revered concept by turning the conventional guest gift on its head in his turn. On the first evening, he is tempted to draw his sword and plunge it into the heart of the sleeping gaint, but he soon realizes that this heroic act

---

2. Friedrich (1987a): 123–25.

would be useless—the massive stone which Polyphemus uses to close the cave from the inside is too heavy for the Greeks to move. So, Odysseus blinds the cyclops after having made him drunk on the wine which Apollo's priest Maron had given him on Ismarus. He therefore makes use of a guest gift to punish the cyclops for breaking the law of hospitality. And this is not the last time the idea of the guest gift is given a new twist.

Twice Polyphemus pours himself more of the wine, a beverage so strong that Maron mixes it one part to twenty with water. While the cyclops is drunk, Odysseus tells him that his name is Outis and initiates probably his most brilliant ruse. Polyphemus falls fast asleep and 'the wine gurgled up from his gullet / with gobs of human meat. This was his drunken vomiting' (9.373–74). Odysseus heats an olive wood stake that he and his men had previously scraped and sharpened in the fire, and, using their combined strength, they thrust its glowing point into the cyclops's eye.

Polyphemus's scream awakens the other cyclopes and brings them to his cave, and Odysseus's cunning comes into play.[3] 'Outis', the name Odysseus has used to introduce himself to the cyclops, is the negation of the Greek indefinite article, *ou tis*, meaning 'not one', 'none' or 'nobody'. When the cyclopes enquire who was attacking him, Polyphemus replies, 'No one [*Ou tis*] is killing me by force or treachery' (9.408). Audiences familiar with Odysseus's trick may also be aware of the irony at the beginning of the cyclops adventure, when the Greeks reach the island in the dark and 'there was none of us [*ou tis*] there whose eyes had spied out the island / and we never saw any long waves rolling in and breaking / on the shore' (9.146–48). The wording 'none of us' [*ou tis*] may make the audience think of the name 'No one' [*Ou tis*] with which Odysseus introduces himself to Polyphemus and tricks him so that Polyphemus finally loses his eyesight.

And that's not all—Homer makes use of a grammatical peculiarity of the Greek language to extend the play with same-sounding words. In some constructions, especially in conditional clauses, the negation *ou*

---

3. See Podlecki (1961); Schein (1970): 79–81; Austin (1972); Goldhill (1991): 31–36.

is replaced by *mē*. *Ou tis* then becomes *mē tis*. Accented differently, but without changing the sound, *mētis* means 'cunning'. The cyclopes' answer begins with a conditional sentence and indicates the means by which Odysseus has overcome Polyphemus: 'If alone as you are none uses violence on you, / why, there is no avoiding the sickness sent by great Zeus; / so you had better pray to your father, the lord Poseidon (9.410–12).

The wordplay is underlined by the fact that Odysseus boasts twice of his *metis*:

> The heart within me
> laughed over how my name and my perfect planning had
>   fooled him.
> [. . .]
> Combining all my resources and cunning [*mētis*],
> as with life at stake, for the great evil was very close to us.
> And as I thought, this was the plan that seemed best to me.
>   (9.413–24)

In retrospect, the questions of the neighbouring cyclopes are also subject to a double meaning: 'Surely no mortal [or: cunning (*metis*)] of the humans against your will can be driving your sheep off? / Surely none [or: cunning (*mētis*)] can be killing you by force or treachery?' (9.405–6). When Odysseus remembers Polyphemus on Ithaca, the wordplay with which he duped the cyclopes resonates one more time: 'but you endured it until intelligence [*metis*] / got you out of the cave, though you expected to perish' (20.20–21).

In Homer's hands, a grammatical rule that plagues students of Greek turns into a play on words in which Odysseus's opponents themselves name the trick to which they fall victim. *Mētis* is both an aspect and a description of the wordplay.[4] It is a clever ruse that the name Outis is at the same time a pronoun indicating 'no one', which in certain sentences has the same sound as the word for cunning. Odysseus simultaneously

---

4. Goldhill (1991): 32.

unveils and conceals his identity; concealing his real name, he adopts a name that, at least in conditional sentences, denotes what is perhaps his most prominent character trait: his wealth of stratagems. *Polymētis*, 'multifaceted', is by far the most frequent epithet used for Odysseus in the *Odyssey*. When Athena praises Odysseus for his strategems in the thirteenth book, she addresses him as 'full of various wiles' (*poikilomētis*).

To escape the cave, Odysseus makes use of one more trick. The blinded Polyphemus positions himself at the entrance to the cave and feels the backs of his sheep as they leave it. Odysseus, however, has tied groups of three sheep together with willow rods and in this way, one companion at a time is safely smuggled out underneath the sheep in the middle. He himself clings to the belly of the largest ram and in this way passes the cyclops who, in a heartrending speech, asks his most beautiful animal why it is the last to go to pasture and not the first, as usual:

> Perhaps you are grieving
> for your master's eye, which a bad man with his wicked
>   companions
> put out, after he had made my brain helpless with wine, this
> Nobody, who I think has not yet got clear of destruction.
>   (9.452–55)[5]

'Nobody' is indeed responsible for the slowness of the ram, though the animal is weighed down by the extra physical weight, rather than feeling any pity for his master.

And Odysseus indeed is not yet safe; in fact, he chooses to put himself in danger one more time. After initially appearing before Polyphemus as a veteran of the Trojan war, he can subsequently only save himself by denying his own identity and becoming 'nobody'. Assuming that the danger has passed, Odysseus reasserts his heroic self,[6] once he is back on board his ship. From there, he reviles Polyphemus, saying Zeus and the gods had blinded him as a punishment for his outrages.

---

5. Newton (1983) emphasizes that the blinded Polyphemus also arouses the reader's pity.
6. Friedrich (1987a).

The boulder which Polyphemus hurls in the direction of the voice misses Odysseus's ship but drives it back towards the shore. Thereafter, back on the open sea, Odysseus calls out once more, from twice the distance this time,

> Cyclops! If any of mortal man ever asks you who it was
> that inflicted upon your eye this shameful blinding,
> tell him that you were blinded by Odysseus, sacker of cities.
> Laertes is his father, and he makes his home in Ithaca. (9.502–5)

Odysseus is only able to introduce himself as a destroyer of cities and with his real name and patrimony after Polyphemus has been overcome by a ruse based on a false name. He has not yet given up his heroic identity, but must resort to rather unheroic means to save his own skin.

Odysseus is to pay a high price for his moment of triumph. When it comes to the gift of hospitality, Polyphemus has the last word: 'So come here, Odysseus, let me give you a guest gift / and urge the glorious Shaker of the Earth to grant you conveyance / home' (9.517–19). Now that Polyphemus knows the real identity of his adversary, he is able to curse him:

> Hear me, Poseidon who circle the earth, dark-haired. If truly
> I am your son, and you acknowledge yourself as my father,
> grant that Odysseus, sacker of cities, son of Laertes,
> who makes his home in Ithaca, may never reach that home;
> but if it is decided that he shall see his own people,
> and come home to his strong-founded house and to his own
>   country,
> let him come late, in bad case, with the loss of all his companions,
> in someone else's ship, and find troubles in his household.
>   (9.528–35)

Polyphemus quotes Odysseus's self-introduction almost verbatim, and his curse is to be fulfilled in its entirety. Odysseus's subsequent wanderings have been the topic of our previous chapter. The fight against the suitors will be the subject of chapter 5.

The Cyclopes between Nature, Civilization and the Golden Age

A closer examination of the cyclopes will serve as a bridge to considering the historical background of the ninth book. The description of the cyclopes has been called a 'paean to the versatility, genius and ambiguity of Greek negation,'[7] and for good reason. Multiple negations make clear in formal terms that the cyclopes are to be understood as the *other* of Greek civilization—they have no laws and hold no assemblies. The assembly Odysseus holds before his voyage to the mainland underlines the contrast between the cyclopes and the Greeks, and demonstrates that the social form of the cyclopes is contraposed to the Greek polis and its institutions. The figure of Polyphemus reinforces the contrast: while the other cyclopes at least live in a family group, he exists as a hermit.

Agriculture, technology and navigation are all unknown to the cyclopes. Homer uses three parables with technical images to emphasize the contrast between them and the Greeks.[8] Odysseus and his companions compare the pole used to blind Polyphemus to a mast (9.321–24) and Homer uses the image of a drill being turned in a ship's beam to depict it being driven into the giant's eye, while the sizzling sound made by the eye is compared to the hissing of a freshly forged axe in cold water (9.383–86). All three images evoke technical skills mastered by the Greeks but not the cyclopes, so that the blinding of Polyphemus appears as a triumph of the achievements of civilization. In addition, the image of the forge may ironically refer to an alternative mythological tradition in which the cyclopes are blacksmiths.[9]

While the similes used for Odysseus's actions stem from the world of technology, Polyphemus is described using images of nature. Odysseus compares his foe not only to a wild animal, a lion, but also to 'a monstrous wonder made to behold, not / like a man, an eater of bread, but more like a wooded / peak of the high mountains seen standing

---

7. Austin (1983): 23.

8. Dimock (1970): 204; Podlecki (1971): 82–83; Segal (1994): 32–33.

9. See Bremmer (2002): 139–40 on the cyclopes as blacksmiths.

away from the others' (9.190–92). That Polyphemus resembles a mountain more than a man underlines how far from human culture, how rooted in nature he is.

The contrast with civilization reaches its epitome in Polyphemus's cannibalism. As formulated in Hesiod's *Works and Days*, for the Greeks, the prohibition against eating one's own species separates man from animal: 'For the son of Cronos has ordained this law for men / that fishes and beasts and winged fowls should / devour one another, for right is not in them; / but to mankind he gave right which proves far the best' (276–80). Not only does Polyphemus devour six of Odysseus's companions, but he also eats them raw. In doing so, he transgresses another basic rule of civilization, according to which humans, unlike animals, eat meat only when it has been cooked.

On the one hand, the absence of civilization brings the cyclopes into conflict with the basic rules of human civilization; on the other, it is reminiscent of a Golden Age.[10] Initially, Odysseus speaks of the cyclopes as beings who,

> putting all their trust in the immortal
> gods, neither plough with their hands nor plant anything,
> but all grows for them without seed planting, without
>   cultivation,
> wheat and barley and also the grapevines, which yield for them
> wine of strength, and it is Zeus's rain that waters it for them.
>   (9.107–11; see also 9.357–58)

Nature bearing fruit without cultivation is a Golden Age topos. To use again Hesiod's words from *Works and Days*, 'for the fruitful earth unforced bare them fruit / abundantly and without stint' (117–18). It is worth remembering that lack of navigation is not only a civilizational deficiency, but also a Golden Age topos whereby people are sedentary and rooted in their homeland!

Although Homer contrasts the life of the cyclopes with Greek civilization, these giants by no means exist in a purely natural state. Polyphemus,

10. Mondi (1983): 23–24; Vidal-Naquet (1986): 21–22.

and presumably the other cyclopes as well, earn their living as shepherds. The ring of stones, spruces and oaks around the cave itself indicates intervention in nature. The cave accommodates a complete dairy:

> Baskets were there, heavy with cheeses, and the pens crowded with lambs and kids. They had all been divided into separate groups, the firstlings in one place, and then the middle ones, the babies again by themselves. And all his vessels, milk pails and pans, that he used for milking into, were running over with whey. (9.219–24)

The ground may be covered with manure, but the division of the stalls reveals a clear system: in the mornings and evenings, Polyphemus milks the sheep and goats, 'each of them in order', and 'put lamb or kid under each one' (9.308–9; 341–42).

One might even make a counter-claim to the technical parables that underline Odysseus's civilizational superiority. Setting aside these metaphors and considering how Odysseus and his companions survive on their voyage, it is apparent that they are vagabonds who live by hunting. On Goat Island they hold a great feast because a god has given them a rich loot. Polyphemus, on the other hand, is a sedentary shepherd. He might therefore be said to have attained a higher stage of human development than Odysseus and his companions during their nostos; compared to wandering hunters, the shepherd with a fixed abode is superior.[11]

Homer paints a multifaceted picture of the cyclopes, which is not adequately encapsulated by a simple dichotomy, such as nature versus culture. Their *otherness*, formally expressed in a dense sequence of negations, is conveyed both in the absence of civilizing achievements and in their proximity to a Golden Age. As a shepherd and the operator of a dairy, Polyphemus domesticates nature, yet reverts to barbarism when he eats raw human flesh. In literary reception, the complexity of the Homeric cyclopes was to be further expanded:[12] Euripides has a cannibal

11. Bakker (2013): 60.
12. For an overview, see Bömer (1982): 405–11.

appear in his satyr play, whose critique of existing social values and argument for a hedonistic life carries echoes of the radical sophists of the fifth century. Hellenistic poetry in turn is dominated by the shepherd, who does appear in the *Odyssey*, but is now more fully developed: Theocritus's *Idyll* 11, for instance, shows Polyphemus being spurned by Galatea, whom Philoxenus appears to have introduced as his lover at the beginning of the fourth century in a dithyramb that has not survived.

The Cyclopes and the 'Great Greek Colonization'

The *Odyssey* is no more a history book than the *Iliad*. While audiences of antiquity generally considered the Trojan War and Odysseus's return home as historical events which Homer narrated with poetic licence, most ancient historians gave up trying to extract a historical core from the Homeric myths. Although at the beginning of the twenty-first century classical philologist Joachim Latacz and archaeologist Manfred Korfmann reanimated Schliemann's belief that he had discovered the Homeric Troy in the Anatolian Hisarlık, the 'Trojan war' which their assertions initiated was eventually won by a broad front of sceptics.[13] Wilamowitz's verdict on Schliemann remains valid. He comments that

> it was to be expected that the world would cheer the discoverer, and it's at least pardonable that the masses, unable to grasp scholarship, took the treasures found as proof of the reality of the Homeric narrative. There'll always be people who plot the course of Hector's death on a map and who hold on to their belief in Hisarlık, regardless of the altitude profile of the terrain. It's not something to ruffle one's feathers, and neither does one take it seriously.[14]

The same might be said about the *Odyssey*: Homer may still inspire the imagination of individual authors, who boldly search for Odysseus's sojourns in the Mediterranean,[15] while most scholars smile at such attempts.

13. See the 'balance sheet' in Ulf (2003).
14. Wilamowitz-Moellendorff (1906): 60.
15. See, for instance, Bittlestone (2005); Berktold (2007).

MAP 1. Map of early Greek colonization. © Peter Palm, Berlin.

And yet, historians are interested in Homer. And rightly so—while the epics don't recount historical events, they are a valuable testimony to early Greek culture and society. Rather than being a direct source, the *Iliad* and *Odyssey* may be termed a 'remnant' (*Überrest*), in Droysen's sense:[16] they

16. Droysen (1977 [1868]): 70

do not bear witness to a past war or a homecoming, but do reflect their own historical background indirectly. The world of the heroes should not be regarded as a simple mirror; rather, the structures of the society in which the Homeric bards performed appear under an archaizing patina and in poetic embellishment.[17] The people's assemblies at Ithaca and Scheria, for example, coincide with the beginnings of an institutionalization of the polis that has been archaeologically attested. And Agamemnon's Mycenaean title of *anax* does not mean that he resembles a Bronze Age king, but rather that he appears as an archaic aristocrat who must assert himself in a permanent competition with his peers.

The ninth book of the *Odyssey* is particularly deserving of the interest of historians, since the experiences of the 'great Greek colonization' are reflected in the Polyphemus adventure.[18] Greek traders were already operating in the wider Mediterranean world in the so-called Dark Ages, but it was not until the middle of the eighth century that a wave of settlements began. One of the first was Pithekoussai in the Gulf of Naples,[19] followed by numerous other poleis in Lower Italy, including Kyme further north, Sybaria on the Adriatic coast and Leontinoi and Katane in Sicily. To the east, the Greeks penetrated into the region of the Sea of Marmara and the Black Sea; to the west, Greek cities arose on the coasts of France and Spain as well as in North Africa.

To use the term 'colonization' for this expansion is problematic, since it invites false associations.[20] Unlike the colonization whereby early modern states seized the New World, the settlement of the Mediterranean was not centrally controlled. The oracle at Delphi seems to have

17. See Grethlein (2010a).

18. Dench (1995): 36–38 and Crielaard (1995): 236–39. See also the interpretation by Dougherty (2001): 134–40, which this chapter endorses in many points. Malkin (1998) perceives the *Odyssey* as proto-colonial and presents a different perspective. For an overview of the 'great Greek colonization', see Boardman (1981); Malkin (2009). For individual studies, see, for instance, Tsetskhladze and De Angelis (1994); Mertens (2006).

19. See Osborne (1998): 258–61 against the tendency of other ancient historians to distinguish Pithekoussai from other colonies as an emporium.

20. Osborne (1998): 269 even holds that 'a proper understanding of archaic Greek history is only possible when chapters on "colonization" are eradicated from books on early Greece'. See also Malkin (2004).

been a hub where information was gathered, but settlements emanated from a multitude of Greek poleis. It is even in doubt whether the foundations had any official character. At least in some cases, it is more likely that they were private initiatives. Often, cities may well not have emerged through a single founding act, but developed from trading posts that were initially intended to be temporary. Whereas in the early modern period, gaining and developing land were important goals of colonization, the settlements of the Greeks were limited to coastal regions and did not involve demanding tribute or laying claim to the hinterland. And unlike with the Spanish and English empires, the new settlements quickly became independent of the mother cities. The term 'early Greek/great Greek colonization' is therefore placed here between inverted commas.

It is no longer assumed that overpopulation forced a 'great Greek colonization'.[21] A mixture of causes is more likely. New settlements, both in the wider Mediterranean world and in Greece itself, offered an opportunity to regulate social tensions as well as promoting population growth. Ambitious aristocrats who had reached the limits of their native cities could rally dissatisfied citizens and distinguish themselves as city founders. Curiosity and a spirit of adventure, accompanied by material needs and a desire for wealth may have driven Greeks to leave their homeland. Targeted commercial interests also seem to have played a major role in the selection of settlement sites. Pithekoussai, for example, is rich in mineral resources and lies opposite Campania, whose coast was frequented by Etruscan merchants.

Odysseus's wanderings and the tall tales he tells on Ithaca point to the Greeks' mobility in the Mediterranean world at that time. In light of the description of Goat Island, the cyclopes can be viewed against the background of a wave of settlements. According to Odysseus, the island was fertile: 'it could bear all crops / in season, and there are meadow lands near the shores of the grey sea, / well watered and soft; there could be grapes grown there endlessly' (9.131–33). In the hypothetical 'it could', the scrutinizing gaze of a city founder finds a fitting

---

21. See, for instance, Osborne (1998).

grammatical form. The island's suitability for trade is also assessed; it has a natural harbour

> with no need for a hawser
> nor anchor stones to be thrown ashore nor cables to make fast;
> one could just run ashore and wait for the time when the sailors'
> desire stirred them to go and the right winds were blowing
>   (9.136–39).

The suitability of the island for settlement is explicitly mentioned when Odysseus asserts that it was deserted,

> For the Cyclopes have no ships with cheeks of vermilion,
> nor have they builders of ships among them, who could have
>   made them
> strong-benched vessels, and these if made could have run them
>   sailings
> to all the various cities of men, in the way that people
> cross the sea by means of ships and visit each other,
> and they could have made this island a strong settlement for
>   them. (9.125–30)

Two details bring to mind Greek foundation stories. Even though the Greeks often settled in places that were already inhabited, the pristine nature of the land is topical in settlement legends. This is also seen when Odysseus says that 'neither again is it held by herded flocks, nor farmers, / but all its days, never plowed up and never planted, / it goes without people and supports the bleating wild goats' (9.122–24).[22] The unplanned arrival under divine guidance is another topos of settlement legends: 'there we sailed ashore and there was some god guiding / us in through the gloom of the night, nothing showed to look at' (9.142–43).[23]

The Polyphemus adventure is not a simple description of the experiences of Greek settlers. As strange as their encounters may at times have been, they did not encounter one-eyed giants. But they did meet with

22. See Moggi (1983).
23. See Dougherty (2001): 129.

peoples who, like the cyclopes, did not sail the sea and who lived by farming cattle, and not in poleis. Above all, the representation of the cyclopes gives expression to fears that arose when venturing into unknown territory. Odysseus's desire to 'find out about these people, and learn what they are, / whether they are savage and violent, and without justice, / or hospitable to strangers and with minds that are godly' (9.174–76) had existential significance for Greek settlers. Would they be received kindly or forced to fight for their right to stay? In the ninth book of the *Odyssey*, such fears find expression in the man-eating fiend Polyphemus.

For ancient Greeks, the prohibition against eating human flesh marked a boundary between animal and human, and between nature and civilization. Polyphemus's cannibalism may also serve another function in Homer. In a study of modern testimonies of Caribbean colonization, Peter Hulme has shown that the idea of cannibalism was used to disguise colonial violence, regardless of whether the natives ate human flesh or not:[24] Europeans justified their own use of violence by making accusations of cannibalism against the indigenous populations. In this way, it is 'native savages' rather than the colonizers who appear as aggressors, with colonization being justified on the grounds that it was an act of civilization. While Odysseus does not intend to establish a colony, his encounter with the cyclopes reflects the fears of Greek settlers, as has been shown. But Odysseus commits the initial aggressive act when he invades Polyphemus's cave, and the cannibalism depicted in the ninth book of the *Odyssey* anticipates the legitimizing function it was to fulfil in early modern colonization.

It should not be assumed from the Homeric portrait of the cyclopes that the Greeks always, or even predominantly, perceived the indigenous peoples they encountered in the wider Mediterranean world as radically different from themselves. The cyclopes, as has been noted, are not completely uncivilized—they practise animal husbandry and live in a natural environment whose fertility reminds of a golden age. Edward Said contends that orientalism has its origins in the Greek idea of

---

24. Hulme (1986); Dougherty (2001): 135–38 on cannibalism in the *Odyssey*.

the barbarian, and that the stigmatization of non-Greeks as barbarians marks the beginnings of the European tradition, as persistent as it is inglorious, of seeing strangers, and especially those from the East, as a negative inversion of one's own values and identity.[25] But the Greek–barbarian antithesis was only formed in the fifth century, under the impression of the Persian Wars, and it is undermined in its founding documents, Aeschylus's *Persians* and Herodotus's *Histories*. For both authors, the Persians were not entirely 'other', but similar to the Greeks in many ways. Above all, both Aeschylus and Herodotus emphasize that Greeks and Persians shared the lot of the *condicio humana*.[26]

In the Archaic period, Greek identity seems to have been based on the idea of association,[27] more than on polarization. Foreigners were integrated through mythical genealogies, and the *Odyssey* and other nostoi helped to create a sense of connection between the Greeks and other populations. For example, according to Hesiod, Etruscan rulers descended from sons that Odysseus fathered with Circe (*Theog.* 1011–18), while the Etruscans themselves revered Odysseus as a founding hero named Uthuze.[28] Just as with other peoples, the shared genealogy provided an ideal framework for peaceful exchange. Above all, religion helped view strangers not so much as a negative 'other' than as distant relatives. While early modern colonizers dismissed indigenous populations on the grounds that they were pagans, the Greeks identified foreign gods with their own.

The *Odyssey*, too, confirms the possibility of associatory interaction with indigenous populations. The episode on Scheria introduces a concept that is contraposed to the idea of antagonistic encounters with natives as portrayed in the ninth book. The Phaeacians represent an antithesis to the cyclopes. The fact that they are themselves descendants of Poseidon and were originally neighbours underlines the gulf that separates the advanced civilization of the one from the rawness of the other. Unlike the one-eyed giants, Alcinous and his people cultivate

25. Said (1978).
26. See Pelling (1997); Grethlein (2012).
27. For Hall (1997; 2002) perhaps a little too strongly stated.
28. Malkin (1998): 160–75.

the land, maintain political institutions and live in a city. Odysseus marvels at the magnificent palace of Alcinous, which is guarded by silver and golden dogs made by Hephaestus. The cyclopes don't have any ships, while the Phaeacians are expert seafarers. And on Scheria, Odysseus not only receives a warm welcome, but is also invited to stay. His initial encounter with Nausicaa is erotically charged; the king's daughter wishes that 'the man to be called my husband could be like this one, / a man living here, if only this one were pleased to stay here (6.244–45). Later, King Alcinous himself offers such a union:

> O father Zeus, Athena and Apollo, how I wish
> that, being the man you are and thinking the way that I do,
> you could have my daughter and be called my son-in-law, staying
> here with me. I would dower you with a house and properties,
> if you stayed by your own good will. (7.311–15)[29]

While Virgil has his hero Aeneas marry the Italic king's daughter Lavinia to lay the foundation for Rome, a love affair between Nausicaa and Odysseus remains an unrealized potentiality, merely hinting that the plot of the *Odyssey* might have taken a different turn. It is different in a post-Homeric epic that has not been handed down, the *Telegony*, which is attributed to Eugammon of Cyrene, a poet of the sixth century BCE. Here, Odysseus sets out again after his return to Ithaca and journeys to Thesprotia, where he marries the king's daughter Callidice. Although the *Odyssey* does not explicitly thematize it, marriage was an important element used by Greek settlers to put their relations with a local population on a friendly footing. The fact that ancient sources do not make explicit reference to such marriages probably shows how naturally settlers attached themselves to native women.[30] The practice is both idealized and presented as potential in Odysseus's encounter with the king's daughter Nausicaa.

While this type of marriage is not mentioned in our sources, it does seem to have found expression in the foundation legends, which often

29. Winkler (1990): 178–80; Austin (1991): 235–43.

30. On marriages between Greek settlers and the local population, see Rougé (1970); van Compernolle (1983); Graham (1984); Coldstream (1993).

tell of an Olympian god consorting with a nymph and founding a settlement in the process.[31] Pindar's ninth Pythian ode gives a striking example:[32] Apollo abducts Cyrene from the valleys of Pelion and brings her to Libya for marriage, as instructed by Chiron:

> To be that woman's husband you
> have come
> to this wild spot, and you intend to bear her
> across the sea to Zeus's choicest garden,
> where you will make her ruler of a city, mustering
> an island people to a bluff ringed round with plains.
> now, though, the mistress of broad meadows, Libya,
> will welcome your illustrious bride in golden halls
> wholeheartedly, and there a share of land
> she will at once hand over, to be held by lawful right,
> one neither lacking fruitful crops
> nor unacquainted with wild beasts. (*Pyth.* 9.51–58)[33]

Although Cyrene does not actually come from North Africa, her union with Apollo takes the form of a wedding. At the very beginning of the ode, Pindar blends marriage and settlement by first mentioning the city of Cyrene, and then, using a relative pronoun, moving on to the nymph of the same name: 'whom the son of Leto with long flowing hair / snatched up' (*Pyth.* 9.5). The sexual act and the founding of the city here coincide; bride and colony merge.

Agriculture is a semantic motif common to colonization and sexuality. The settlers were obliged to cultivate the land, and agricultural metaphors were often used to refer to marriage.[34] Comparing sexual relations with agriculture made marriage into an analogue of settlement. Odysseus underlines this by turning the metaphor around.[35] Stating that the island was deserted, he says that it is 'widowed and without men' (9.124). Here

---

31. Gierth (1971): 9–16; Dougherty (1993): 61–80.

32. For an interpretation of the colonization motif, see Miller (1997): 152–65.

33. Translation by Andrew M. Miller (with translator's lineation): see Miller (2019).

34. See duBois (1988): 39–64.

35. See Xian (2017a).

it is the relationship between man and woman, and specifically, widow-hood, which illustrates the fallow of potential settlement land. The foundation legends propagate the similarity between colonization and marriage—foundation is told in terms of procreation. At the same time, the analogy produces metaphors that introduce settlement and women as reciprocal images.

For Carol Dougherty, the parallel has a deeper ideological purpose.[36] In Greek culture, marriage is understood both as an elevation of women from a state of nature to civilization and—from the female perspective—as an act of violence. Dougherty argues that this ambiguity is exploited in the 'colonial discourse'; the metaphor of marriage helps to portray the violence of taking land by force and driving out the indigenous inhabitants as a process of civilization. As previously mentioned, however, care must be taken not to equate the 'great Greek colonization' with early modern colonization. While there were cases such as Syracuse, where the Greeks did subjugate the indigenous inhabitants, in other settlements they came to a peaceful arrangement. The name Megara Hyblaea, for instance, recalls the Sicilian king Hyblon granting the Greek settlers their land. In many places, the Greeks lived amicably, or at least without military conflict, alongside the Italic, Phoenician and other peoples. Legends that represent the founding act as a sex act do not seem to justify violence, so much as reflect marriages with native women. They anchor historical practice in myth and elevate it poetically.

As the example of the Polyphemus adventure shows, the relationship between the Homeric epic and history is multifaceted. Determining Odysseus's route through the Mediterranean is a vain endeavour, especially since mythical topography should not be confused with geographical topography. When it comes to bearing witness to its own time, however, the *Odyssey* is a valuable document that complements archaeological findings. Odysseus is not a settler; he wants to return to Ithaca at any price. Yet his adventures are influenced by the experiences of the Greeks as they penetrated the Mediterranean world. While the nightmarish figure of the cannibal Polyphemus personifies settlers'

36. Dougherty (1993): 61–80; (2001): 130–34.

fears, the unrealized marriage to Nausicaa hints at a practice that was central to establishing friendly relations, which is also represented in the founding myths. Even without recounting stories relating to settlements, the *Odyssey*, refracted in the mirror of the epic imagination, reflects the adventure of the 'great Greek colonization'. At the same time, however, it did play a role in the historical process of settlement. From Odysseus's amorous encounters, ruling dynasties were derived which allowed the Greeks to integrate the peoples they encountered into their genealogies. For instance, the Etruscan kings traded as descendants of Odysseus and Circe, as previously mentioned. The *Odyssey* doesn't just depict a Greek asserting himself in foreign lands; it also itself served to build bridges between the Greeks and other peoples.

Homer also influenced history in other ways. Genealogies anchored in the epic not only created connections, but could also be used to support specific claims. Herodotus, for example, reports how a Spartan envoy affirmed his claim to the supreme command of the Greek army against Xerxes by referring to Agamemnon, progenitor of Sparta (7.159)—the myth is here used to maintain a historical argument.[37] The Homeric code of honour determined the behaviour of aristocrats in particular, and not only in the Archaic period. Alexander the Great is a later example of the normative power of the Homeric epic. He seems to have felt and enacted himself as Achilles *redivivus*, to the very tips of his fingers.[38] He adapted his appearance to images of Achilles and at Troy offered special honours to his tomb, while he had his own dearest companion Hephaestion garland the tomb of Patroclus. After Hephaestion's death, Alexander honoured him with funerary games, and, like Achilles, shaved his hair over his friend's grave (Arrian 1.12.1; 7.14.4).

Homer also provided the Greeks with patterns of interpretation they could use to process their own experiences. In the fifth century, the Greeks viewed the Persian Wars above all against the background of the Trojan War. Time and again, in tragedy and historiography, as well as in inscriptions and paintings, they compared their wars with the Persians

37. See Grethlein (2010b): 160–73.
38. See, for instance, Ameling (1988); Stewart (1993): 78–86.

to the Greek alliance against Troy.[39] The comparison ultimately meant that the Trojan War was reinterpreted as a conflict between barbarians and Greeks. The *Odyssey*, too, served the Greeks as a foil for their experiences. When Xenophon recounts the attempt of ten thousand mercenaries to make their way to Greece from the depths of Asia Minor in the *Anabasis*,[40] he refers both explicitly and implicitly to Odysseus's nostos. Odysseus himself was repeatedly used as a model, such as when the tragedians turned him into a proto-sophist. In Sophocles's *Philoctetes*, for example, Odysseus argues with both rhetorical brilliance and a ruthlessness that would have done credit to the star orators of the fifth century.

While the *Iliad* and *Odyssey* are not history books, ancient Greek history can hardly be comprehended without Homer. There may have been no Trojan War and no returnee named Odysseus, yet Homer is an important witness to the world of archaic Greece, as shown, for instance, in the *Odyssey*'s reflection of 'early Greek colonization'. Both the Polyphemus adventure and encounter with Nausicaa incorporate the Greeks' experiences as they roamed the Mediterranean world. These two episodes deal with opportunities and dangers, hopes and nightmares of Greek settlers. As previously shown in the Apologoi, narratives not only process experiences, but in turn produce an effect. The Homeric epics have shaped Greek history in many ways; they served as examples, were tapped into as a source for traditions and provided patterns of interpretation.

The Blinding of Polyphemus in Archaic Vase Painting

The Polyphemus adventure prompts not only reflections on the relationship between epic and history, but also an examination of the reception of the *Odyssey* in the visual arts. The blinding of the cyclops is the earliest Odyssean motif in vase painting.[41] A number of images date back to

39. See Boedeker (1998)
40. Tuplin (2003).
41. See the catalogues in Touchefeu-Meynier (1968): 10–41; (1992): 956–57.

the second half of the seventh century and show Odysseus and his companions driving a stake or staff into Polyphemus's eye, and it is not until the middle of the sixth century that other Odyssean scenes appear. From this period onwards, images depicting the Sirens and Odysseus's ship, or Circe transforming his companions into animals, for example, are found. Other spectacular motifs, such as Scylla, don't appear until the fifth century.

Recently, some scholars have questioned whether the illustrations from the seventh century actually depict Odysseus and Polyphemus.[42] They argue that the blinding of a one-eyed monster is a common fairy-tale motif, and that deviations from the Homeric narrative suggest that the images depict a fairy tale rather than Odysseus's adventure. But while one may welcome critique of a tendency in older research to identify narrative images with Homeric scenes almost at any price, in this case, the scepticism is not justified. Image and poetry are two distinct media, each with its own possibilities and conventions of representation. Especially in the oral culture of the Archaic period, images did not act as text illustrations. Rather, they were representations of stories in their own right—stories that also happened to be the subject of poetry.[43] There may well be differences in the depiction, be it that the number of attackers differs from that mentioned in Homer, or that the depicted weapon looks more like a spear than the trunk of an olive tree.

Above all, there is one detail in some of these images which vouches for the Homeric origin of the motif.[44] The inclusion of a drinking vessel identifies the one-eyed giant as Polyphemus. By incorporating the cup, the artists are trying to depict more than just a scene; the cup suggests that the attackers have made the giant drunk before they dared approach him. While fighting a one-eyed adversary may be a common fairy-tale motif that comprises many versions, intoxication does not play a role in any of them. Only Homer introduces wine into his story and thereby

42. Snodgrass (1998): 89–100; Burgess (2001): 94–111.
43. Squire (2009): 122–39.
44. Giuliani (2003): 110–12.

FIG. 8. Fragment of an Argive krater, showing the blinding of Polyphemus, ca. 670 BCE, Archaeological Museum, Argos. Photo: Bridgeman Images.

gives it an ironic twist: Odysseus uses the gift of hospitality to punish Polyphemus for having violated it. It can therefore safely be stated that these images do depict the blinding of Polyphemus.

The survival of images from the Archaic period is as fragmentary as is that of texts. Only a fraction of the images that circulated at the time still exist, and caution is needed when tracing developments. Yet even if we cannot say with certainty that the Polyphemus episode was the first Odyssean motif in pictorial art, its popularity can be considered proven. The images dating back to the seventh century originated in different regions of the Greek *oikumene*. The blinding of Polyphemus is found on an Attic giant amphora from Eleusis, a krater from Argos and another from Etrurian Caere, a pithos from southern Etruria and a bronze plate from Samos. The wide geographical distribution attests to the attraction which the Polyphemus adventure held for visual artists everywhere.

How can this popularity be explained? Scholars have pointed to the charm and wit of the story as well as to its structural significance within the *Odyssey*: by blinding Polyphemus, Odysseus draws upon himself the wrath of Poseidon, who causes his wanderings.[45] The idea that the Polyphemus episode reflects the Greeks' colonial experiences holds particular interest. Tonio Hölscher interprets Polyphemus and other monsters popular in archaic art as symbols for the foreign lands into which the Greeks ventured.[46] Like the centaurs and fabulous wild animals that represented nature, and against which the polis and its culture distinguished itself, Polyphemus embodied the *otherness* of distant peoples. According to Hölscher, the 'other' acted as a negative foil and was used to contour a pan-Hellenic identity: 'The realm of this "Hellenic" culture demarcated itself against the savagery of foreign peoples at the edges of the Greek world.'[47] By attempting to explain the popularity of the Polyphemus motif within the scope of history, this thesis not only goes beyond literary explanations, but acquires plausibility through the Homeric narrative, in which the imaginative world of Greek settlers was anchored, as has been shown.

And yet, the colonial interpretation as formulated by Hölscher is not without its problems. The sense of a collective Greek identity was far less present than his thesis presupposes. While the *Iliad* and a number of cult sites testify to the emergence of the pan-Hellenic idea, it is more likely that the Greeks saw themselves primarily as members of a polis or ethnic group. The comparatively low importance of pan-Hellenic identity is shown in the history of the term. When Homer speaks of 'Hellenes', he means the inhabitants of a region south of Thessaly and adjacent to Phthia, probably the valley of the river Spercheios, as Thucydides notes (1.3.1–3). It is only later, in the sixth century, that 'Hellenes' seems to have become established as a name for Greeks.[48] As previously discussed,

---

45. See Touchefeu-Meynier (1992): 957 on the beauty of the story; Schefold (1993): 163 on the importance of Polyphemus's adventure to the plot of the *Odyssey*. See also Kannicht (1982): 85–86 on artistic possibilities.

46. Hölscher (1998): 56–68; (1999): 20–24.

47. Hölscher (1998): 57.

48. See Stier (1970); Hall (2002): 123–71.

FIG. 9. Aristonothus krater, showing the blinding of Polyphemus, ca. 670 BCE, Musei Capitolini, Rome. Photo: akg-images/De Agostini Picture Library/ G. Dagli Orti.

before the Persian Wars, collective identity developed on a basis of association more than of polarization. The tendency not to identify the foreign with a negatively-charged 'other' is tangible in the Homeric epic—the Trojans hardly differ from the Greeks, and it is only in the fifth century that they come to be referred to as barbarians.[49]

49. On the Trojans in Homer, see Stoevesandt (2004).

The difficulty which attends an interpretation of Polyphemus as a paradigm for the 'other' of Greek culture is encapsulated in its supposedly strongest evidence, the Aristonothos krater. The front of the vase shows the blinding of Polyphemus: five men drive a long rod into the cyclops's eye. Polyphemus is sitting on the ground and supports himself with his left hand. In the background, the implements of his dairy can be seen. The other side of the krater depicts two ships meeting: the one on the right is a rowing vessel with three armed warriors on board and a smaller figure at the stern; the one on the left is a vessel with rigging but without sails, its bow pointing upwards. It also features three armed warriors and there is a small figure on the top of the mast. The scene is obviously a sea battle.

It is tempting to look for connections between the images on the front and back. In one interpretation, the Aristonothos krater is an Etruscan appropriation of the Odysseus myth in which Odysseus's triumph is reflected in the victory of an Etruscan ship over a Greek one.[50] This supposition, however, is contradicted by the distribution of the images—the Greek rowing boat is on the right-hand side, the space that Odysseus and his companions also occupy. It has therefore been suggested that the juxtaposition is, rather, a demonstration of Greek superiority.[51] Odysseus's encounter with the primitive Polyphemus serves as a foil for the encounter between Greek settlers and Etruscans. However, this is also problematic—can the Etruscans really be equated with Polyphemus, despite the tradition whereby the Etruscan ruling dynasty is descended from Odysseus? Above all, however, the krater comes from Etruria, and the question arises of how such a chauvinistic representation would have been received there.

These opposing interpretations are based on the assumption that the rowing vessel is Greek and the sailing ship Etruscan, or barbarian in a more general sense. However, there is no iconographic reason for identifying the sailing ship as Etruscan. It is not certain that the difference between the ships indicates any ethnic alterity, especially as the soldiers

50. Torelli (1986): 171–72; (1996): 568.
51. Dougherty (2003).

on both vessels are carrying the same weapons—weapons usually being an important iconographic means of characterizing a figure as foreign. The differing depiction of the ships might simply represent an artistic means of illustrating conflict.

A fundamental question to consider is how closely the two images correspond, and whether one of them lends itself to being labelled 'primitive'. On the front, five men are attacking a giant lying on the ground. On the reverse, two boats, each shown with three larger warriors and a smaller figure, face each other. Even leaving aside the scant formal correspondence, the following question arises: to what extent can Polyphemus, whose savagery is perceived not least in the fact that he does not go to sea, symbolize the primitiveness of men on a ship? If the front and back do throw light on each other, the degree of civilization cannot be the *tertium comparationis*.

It therefore proves difficult to use the Aristonothos krater as a reference for an ethnic interpretation of the Polyphemus myth. The creation of the vessel itself illustrates a different kind of interaction between the western Greeks and the established population.[52] An inscription above Polyphemus's head identifies the potter as Aristonothos; that is, as a Greek. But the krater was found in the necropolis of the Etrurian city of Caere; and while the style seems to show influences from Argos, the clay and colours indicate a local product. The krater, therefore, is an example of mutual exchange and an interpenetration of cultures in new settlement areas: an object used in Etruria and made of local materials was painted by a Greek artist using techniques of his homeland.

The retrospective view makes it tempting to see Polyphemus as a symbol for the 'other' which foreign cultures represented to the Greeks. But the Greek–barbarian dichotomy, as formative as it was to be, only took shape and gained force in the fifth century. It is unlikely that Polyphemus was used to portray peoples encountered in the eighth and seventh centuries as uncivilized and to derive a negative reference point for a pan-Hellenic identity. Rather, Polyphemus is one of the mythical creatures who, according to Greek perception, populated the edges of

52. Ibid.: 50–52.

the world and made it unsafe. It therefore was indeed the 'great Greek colonization' that made Polyphemus so attractive; not as a figure of ethnic alterity, however, but rather as an expression of the fear of the unknown. Polyphemus's historical significance is seen not so much in the formation of Greek identity as in the advance into new worlds.

Additionally, there is an aesthetic aspect which lends fascination to the motif of the blinding of Polyphemus, and which enables archaic vase painting to be seen from a fresh perspective.[53] The Eleusis amphora, which probably dates from the first half of the seventh century and is the earliest evidence of the motif, makes this particularly clear. This proto-Attic vessel, now in the Archaeological Museum of Eleusis, has impressive dimensions—it is almost a metre and a half in height. Nevertheless, the amphora has had to be cut open and reassembled, for a boy to be interred inside it.[54]

Three scenes are depicted on the front. The neck shows Odysseus and two of his companions blinding Polyphemus; the register just below the neck shows a lion chasing a boar; and the belly depicts the pursuit of Perseus by two gorgons with a third, decapitated, lying horizontally in the air and stretching towards the ornate back of the vessel. The distribution of white and black paint creates an intense dialogue between the three scenes. In the first scene, the attacker at the front is obviously Odysseus. He is highlighted in white and forms a vertical axis with the lion's head, which appears on a light clay background, and with Athena, who stands between the gorgons and Perseus and is also depicted in white. Black is used to align Polyphemus with the body of the lion as well as with Perseus. This corresponds to the other side, where the colour of Odysseus's two comrades relates to the boar and the two gorgons. The connections are intensified through the repetition of forms. The legs of the four figures on the belly of the amphora form triangles, which take up the lines of an ornamental band below and are repeated in the legs of the animals, as well as the legs of the men on the

---

53. See J. Grethlein (2015c); (2016); (2017).

54. See Mylonas (1957) on the amphora, and Osborne (1988) for an interpretation that focuses on its use as a sarcophagus and the images as a confrontation with death.

FIG. 10A. Proto-Attic amphora, showing: (neck) the blinding of Polyphemus; (shoulder) animal fight; (belly) Gorgons and Perseus, ca. 670 BCE, Ephorate of Antiquities of West Attica, Athens. © Hellenic Ministry of Culture and Sports.

FIG. 10B. Detail of Fig. 10a.

shoulder of the vase. The legs of lunging figures form triangles on count-less vases, but the repetition of the shape along the vertical axis of the entire vase is unusual.

These formal parallels invite the viewer to compare the individual images. The juxtaposition of the scene from the *Odyssey* with the animal scene reminds one of animal parables used by Homer to illustrate duels on the battlefield. Odysseus is placed on the same side as the boar, which is physically inferior to the lion, just as Odysseus is in relation to the cyclops. Homer compares Odysseus to a boar (*Il.* 11.414) and Odysseus owes a scar to an encounter with a boar while out hunting in his youth (*Od.* 19.392–466). At the same time, the white paint also connects Odysseus to the stronger animal, the lion, whose head has the light colour of the clay background, and this may indicate that, although physically inferior like the boar, he will nevertheless triumph over his opponent like the lion.

The correspondence between the Polyphemus scene and that of the gorgons' pursuit of Perseus deserves special attention. Both images place hero and monster in a violent confrontation, but in reverse. The roles of the characters are reversed—three men attack the cyclops while Perseus is chased by three gorgons, although only two are still in pursuit, since one has been killed. The reversal is emphasized by the already mentioned formal connections: Polyphemus and Perseus, who are both painted black, form a vertical axis. The gorgons are placed below the human attackers and are linked to them by the triangles formed by the legs.

Both scenes revolve around the eye and the gaze, albeit in different ways. The gorgons' gaze petrifies others, while Polyphemus loses his sight. In one scene, the power of the gaze is potentiated, while in the other, the fragility of sight is highlighted.[55] The eye is at the centre of the battle between man and monster. In one case, the terror which the monster exerts is grounded in the gaze; in the other, the hero breaks the monster's power by depriving him of sight. The contrast between petrifying gaze and extinguished eyesight draws attention to the fact that both scenes thematize the gaze as a means of control. The significance of the gaze will be discussed further in the next chapter, which deals with the final part of the *Odyssey*, the killing of the suitors.

The eye, of course, is also the organ with which the viewer perceives the amphora. Pictorial representations of the gaze are therefore potentially reflexive. The gaze in a picture can mirror the observer's gaze, or it can form a contrast to it. Michael Fried demonstrated this for classical

---

55. On the reflexivity of the gorgon in vase paintings, see Mack (2002); Grethlein (2015c): 96–105; (2017): ch. 6.

FIG. 11. Jean Siméon Chardin (1699–1779), *Soap Bubbles*, ca. 1734, oil on canvas, 61 × 63 cm, The Metropolitan Museum of Art, New York, Wentworth Fund, 1949. Photo: akg-images (public domain).

eighteenth-century French painting when he analyzed the depiction of the gaze in Chardin, Greuze and other artists in the context of contemporary art-historical treatises.[56] For instance, a famous painting by Chardin shows a young man leaning out of a window. Totally absorbed, he gazes at a soap bubble he is blowing. A little boy, who can only just peer over the window ledge, watches him attentively. The absorption of the two brings to mind Diderot's description, according to which a good painting succeeds in captivating the viewer—the gaze of the

56. Fried (1980).

soap blower and the little boy reflects the effect that a painting should have on the viewer.

On the Eleusis amphora, too, the gaze is reflexively charged. But unlike Chardin's painting, the two scenes on the amphora's neck and belly create a contrast between the gaze as depicted on the vase and the observer's gaze at the scene. In the iconography of ancient vase painting, gorgons are among very few figures that are almost always depicted *en face*. They look directly at the viewers and invite them to return the gaze. Further, the frontal representation produces a paradox that emphasizes a particular mode of pictorial vision. The gorgons do not petrify the object of their gaze, the viewer; they are themselves rigidified—in the painting. The fact that later poets such as Ovid refer to the gorgons' victims as images or statues (*Met.* 5.198–99; 206; 226–99) makes this reversal clear. Fixed as an image, the gorgon's gaze cannot transform those who behold it into statues. This highlights the peculiar way in which an image is perceived: we see something where it is not; images make visible, but not present. An image is always seen with the awareness that it is a representation.[57] Not even the deadly gaze of the gorgon can harm the observer. In the words of Hans Jonas, an image 'can represent danger without endangering, harm without harming, the object of desire without satiating. That which is represented in a picture is lifted from the causal intercourse of things and transferred to a nondynamic existence, which is the very existence of the picture.'[58] In the frontal representation of the gorgon, the viewer experiences the picture's representing without creating physical presence.

A similar reflection is inherent in the Polyphemus scene. The cyclops loses the very organ with which the viewer perceives the image, and the scene negates what both depiction and perception are based on. It thereby emphasizes how it is itself perceived. Polyphemus's loss of sight draws attention to the imperturbability of the gaze with which the

57. This aspect is underestimated by the current trend to emphasize the 'agency' of images; see Grethlein (2017): ch. 5.

58. Jonas (1994): 111. Wollheim (1980); (1987): 53–79 offers an 'as if' model for seeing pictures using the concept of 'seeing in'.

FIG. 12. Skyphos, showing the blinding of Polyphemus, ca. 500 BCE, Staatliche Museen zu Berlin (SMB), Collection of Classical Antiquities. Photo: bpk/Johannes Laurentius.

viewer perceives the image. The last moment in which Polyphemus can still see is captured by the picture, and has been so for centuries, even millennia. While the gorgons' frontal gaze creates an awareness of the gap between image and reality, Polyphemus's blinding contrasts that which is depicted with the perception of it: gazing at the image means beholding the extinction of a gaze. With the motif of the gaze, both scenes highlight the distinct 'as-if' mode of seeing pictures. The observer sees what is depicted in the awareness that it does not exist where it is seen. What is seen is a representation, and the viewer is separated from it by an unbridgeable gulf.

On the Eleusis amphora, the frame of the image on the neck deepens this engagement with the viewing of an image.[59] The figures extend beyond the lower and upper frames. While this is also found on other archaic vases, the upper frame's dual function is remarkable here: it simultaneously represents the spear which the Greeks drive into the

59. For a different interpretation of the concept discussed here, see Osborne (1988): 4. On the concept in Greek vase painting in general, see especially Hurwit (1977).

cyclops's eye. The spear is visually separated from the border only between Polyphemus and the figure at the forefront, so that the instrument with which Polyphemus is blinded also constitutes the frame of the image for the viewer. The close interlocking of depiction and depicted marks the contrast between looking *at* the picture and looking *within* the picture. The spear may also be the frame of the overall image that is seen, but the viewer's gaze is in contrast with the sight that is being extinguished in the image.

Later vases develop the reflexivity of the Polyphemus motif further. Black figures on a skyphos dating back to 500 BCE, on display in the Berlin Antikensammlung, show Odysseus and two companions driving a staff into Polyphemus's eye from below, with the huge cyclops leaning against a rock. His posture—the left hand is resting against his body while he grips the back of his head with his right—shows that he is not prepared for the attack. His head is turned away from the attackers, which also emphasizes his surprise. The depiction of the giant with two eyes does not indicate that this is a different narrative; it is more likely due to the pictorial scheme for frontal depictions.[60] By turning his head, Polyphemus returns the viewer's gaze. This meeting of the gaze increases the contrast between representation and represented: at the very moment when the cyclops's eye is extinguished, he meets the viewer's eye. Polyphemus gazes out of the picture to encounter the viewer's gaze, and the relation of the image to the viewer's perception of it lends sharpness to the reflexivity of the motif, reminding us of the contrast between the viewer's ability to perceive and the depiction of the negation of sight.

A pseudo-Chalcidian amphora from the end of the sixth century, which also features black figures, thematizes Polyphemus's gaze in a different but no less forceful way. The cyclops's eye is here hidden behind the attackers' weapon, and its invisibility visualizes the blinding for the viewer—Polyphemus's loss of (active) sight is iconographically expressed by the eye's (passive) imperceptibility. In addition, the neck of

60. Giuliani (2003): 164–65.

FIG. 13. Pseudo-Chalcidian amphora, showing the blinding of Polyphemus, ca. 530 BCE, The British Museum, London. Photo: bpk / Trustees of the British Museum / British Museum Images.

the vessel features a mask of Silenus with two large eyes staring out at the viewer. Such masks, which are not uncommon on Chalcidian vases, are a Dionysian motif. On this amphora, it acquires additional meaning: the eyes draw attention to the act of seeing and underline that the organ which Polyphemus is losing is also that with which we perceive the image. The vase turns the gaze on the viewer and brings to mind the contrast between seeing and the depicted negation of seeing.

The classification of the Eleusis amphora as 'proto-Attic' reveals the tendency of art historians to view seventh century vase painting primarily as a developmental stage before later, more sophisticated art. As important as such teleological models are to an understanding of art history, there is a risk that they may lead to the complexity of earlier epochs being underrated. The Polyphemus motif suggests that the art of the seventh century was possessed of a high degree of reflexivity, comparable to the reflexivity of the Homeric epic. As discussed in the chapters 2 and 3 above, the narratives embedded in the plot and reactions to them act as a mirror for the *Odyssey* and its reception. Similarly, the depiction of Polyphemus's blinding is an invitation to reflect on the act of seeing images. There is a correlation between narrative reflections on the reception of stories and the 'theory' of viewing images. While the former highlight the audience's immersion in narrative, the latter emphasizes that that which is seen is a representation. In this way, both aspects of the 'as if' situation, which characterizes both the reception of images and narratives, come to the fore. We become engrossed in the narrated action or painted scene without forgetting that it is a representation.[61]

The interest in the gaze in early Greek vase painting is by no means limited to the Polyphemus motif. Eyes are a common ornament, which is often used to anthropomorphize the vessels themselves.[62] This is most evident in the black-figure eye cups made in Athens and Chalcis, especially in the last third of the sixth century.[63] When a symposiast drank from it, the cup turned into a mask: the eyes are featured on the cup, the upturned bottom appears as a mouth and the handles become ears to complete the image that appeared in front of the face of the sipping symposiast. And even before eye cups, there were numerous vessels that

61. See Grethlein (2017) for an attempt to determine the commonalities and differences between the narrative and figurative 'as if' in the context of ancient material.

62. On eyes in early Greek vase painting, see Steinhart (1995); Moser von Filseck (1996); Haug (2015). On the effect of anthropomorphizing, see Martens (1992): 284, 359.

63. See, for instance, Ferrari (1986); Kunisch (1990).

FIG. 14. Attic eye cup, ca. 520 BCE. © The Fitzwilliam Museum, Cambridge.

took on the character of a face by depicting eyes on them. Figure 15 shows a Boeotian krater from the Staatliche Antikensammlungen in Munich, which has eyes depicted under the handles, as is also the case with other vessels. Whether or not the eyes here fulfil an apotropaic function, as older research claims, they also meet the viewer's gaze and thematize the sense used to perceive.

Greco-Roman antiquity is considered ocularcentric—a culture focused on the eye and seeing. Scholars of antiquity have identified a lively artistic preoccupation with the gaze, especially in the Imperial period. Art historians have discovered the construction of subjectivity in the gaze of figures in Pompeian wall paintings, while philologists have investigated and discussed in detail the role of the gaze in the novel of Achilles Tartius, in which the act of seeing plays a major role in terms

FIG. 15. Boeotian krater, ca. 700 BCE, State Collection of Classical Antiquities and Glyptothek, Munich. Photo: Renate Kühling.

of representing desire.[64] The descriptions of artworks by Philostratus, who simultaneously blends and plays off image and text against each other as different forms of representation, is particularly virtuosic.[65] The first scenes of the *Odyssey* to be depicted on vases show that an interest

64. See, for instance, Elsner (2007); Morales (2004).
65. See, for instance, Squire (2013).

in the gaze can be traced back to the Archaic period. Artists of the seventh century exploited the potential for reflexivity that is inherent in the motif of the eye. The next chapter will return to Homer's narrative and explore Homer's interest in the gaze. This is a significant theme in the *Odyssey*, although, since narrative is a different medium, it functions in a different way.

5

Homecoming, Recognition and Narrative

AFTER THE PREVIOUS chapter's detour into history and art history, this chapter returns the plot of the *Odyssey*. When thinking of Odysseus, it is the spectacular adventures related in the Apologoi that primarily come to mind: aside from the blinding of the cyclops, there is the adventure in which he must traverse the perilous passage between Scylla and Charybdis, for instance, and his encounter with the Sirens' song, as beguiling as it is deadly. Yet Odysseus's experiences once he is back on Ithaca occupy half of the epic. He returns to his homeland in the thirteenth book, but the nostos does not end there. His court is besieged by haughty young men and his wife is about to marry one of them. The homecoming, the third part of the *Odyssey* after the Telemachy and Escape to the Phaeacians, relates how Odysseus ultimately reclaims his ancestral place with the aid of Athena, using cunning as well as force.

At the port of Phorcys, where the Phaeacians have left a somnolent Odysseus with his host gifts, he meets a youth who reveals himself as Athena and who tells him how to succeed in wreaking revenge on the suitors.[1] He is to conceal his real identity and to put the inhabitants of Ithaca, including his wife Penelope, to the test. Athena transforms him into an old beggar:

1. On the location of Phorcys, see Xian (2017b).

But come now,
let me make you so that no mortal can recognize you.
For I will wither the handsome flesh that is on your flexible
limbs, and ruin the brown hair on your head, and about you
put on such a clout of cloth any man will loathe when he
     sees you
wearing it; I will dim those eyes, that have been so handsome,
so you will be unprepossessing to all the suitors. (13.396–402)

Before Odysseus sets off for his palace in disguise, he visits the swine-herd, whose farm appears like a rural idyll. It is far removed from the splendour of the palace on Scheria, and hardly a *locus amoenus* like Calypso's island, yet the farmstead is well ordered; the pigsties are adjacent to the house and enclosed by a stone wall secured by oak posts. Eumaeus welcomes the beggar cordially and without hesitation, gives him plenty to eat and provides him with warm blankets and animal skins. On the following day Telemachus, whom Athena has led past the suitors' ambush and safely back to Ithaca, arrives at Eumaeus's homestead and on Athena's instructions, Odysseus reveals his true identity to his son. He initiates Telemachus into his plan to kill the suitors with the aid of the goddess, whereupon father and son go to the palace separately to avoid suspicion. On the way, Odysseus meets the goatherd Melanthius and experiences the first of many taunts to come.

At the palace, the suitors mock Odysseus, whom they see as a beggar who is as useless as he is unattractive, and threaten to drive him from Ithaca. Antinous, spokesman of the young aristocrats, scolds,

What spirit brought this pain upon us, to spoil our feasting?
Stand off, so, in the middle, and keep away from my table,
or otherwise you may find yourself in a sorry Cyprus
or Egypt, you are so bold a one, and a shameless beggar.
    (17.446–49).

When Odysseus replies that Antinous was not in his right mind, the latter hurls a stool at him. It is only after Odysseus has defeated the beggar Iros in a duel that he is permitted to stay and dine with the suitors.

And even then, the young men continue to harass him. Eurymachus, another ringleader, also aims a stool at Odysseus, while Ktesippos hurls a cow's hoof. The maidservants, especially Melantho, also disapprove of and insult the beggar, but Telemachus insists that he be entertained as a guest.

Odysseus witnesses how Penelope appears before the suitors. She announces that, since Telemachus has become a man, she will obey her husband's parting words to her and remarry. In the evening, Penelope meets the 'beggar', who tells her about his life and claims to have seen Odysseus, saying that his return home was imminent. Penelope, even though she had heard the same thing in a dream, does not believe him; however, she intends the beggar to be well looked after. When the servant Eurycleia, Odysseus's old nurse, washes his feet, she recognizes him by a scar on his leg, but Odysseus is quick to intervene and prevents her from telling Penelope, since his identity must remain a secret.

The next day, Penelope invites the suitors to take part in a trial. Whoever manages to take up Odysseus's bow and use it to shoot through twelve hatchets will become her new husband. None of the suitors succeeds in even drawing the bow, while the beggar, ridiculed by all, draws it effortlessly and shoots through the twelve axes. He kills Antinous with the second arrow and reveals himself to the suitors as the rightful master of the house. Odysseus, Telemachus and the two loyal shepherds Eumaeus and Philoetius exploit the young men's panic and a bloodbath follows. Even when the suitors regroup and get hold of weapons, they are unable to withstand the onslaught of their opponents, who are actively supported by Athena in the form of Mentor.

After bathing and rejuvenated by Athena, Odysseus appears before his wife once more. Penelope remains suspicious and only recognizes her husband when he speaks of the special construction of their marriage bed, which he had once built himself. After twenty years of separation, Odysseus and Penelope give themselves over to love and tell each other what they have gone through. On the following day, Odysseus seeks out his father Laertes, who, neglected and despondent, lives in the countryside. With their faithful servants and Athena by their

FIG. 16. Campanian bell krater, showing Odysseus, Telemachus and Eumaeus fighting the suitors, ca. 330 BCE. Photo: akg-images/Album/Oronoz.

side, Odysseus, Laertes and Telemachus then confront the vengeful relatives of the slain suitors from Ithaca. Odysseus's men quickly gain the upper hand, but Athena ends the battle precipitately and restores peace on Ithaca.

On Scheria, Odysseus was able to process his experiences. As a narrator, he looked back on misfortunes that had threatened to overwhelm him, but which, assembled into a narrative, lost their terror. On Ithaca,

Odysseus reclaims his former identity. Step by step, he reassumes earlier roles, revealing himself first as Telemachus's father, then as master of the house to Eurycleia, the shepherds and the suitors, and finally as Penelope's husband and Laertes's son. Narration proves to be a central aspect of Odysseus's return. Before examining this more closely, however, the theme introduced in the previous chapter will be explored further—the role of the gaze in Odysseus's homecoming. Compared to the visual semantics of the nostos, seeing, ironically, plays no role in his homecoming or in scenes where he is recognized. Instead, the gaze is used as an expression of control and aggression, and the confrontational gaze underlines how Odysseus moves from being a passive, suffering hero to an active, violent one as the plot develops. The fact that seeing fails to be the means by which identity is verified draws attention to the importance of narrative in the anagnorisis (recognition) scenes, which deal with the recognition of Odysseus. His encounters with Eurycleia, Penelope and Laertes illustrate how strongly identity is shaped by narrative. Thereupon, however, Odysseus's tall tales illustrate how narratives can serve to manipulate when used as a way of establishing identity. These tales also demonstrate that the dividing line between truth and falsehood is by no means clear-cut or without significance to important aspects of narration.

The Eyes of Odysseus

Seeing and Recognition

Homer uses expressions related to seeing throughout Odysseus's homecoming. At the beginning of the *Odyssey*, for example, Telemachus is in conversation with Athena alias Mentor, and expresses the wish that 'if they were ever to see him coming back to Ithaca / all the prayer of them all would be to be lighter on their feet / instead of to be richer men for gold and clothing' (1.163–65). From Odysseus's perspective in particular, the nostos acquires visual connotations. Time and again, he longs to 'see his own people, / and come home to his strong-founded house and to his own country' (9.532–33; see also 4.475–76; 5.41–42; 114–15;), to see his wife (8.410; see also 11.161–62) and his property, his servants and 'great high-roofed house' (7.224–25). The close connection between seeing and the nostos even finds expression in formulaic language, in phrases such as to 'see my day of homecoming' (5.220; see also 3.233; 6.311; 8.466).

The plot of the *Odyssey* does not unfold the linguistic link between homecoming and vision, but rather dissolves it. After their first visit to Aeolus, the Greeks seem to reach Ithaca swiftly. Odysseus tells the Phaeacians that 'we sailed on, night and day, for nine days, / and on the tenth at last appeared the land of our fathers, / and we could see people tending fires, we were very close to them' (10.28–30). But then he falls asleep and his suspicious companions open Aeolus's gift, which is a great bag that contains all the unfavourable winds. As these winds escape, the ship is blown far off course. Unlike Agamemnon, who 'stepped rejoicing on the soil of his country' (4.521), the sight of home does not mean homecoming for Odysseus. When he finally does set foot on Ithaca, in the thirteenth book, he does not even recognize his island, because Athena has shrouded it in mist. His homecoming, therefore, is not attended by the discerning gaze which the visual expressions used for the nostos would lead us to expect.

Odysseus's transformation into an old beggar means that the gaze hardly plays a role in the recognition scenes,[2] and Homer does not fulfil the visual connotations of the nostos for the Ithacans either. Significantly, the only one who recognizes Odysseus on sight is his dog.[3] The hunting dog Argos is the first to spot him returning and remains the only one to recognize him instantly. No sooner has he pricked up his ears to greet his master than he dies. Previously, the agitation with which Eumaeus's dogs react to Athena in the guise of Mentor had illustrated these animals' sensitivity to the true identity behind a disguise. Argos additionally has a special relationship with his master, and resembles him in his present state: disregarded, he sleeps on a dunghill, neglected and tormented by fleas.

2. On the recognition scenes, see Erbse (1972): 55–109; Richardson (1983); Murnaghan (1987); Pucci (1987): 83–97; Goldhill (1991): 5–24.

3. On the dog Argos, see Rose (1979); Goldhill (1988): 9–19; Steiner (2010): 116–18.

The scene with Argos is one of the most poignant in the *Odyssey*, and serves to question the value of appearances. Odysseus says to Eumaeus,

> The shape of him is splendid, and yet I cannot be certain
> whether he had the running speed to go with this beauty
> or is just one of the kind of table dog that gentlemen
> keep, and it is only for show that their masters care for them.
> (17.307–10)

Here, as in other passages, it becomes clear that appearances may not indicate actual value. In the same vein, 'there was no real strength' in the beggar Iros, though 'his build was big to look at' (18.3–4). Odysseus flatteringly says to Antinous that 'you seem to me, of all the Achaians, / not the worst, but the best. You look like a king' (17.415–16), while the latter's noble appearance conceals the most sacrilegious of the suitors.

Other scenes of recognition are also designed to undermine the significance of appearances and to deprive the gaze of importance in Odysseus's homecoming. Telemachus is the first to whom Odysseus reveals himself. Strictly speaking, this is not anagnorisis, since Telemachus, having no memory of his father, is unable to recognize him.[4] And yet, the scene destabilizes the meaning of the gaze. Having transformed Odysseus into a decrepit old man, Athena now gives him the appearance of a radiant young one. This metamorphosis confuses Telemachus; he suspects that he is looking at a god in disguise, causing Odysseus to explain,

> but here you see the work of Athena, the giver of plunder,
> who turns me into whatever she pleases, since she can do this;
> and now she will make me look like a beggar, but then the
>> next time
> like a young man, and wearing splendid clothes on my body.'
> (16.207–10)

It is not what he sees, but what he hears, that convinces Telemachus of his father's identity.[5]

---

4. Erbse (1972): 106–7.
5. See Pucci (1987): 95.

The anagnorisis scene with Eurycleia in turn plays off the sense of touch against the sense of sight.[6] Penelope remarks that the feet and hands of the beggar resemble those of Odysseus (19.358–59) and Eurycleia even states that 'there have been many hard-travelling strangers who have come here, / but I say I have never seen one as like as you are / to Odysseus, both as to your feet, and voice and appearance' (19.379–81). Nevertheless, it is the touching of a scar which shows Eurycleia who is before her (19.467–68; 474–75). The fact that Odysseus moves away from the fire so that Eurycleia would not notice the scar by its light shows that it marks him visually. It is remarkable that Homer lets Eurycleia detect his identity by touch. Unlike sight, which is a remote sense, touch requires direct physical contact. It might be said that the tactile sense is particularly apt here due to its intimacy, since it is the wet nurse who recognizes the man she had cradled and nursed as an infant.

The scar also plays a role in two other anagnorisis scenes. Odysseus shows his leg to the shepherds Eumaeus and Philoetius, and later to Laertes. The scar is seen, but this does not trigger recognition; it is merely felt to support the beggar's claim to be Odysseus. It is not so much by the scar that Odysseus makes himself known, as by his speech. Similarly, Odysseus does not recognize Eumaeus and Philoetius from their appearance, but from their answers to his questions, which show him whose side they would be on if their master were to return.

The most detailed of the anagnorisis scenes, the meeting of Odysseus and Penelope in the twenty-third book,[7] makes the limited use of the gaze in the second half of the *Odyssey* particularly clear. Penelope does not recognize her husband until after the revenge on the suitors. Before exploring this scene further, an influential strand of research must be mentioned, which holds that Penelope does recognize the identity of the beggar earlier—consciously, according to some scholars, and unconsciously according to others.[8] Both these propositions arise from

6. On the Eurycleia scene, see Köhnken (1976); Lynn-George (1988): 1–27; Rohdich (1990): 35–46.

7. On this scene, see, for instance, Murnaghan (1987): 118–47; Katz (1991): 155–91; Zeitlin (1996): 19–52.

8. On this issue, see also Grethlein (2018).

the difficulty of interpreting Penelope's behaviour. Penelope is not well disposed towards the suitors. She promises to marry one of them only after she has finished the shroud she is weaving for Laertes, and, until she is betrayed by her maidservant, spends her nights unravelling what she had woven during the day. In the eighteenth book, however, she seems deliberately to arouse the desire of the suitors, and in the nineteenth book initiates the trial by bow in order to determine her new husband. How can this action, aimed at a new marriage, be reconciled with her unbreakable loyalty to Odysseus? While some analysts have attributed the discrepancy to a superimposition of different traditions,[9] others have seen the text as coherent, and interpreted Penelope's behaviour along psychological lines.[10] If Penelope does know or at least suspect the beggar's real identity, then, they argue, her behaviour can be interpreted as an attempt to support her husband without destroying his incognito.

Indeed, in the second Nekyia, when the souls of the suitors enter the underworld, the shade of Amphimedon claims that Penelope had organized the bow trial on Odysseus's behalf (24.167–69). However, this can be seen as nothing more than a character's conjecture and an attempt at an explanation of why the suitors had been so entirely unprepared for Odysseus's revenge. In the main narrative, there is no indication that Penelope sees through Odysseus's disguise. On the contrary, Athena intervenes to prevent Eurycleia from telling Penelope that Odysseus stands before her (19.476–79), and in a prayer Penelope asks the gods to kill her, so that she 'could meet the Odysseus I long for, even under the hateful / earth, and not have to please the mind of an inferior / husband' (20.81–83). And she does not recognize Odysseus even after the suitors have been killed. These and other passages indicate that Penelope does not in fact see through Odysseus's disguise.

9. See, for instance, Hölscher (1967b).

10. See Harsh (1950) for her full recognition of the beggar's identity; Amory (1963) for an unconscious recognition; Russo (1982) for a more cautious interpretation of the beggar reminding Penelope of Odysseus in various ways. See also Austin (1975): 205–38; Winkler (1990): 142–56. For a critique of this tradition, see Murnaghan (1987): 135–39; Katz (1991): 93–113.

Psychologizing misinterpretations of the Homeric Penelope are due to expectations relating to the plausibility of narratives. The modern novel introduced the concept of psychological plausibility, and readers tend to expect the attitudes of characters to reflect their feelings and their actions to spring from their motives. Even when authors such as Chandler or Hemingway give little insight into the inner life of characters, it is nevertheless inferred. But as previously seen in connection with the character of Telemachus, the interest in an individualizing portrayal of characters is much less pronounced in the Homeric epic, and indeed in many ancient narrative genres, than it is in the modern novel. This is not to suggest that ancient authors and their audiences had a more primitive conception of the human being; rather, it is due to a form of storytelling that derives its power from the plot, rather than from the inner life of characters.

Penelope's appearance before the suitors to initiate the bow trial is therefore not to be understood in psychological terms, but rather as part of the plot. Penelope does not change her mind; she is not subconsciously attracted to the suitors, nor unstable, nor unable to commit to a definite purpose. Her entrance in the eighteenth book and the bow trial both serve to bring about the decisive battle between Odysseus and the suitors. Her initiative creates tension: no sooner has Odysseus returned to his court than he is compelled to act. How will the frail beggar manage to prevent his wife's remarriage to one of these young aristocrats? It serves no purpose to attribute processes of consciousness to Penelope that are not even hinted at in the text, and which, in fact, are contradicted. A gripping plot is at the centre of the Homeric narrative, rather than any subtle illumination of the characters' inner worlds.

Penelope only recognizes Odysseus in the twenty-third book. Her ultimate recognition of him highlights even more clearly than the other anagnorisis scenes that it is not seeing that establishes or confirms Odysseus's identity. Eurycleia wakes Penelope with the words, 'Wake, Penelope, dear child, so that, with your own eyes, / you can see what all your days you have been longing for. / Odysseus is here, he is in the house' (23.5–7). As husband and wife sit facing each other in the glow of the fire, the time has come for a thorough examination:

he was seated by the tall pillar,
looking downward, and waiting to find out if his majestic
wife would have anything to say to him, now that she saw him.
She sat a long time in silence, and her heart was wondering.
Sometimes she would look at him, with her eyes full upon him,
and again would fail to know him in the foul clothing he wore.
    (23.90–95)[11]

Even though Athena has changed Odysseus back and rejuvenated him,
however closely Penelope regards him, she still does not recognize him.
Seeing therefore does not suffice for Penelope to determine the identity
of her husband. When Telemachus reproaches her for her motionless-
ness, she replies,

But if he is truly Odysseus,
and he has come home, then we shall find other ways, and better,
to recognize each other, for we have signs that we know of
between the two of us only, but they are secret from others.
    (23. 107–10)

Penelope only recognizes Odysseus when he passes a test of her de-
vising, and in which she proves herself equal, if not superior, to her
shrewd husband. She asks Odysseus to carry their bed from the bed-
room to the vestibule and to sleep there. No sooner has she said this
than Odysseus becomes uncharacteristically agitated and accuses his
wife of infidelity. The bed, which he had built, was constructed around
a tree and is immovable. If it was no longer in place, then another man
must have taken possession of the bedroom and Penelope must have
been unfaithful. Once Odysseus has proved himself familiar with the
bed's construction, Penelope begins to cry, falls around his neck and
kisses his head. Her test adroitly links the question of Odysseus's iden-
tity with the question of her own fidelity[12]—the bed which proves the
former to her also testifies to the latter.

11. I see no reason to regard *esidesken* (23.94), transmitted in all manuscripts and here mean-
ing 'would look at', as corrupted. See Russo, Fernandez-Galliano and Heubeck (1992), ad loc.
12. Zeitlin (1996): 24; see also Whitman (1958): 304.

FIG. 17. Melic relief, showing Odysseus and Penelope, ca. 450 BCE, The Metropolitan Museum of Art, New York. Photo: bpk (public domain).

There will be occasion to return to Odysseus's bed later in this chapter. For now, it will suffice to note that Penelope's recognition underlines the inadequacy of seeing more than do the other anagnorisis scenes. Even the scrutinizing eye, the intense gaze of the wife, is unable definitively to identify the husband. The exterior, or that which the eye beholds, is not enough to establish with certainty what someone's qualities are, including their physical strength. Antinous may look noble and Iros appear strong, yet the one is unscrupulous and sacrilegious, and the other hopelessly inferior to the apparent beggar wrapped in rags. In the repeated transformations of Odysseus by Athena, the gulf between reality and appearance, which the *Odyssey* reveals, gains its sharpest expression.

The anagnorisis scenes therefore contribute to Homer's ironic play with the nostos. As has been shown, Homer refers to the nostos in visual terms and metaphors: the suitors will see Odysseus, Odysseus will see his family and the day of his homecoming. Yet he refuses to allow the linguistic link between the gaze and the homecoming to become established in the plot. First Odysseus sees Ithaca without returning home, and when he does return, he does not recognize the land. Subsequently, he remains incognito himself; neither his loved ones nor his enemies recognize him and only a dog penetrates his disguise. In the nostos, linguistic expression and action diverge: the action does not bring to fruition the connection between seeing and the nostos, and thwarts the expectations which visual references, such as 'seeing him coming back to Ithaca', 'seeing his own people' and 'seeing the day of homecoming', invite.

The Gaze and Aggression

Before examining what may prove central to the anagnorisis scenes, if it is not seeing, the gaze is worth some brief further exploration. In the *Odyssey*, the gaze is multifaceted—it is a means of recognition, even if inadequate; it conveys admiration, as when Hermes marvels at the fauna on Calypso's island, or when Odysseus beholds Alcinous's magnificent palace. It also serves to express control and aggression. The confrontational and subjugating gaze deserves particular attention. It is apparent in the confrontation between Odysseus and the suitors, and reaches from the Apologoi to the Mnesterophony, the murder of the suitors.

As previously discussed, in the nineteenth book, Penelope does not know that the beggar she is talking to is her husband. Yet their conversation does contain elements of recognition, one might say, of Odysseus as he had been in the past.[13] When Penelope demands proof that the beggar had really seen Odysseus, the beggar describes among other things a brooch that held Odysseus's cloak together:

> but the pin to it was golden and fashioned
> with double sheaths, and the front part of it was artfully
> done: a hound held in his forepaws a dappled
> fawn, gazing at [*laōn*] it as it struggled; and all admired it,
> how, though they were golden, it gazed at the fawn and strangled it
> and the fawn struggled with his feet as he tried to escape him.
>   (19.226–31)

13. Murnaghan (1987): 167.

This description links two distinct gazes: the astonished gaze of the viewer, which resembles the gaze that is admiringly directed at the miracles of Aeaea and Scheria, is here directed at a second gaze, that with which the dog beholds (*laein*) the fawn.[14] The dog's gaze expresses domination in relation to the struggling prey. The brooch's ecphrasis has also been interpreted as a subtle anticipation of the murder of the suitors: in some passages, the suitors are compared to fawns, and Odysseus to dogs. The dog's taking hold of the fawn therefore foreshadows Odysseus's revenge.[15] Further, the dog's gaze finds a parallel in the Mnesterophony. Homer develops the connection between the gaze and aggression which the brooch figuratively captures. Odysseus scrutinizes the suitors at night, anticipating his future control of the house, and subsequently, he fixes his opponents with a peculiar gaze before killing them.

In the eighteenth book, Odysseus offers to take care of the torches at nightfall and sends the servants away in a commanding tone that ill becomes a beggar but is well suited to his real identity as master of the house. Melantho, who is in an amorous relationship with Eurymachus, sharply rebukes the beggar, but the latter intimidates her by threatening her with Telemachus. The servants leave the megaron, while Odysseus 'took his place by the burning cressets, and kept them lighted, / looking after them all himself, but the heart within him / was pondering other thoughts, which were not to go unaccomplished' (18.343–45).

Here, the torches on the wall illuminate Odysseus; on the following day, Athena will make him and Telemachus appear in the glaring light of a torch to announce their impending victory (19.33–40).[16] By combining the image of light with his thoughts, the silent gaze anticipates

14. *Lae* has also been translated as 'grip' (e.g., Lorimer 1950: 514 n. 3), and 'bark' (Leumann 1950: 233–34); but there is no supporting evidence for these meanings and the etymological justification is not convincing. Note that Lattimore in fact translates *laōn* as 'preyed on' (adapted in the extract quoted above). The only other instance, the 'Homeric Hymn to Hermes' (360) denotes the gaze of an eagle. The probable relationship with words like *alaos* and *alaoō* confirms this meaning. See Prier (1980).

15. Rose (1979): 224; Rinon (2008): 61. Felson-Rubin (1994): 58 interprets the image as an erotic chase, perhaps that of Odysseus after Penelope.

16. See Russo, Fernandez-Galiano and Heubeck (1992), ad 18.317–18; Bremer (1976): 155. Austin (1975): 251 n. 6 sees Odysseus in this scene as an incarnation of the sun god, of whom it is said that 'he sees all and hears all'.

Odysseus imminently taking control of house and foe. The suitors who have been humiliating him at leisure are the object of his gaze without even being aware of it. Asleep, they are defenceless before the eyes of the true master of the house. Odysseus will let them 'see the light of the sun', but his thoughts already dwell on his bloody revenge.

While the nocturnal scrutiny of the suitors in the megaron expresses domination, Odysseus beholds Melantho with another kind of gaze, one which also applies to his revenge on the suitors. In Lattimore's translation, Odysseus looks at her 'darkly' (*hypodra idōn*, 18.337) as he rebukes her. According to the most likely etymology, *hypodra* implies 'looking up from below',[17] to denote a look with eyebrows drawn together to express anger. Together with the participle *idōn* (seeing), *hypodra* makes a formula which Homer uses to introduce direct speech. An examination of the formula *hypodra idōn* in the Homeric epic reveals that 'the speaker, whatever his message, transmits by his facial demeanour that an infraction of propriety has occurred; he deplores the wilful traducing of rules of conduct governing relations between superordinates and inferiors'.[18] Although based primarily on an analysis of the *Iliad*, this also applies to *hypodra idōn* in the *Odyssey*. In the latter narrative context, the formula acquires a more specific meaning: it not only expresses disapproval, but is also linked to the use of physical violence. In the *Odyssey*, the 'gaze from below' indicates aggression that precedes an attack.

There are nine instances of *hypodra idōn* in the *Odyssey*. On two occasions, Odysseus is himself the victim of the hostile gaze that heralds physical violence. Antinous looks at Odysseus 'from under his brows' and rebukes him for begging, before hurling a stool at his shoulder (17.458–65). Soon after, it is Eurymachus who aims a stool at him after scolding and 'looking darkly' at him (18.387–98). In the seven remaining instances of *hypodra idōn*, Odysseus is the aggressor. It is striking that six of them occur in Books 18 to 22, with Odysseus menacingly fixing his opponents: Melantho (18.337; 19.70); the beggar Iros (18.14);

---

17. 'von unten blickend': *Lexikon des frühgriechischen Epos*, ed. by B. Snell (1955–2010), Göttingen [*LfgrE*], s.v. (Sullivan).

18. Holoka (1983): 16. Cairns (2003): 44 emphasizes that the superior status of a speaker is only reflected in his entitlement to rebuke his counterpart.

Eurymachus (22.60); Leiodes (22.320); and the group of suitors (22.34). All of these are subsequently eliminated by Odysseus and his allies. The aggression inherent in this type of scowling gaze is bound to be discharged—even if not always straightaway.

The encounter between Iros and Odysseus only turns violent after Antinous and Eurymachus order them to fight, and Melantho is not punished until the twenty-second book (22.465–73), along with the other maidservants. In the twenty-second book, the connection between the gaze and aggression is palpable. After shooting the first of the suitors, Antinous, Odysseus looks 'darkly upon them' and reveals his identity, so that 'the green fear took hold of all of them, / and each man looked about him for a way to escape sheer death' (22.42–43). Desperate for salvation, the remaining suitors avoid Odysseus's gaze. Eurymachus blames Antinous for their doings and pleads for the rest to be spared, only to be rewarded with another 'dark look' and to be killed by Odysseus after a further exchange of words.

Thereafter, Odysseus rejects the seer Leodes's supplication:

> Then looking darkly at him spoke resourceful Odysseus:
> 'If you claim to be the diviner among these people,
> many a time you must have prayed in my palace, asking
> that the completion of my sweet homecoming be far off
> from me, that my dear wife would go off with you, and bear you
> children. So you cannot escape from sorry destruction.'
> So he spoke, and in his heavy hand caught up a sword
> that was lying there on the ground where Agelaos had dropped it
> when he was killed. With this he cut through the neck at the
>   middle,
> and the head of Leodes dropped in the dust while he was still
>   speaking. (22.320–29)

The rapid succession of looking and killing manifests the gaze as an act that encompasses aggression and subjugation, which is also inherent in the ecphrasis of the brooch. In the *Odyssey, hypodra idōn* becomes a formula which couples the aggressive potential of the gaze with the use of physical violence.

The link between gaze and attack forms when Odysseus chooses the bow as the weapon with which to commence the slaughter.[19] While he is not associated with this weapon in the *Iliad*, here he not only boasts of his prowess with it (8.215–22) but also demonstrates his skill. He turns the bow trial into the prelude to his revenge and kills the first suitors with the bow they had failed to draw. In this way, Odysseus uses a gift of hospitality to punish a breach of the law of hospitality, just as he had used Maron's wine to punish Polyphemus for his transgressions. The bow is a weapon that requires a keen eye, as Homer well knew. During his visit to the underworld, Odysseus encounters another famous archer, Heracles:

> All around him was a clamor of the dead as of birds scattering
> scared in every direction; but he came on, like dark night,
> holding his bow bare with an arrow laid on the bowstring,
> and forever looking, as one who shot, with terrible glances
>   [*deinon paptainōn*]. (11.605–8)

Here [*deinon*] *paptainōn*, translated as 'looking with [terrible] glances', refers to the movement of the eyes before they fix on an object as a target.[20] Nevertheless, Heracles's gaze instantly seems to turn into shots, again underlining the aggressive potential of the eye.

The only other hero who looks around 'with terrible glances' in the *Odyssey* is Odysseus himself. As the suitors enter the underworld, Amphimedon describes their battle against him: 'He stood on the threshold, and scattered out the swift shafts before him, / glaring terribly, and struck down the king Antinous' (24.178–79). Gaze and shot all but coincide; the rapid sequence of glaring and striking epitomizes the aggressive potential of the eye. When Odysseus handles the bow and a suitor sneers that 'this man is an admirer of bows, or one who steals them' (21.397), he fails to recognize the power inherent in Odysseus's gaze. Odysseus is no contemplative connoisseur of the bow; he takes hold of

19. On the bow, especially its comparison with the cithara, see Segal (1994): 53–57; 98–100; on its genealogy, Grethlein (2008): 42–43.

20. *LfgrE*, s.v. (Beck). Hainsworth's assertion (1993) that *paptainōn* expresses 'a symptom of fear' is obviously wrong (on *Il.* 12.333).

the weapon so as to translate the aggression of his gaze into force and to initiate the slaughter.

This confrontational gaze appears mainly in the Mnesterophony, although it is also seen in the Apologoi. There, however, Odysseus is the victim of violence in various ways, rather than exercising control. Two adventures, his encounter with Polyphemus and his journey past Scylla, are particularly striking in this respect.

At the beginning of the Polyphemus episode, there is another type of gaze, which appears in Odysseus's desire to see the cyclops and to find out if the latter will bestow gifts on him. It causes him to disregard his companions' caution, and the cave becomes a prison where the Greeks are at the mercy of a giant who neither cares about the laws of hospitality nor fears Zeus's punishment. As has been shown, Odysseus's cunning play on the word *outis* is perhaps the most impressive element of this adventure, since the giant's blinding is the prerequisite for their escape; it is only after the Greeks have rammed the red-hot olive trunk into Polyphemus's eye and he can no longer see that Odysseus and his remaining companions are able to get out of the cave. Later, when Odysseus taunts Polyphemus from his ship, the latter hurls huge boulders into the sea, but not being able to see, misses his target.

The cyclops story shows Odysseus not as the subject but as the object of an aggressive gaze. Polyphemus only has one eye and he uses it to control his prisoners. It is only after the cyclops has lost this means of control that the Greeks are able to escape. Clinging to the belly of a ram, Odysseus is able to pass Polyphemus, who, unable to see the sheep as they pass him, touches their backs. Previously, the cyclops could mistreat, taunt and devour his captives at will, but without his sight he has lost control over them. This loss of control signifies *ex negativo* the power of sight.

The semantics of the confrontational gaze also come into play in the Scylla episode.[21] This scene has mainly been discussed regarding Odysseus's attempt to attack the monster. He ignores Circe's warning about Scylla, who cannot be fended off, let alone fought: 'I put on my

---

21. On Scylla in and after the *Odyssey*, see Hopman (2012b).

glorious armor and, taking up two long / spears in my hands, I stood bestriding the vessel's foredeck' (12.228–29). As Circe predicted, his daring has fatal consequences—Scylla seizes six of the men and devours them. The Iliadic vocabulary which Homer uses to describe the armouring process highlights the gulf between the heroic struggle at Troy and the adventures of the *Odyssey*, 'the incommensurability between the fantasy world and Iliadic heroism',[22] and makes palpable Odysseus's helplessness when confronted by creatures like Scylla.

It is remarkable that Odysseus, having climbed on deck in full armour, is unable to see her:

> I expected Scylla of the rocks to appear first
> from that direction, she who brought pain to my companions.
> I could not make her out anywhere, and my eyes grew weary
> from looking everywhere on the misty face of the sea rock.
> (12.230–33)

Odysseus only sees Scylla as she seizes six of the men: 'Right in her doorway she ate them up. They were screaming / and reaching out their hands to me in this horrid encounter' (12.256–57); and he adds that 'that was the most pitiful scene that these eyes have looked on / in my sufferings as I explored the routes over the water' (12.258–59).

The terror of Scylla is evident not only from the ineffectiveness of the heroic armour, but also from the fact that she can only be perceived once she strikes—an enemy who cannot be seen cannot be fought. Paradoxically, Scylla's partial invisibility contributes to making this 'the most pitiful scene that these eyes have looked on'. While Odysseus escapes Polyphemus by depriving him of sight, his helplessness against Scylla stems from the fact that the monster eludes his sight, which he could otherwise use to locate and subjugate her. Odysseus is not physically blinded by Scylla, but the imperceptibility of her attack disorientates him in a way that is similar to what he himself inflicts on Polyphemus.

In the Apologoi, Odysseus is the victim of the confrontational gaze and barely manages to save his own life. As a means of gaining control

22. Reinhardt (1948): 70; see also Whitman (1958): 300.

by exercising aggression, the gaze traces Odysseus's development from a passive to an active hero.[23] When he tells the Phaeacians of his adventures, it is above all his ability to endure suffering that makes him heroic: the long-suffering protagonist is confronted by overpowering supernatural forces, suffers shipwreck, loses his companions; yet still holds on to the nostos. In the Mnesterophony, the tide turns, and Odysseus becomes the aggressor. As Polyphemus had previously done to him in the cave, he imprisons the suitors in the megaron of his palace; then he slaughters them without mercy.

Yet the development from passive to active hero is not a linear one. Odysseus does know how to vanquish opponents in the Apologoi, shown not least in the blinding of the cyclops. Conversely, he has much to endure on Ithaca, where he is subjected to verbal abuse as well as violence, and in the eighteenth book he is the target of a confrontational gaze. However, overall it may be said that during his voyaging, Odysseus proves himself by defying attempts on his life, while on Ithaca he reclaims his ability to be proactive. He empowers himself in the Mnesterophony, increasingly taking the initiative rather than being on the defensive. This development is manifest in the narrative role of the aggressive gaze, which Odysseus only assumes once he is back on Ithaca, and after he has eliminated the controlling eye of a cyclops and experienced the impossibility of fighting an invisible opponent.

Two fishing analogies illustrate this change from a largely passive to an active hero. In the third chapter, a parable depicts Scylla as she seizes six men with her six arms:

And as a fisherman with a very long rod, on a jutting
rock, will cast his treacherous bait for the little fishes,
and sinks the horn of a field-ranging ox into the water,
then hauls them up and throws them on the dry land, gasping
and struggling, so they gasped and struggled as they were hoisted
up the cliff. (12. 251–56)

---

23. On Odysseus as a passive and active hero, see Cook (1999), who, however, does not refer to the process of transformation.

Homer here develops a brief comparison between the Laestrygonians, who throw stones at Odysseus and his men, and men who harpoon fish (10.121–24). The other fishing analogy relates to Odysseus as he views the slain suitors:

> but he saw them, one and all in their numbers, lying fallen
> in their blood and in the dust, like fish whom the fishermen
> have taken in their net with many holes, and dragged out
> onto the hollow beach from the grey sea, and all of them
> lie piled in the sand, needing the restless salt water;
> but Helios, the shining Sun, bakes the life out of them.
> Like these, the suitors now were lying piled on each other.
>   (22.383–89)

In the first illustration, an individual angler uses a fishing rod; in the second, fish are caught in a net. In the first, the *tertium comparationis* is the writhing of fish and men; in the second, it is dead bodies that lie piled up. These are the only two detailed fishing analogies in the *Odyssey*, which invites a comparison that reveals the change: in the first, Odysseus is forced to watch his companions being harpooned like fish; in the second, he is the fisherman who contemplates his catch at his leisure. The long-suffering hero has reverted to being the proud city-destroyer.

Narrative and Identity

In the last third of the *Odyssey*, the gaze plays a significant role. It traces Odysseus's change from a long-suffering to an active hero, from victim to perpetrator. The depictions of the nostos give the impression that the gaze must necessarily play a role in his recognition on Ithaca; however, this turns out not to be the case, as has been shown. Appearances don't reveal who he is, and the three detailed recognition scenes demonstrate that it is something else that establishes his identity instead. At the centre of the anagnorisis scenes involving Eurycleia, Penelope and Laertes there are narratives. A brief survey of these three scenes will show that recognition is not the same as simple identification, and that it refers rather to identity that is expressed in narratives—indeed, identity that is defined by narratives.

Eurycleia

Eurycleia washes the beggar's feet on Penelope's orders. Odysseus avoids the glow of the fire, but when Eurycleia touches his scar, she recognizes him. An artfully structured digression begins at this point, which outlines the story of the scar (19.392–466). Homer initially moves back in time, briefly mentioning that Odysseus had got the scar in his youth during a visit to the house of his grandfather Autolycus, then digresses to add how Autolycus had visited Ithaca after the birth of his grandson and gave him the name Odysseus. His invitation that Odysseus should come to Mount Parnassus when he was older to receive rich gifts from him is used as a springboard to move forward in time and recount Odysseus's subsequent visit to his grandfather in detail. Autolycus hosts a grand banquet in honour of him. When they hunt together on the following day, Odysseus kills a wild boar, but is severely wounded in the leg and only able to return home once the wound has healed. On Ithaca, Odysseus tells his parents about the hunt. His explanation of how he had come by the scar brings Homer back to the narrative present, the point when Eurycleia touches the scar.

The scar digression has come to be known beyond classical philology through Erich Auerbach. In the first chapter of his book *Mimesis*, Auerbach contrasts the episode with the biblical narrative of Isaac's sacrifice. According to him, the Old Testament narrates its story selectively and manages perspectives skilfully, while the Homeric epic does not distinguish between background and foreground information: the detailed narration of the scar was unrelated to the plot and illustrated that Homer knew 'only a foreground, only a uniformly illuminated, uniformly objective present'.[24] This was why the Homeric epic, unlike the stories of the

24. Auerbach (2003 [1946]): 7. On critique by classical philologists, see Lynn-George (1988): 1–27; de Jong (1999). Bakker (2005): 56–70 offers a defence from the perspective of oral poetry research.

Old Testament, lacked tension. But however often this reading is quoted, Auerbach's contention does not do justice to the scar digression, nor to the complexity of Homeric narrative. The detailed description of the hunt is not due to a narrative style that indiscriminately focuses on each moment that comes up, to describe each in detail. Like other digressions in the Homeric epic, this tangent serves to lend weight to its subject, in this case the scar. The detailed narrative turns the thing that first reveals Odysseus's identity to Eurycleia, and later to the shepherds and Laertes, into a significant object, and underscores its narrative importance.

Moreover, the digression does indeed create tension and achieves what Auerbach denies the Homeric epic, both here and elsewhere. He criticizes the scar narrative being inserted at this point; however, if Homer had inserted it when the scar was first mentioned, it would have appeared to be Odysseus's memory. Auerbach notes that 'the excursus does not begin until two lines later, when Eurycleia has discovered the scar—the possibility for a perspectivistic connection no longer exists, and the story of the wound becomes an independent and exclusive present'.[25] Yet the placement of the digression is, in fact, highly effective: it occurs after identification and before reaction, so that it is bound to increase the audience's attention by delaying to answer whether Eurycleia reveals Odysseus's identity and Penelope learns that the beggar is her husband in disguise.

Finally, the digression is designed to relate to the narrative context and interwoven with the plot in several ways. In it, Eurycleia, who has just recognized Odysseus, has a prominent place. It is she who asked Autolycus to name the child. Significantly, when Homer retells the story of the scar in the anagnorisis scene with Laertes, Eurycleia is not mentioned. The appearance of Autolycus, which is described in detail, is also relevant to the plot. The introduction of Autolycus as 'his mother's noble father, who surpassed all men / in thievery and the art of the oath' (19.395–96) recalls how Odysseus, himself a 'sharp one, and a stealthy one' (13.291), introduces himself to the Phaeacians: 'I am Odysseus son of

---

25. Auerbach (2003 [1946]): 7.

Laertes, known before all men / for the study of crafty designs' (9.19–20). The characterization of the grandfather mirrors the skills Odysseus uses to regain control of Ithaca. Autolycus chooses the name Odysseus because he is himself *odyssamenos*. If this participle is understood medially and translated as 'one who is full of wrath', then the name describes Odysseus's current condition; if it is read passively as 'one who is hated', the etymology describes the resentment of the gods, which haunts Odysseus on his wanderings.[26] But above all, the explanation of the name draws the audience's attention to the fact that Odysseus is still hiding behind a false identity.[27] Just before he reappears as Odysseus, Homer offers a dazzling etymology of a name in which the plot of the *Odyssey* is refracted as if in a prism.

Because the scar digression appears after Eurycleia's discovery, it has been suggested that it represents the thoughts that flash through her mind.[28] While the scar might well remind her of Odysseus's visit to his grandfather, however, it is implausible to assume that the intricate and detailed narrative that follows should be a reflection of her thoughts. And the question is not whether she is aware of all the elements the digression reveals, but whether she is likely to think of all those details at the moment when she recognizes her master. It is improbable that details such as Autolycus enjoying Hermes's favour due to having offered him many sacrifices, or the banquet Autolycus hosts in honour of his grandson, which is described in detail, or the five-year-old heifer that is slaughtered, would pass through Eurycleia's mind. Rather, these details can be attributed to the omniscient narrator.

Although the scar digression does not reflect Eurycleia's thoughts, it does include a detailed narrative of which the scar must necessarily remind her. The scar is not just a mark that identifies Odysseus; it also evokes a significant story. Odysseus's visit to Autolycus has the unmistakable features of a rite of passage: on the threshold of manhood, he sets out and performs his first independent act in a foreign land. He

26. On the etymology, see Rank (1951) 51–63; Strauss Clay (1983): 59–62.
27. Rutherford (1992) ad 19.390–91.
28. De Jong (1985); Peradotto (1995): 125–26; contra Doherty (1995): 155–56.

risks his life and sustains an injury that will mark him for life. When he returns, he is ready to assume a new position in his community. The scar narrative therefore outlines a key moment in Odysseus's life: his progression from child to man, from youth to hero.

Recognizing Odysseus by the scar therefore creates a link between simple identification and identity. This link is by no means self-evident, since a person could also be recognized by peculiarities that either do not reflect their essence or do so only superficially. Odysseus's scar, however, recalls an experience that laid the foundation for his heroic personality. Eurycleia does not simply identify Odysseus, but recognizes him as the hero who, barely out of boyhood, killed a huge boar single-handedly. The fact that she recognizes him by the sense of touch is appropriate to their intimate relationship, and the digressive narrative, similarly, corresponds to Odysseus's relationship to the one who recognizes him. Homer not only narrates how Eurycleia places the infant on Autolycus's knees; Odysseus's later visit to his grandfather marks the point when the boy leaves home, where nurse and servants preside over him, and enters the heroic world.

Above all, the scar digression illustrates how identities are established through narrative. The scar narrative encapsulates Odysseus's identity as a hero by tracing his entry into the heroic world, while the digression itself thematizes the role of the narrator. Once the wound has healed, Autolycus and his sons send Odysseus back to Ithaca:

> there his father and queenly mother
> were glad in his homecoming, and asked about all that had
>   happened,
> and how he came by his wound, and he told well his story,
> how in the hunt the boar with his white tusk had wounded him
> as he went up to Parnassos with the sons of Autolycus. (19.462–66)

Once he returns home, Odysseus recounts his adventure, as he also does in the Apologoi. He uses narrative as the medium with which to process the experience: it is the narrative rather than the experience itself that acquires form and meaning, in turn to shape his identity and determine who he is.

Penelope

In the recognition scene involving Penelope, the bed links husband and wife in specific ways, as previously shown. It testifies to the wife's fidelity while corroborating the husband's identity. In choosing the bed, Penelope introduces an excellent touchstone. While the bow, which had been a host gift, proves Odysseus's identity to the suitors by showing him as someone who is firmly anchored in heroic society and who knows how to fight, this does not suffice for Penelope. She is no more convinced by the archery trial than she is when she hears from Eurycleia about Odysseus's scar.[29] The bed, however, brings into play an object that is specific to Odysseus in his role as her husband. It is not only the place where the marriage is consummated, but embodies the character of marriage itself. The bedpost is made of an olive tree whose 'long leaves' were 'growing strongly in the courtyard' (23.190–91), but which has been pruned and straightened. This positions the bed conceptually between nature and culture, akin to the institution of marriage, which lends a cultural form to the natural act of procreation.[30]

Homer even subtly links the bed with the person of Odysseus. The silver and gold ornamentation as well as the ivory on the bed recalls a parable which pictures Athena's rejuvenation of Odysseus just a few verses earlier:

> And as when a master craftsman overlays gold on silver,
> and he is one who was taught by Hephaestus and Pallas Athena
> in art complete, and grace is on every work he finishes;
> so Athena gilded with grace his head and his shoulders.
> (23.159–62)

Homer here compares Odysseus to artefacts which in their materiality resemble the bed that becomes a hallmark of his identity.[31]

The bed is emblematic of their marriage in spatial as well as material terms. When Penelope fails to recognize Odysseus, she refers to 'signs

29. Murnaghan (1987): 115–16.
30. Starobinski (1975); Katz (1991): 181; Zeitlin (1996): 20–23.
31. Zeitlin (1996): 41.

that we know of / between the two of us only, but they are secret from others' (23.109–10). Details of the bed are known only to the couple—it was built after the bedchamber was completed and stands at its centre, just as the bedchamber itself seems to form the core of the house; the house is built within a court that is enclosed in turn. The position of the bed inside several concentric circles shields it from the outside world and images the intimacy of marriage, the togetherness that excludes others and simultaneously forms the core of the family.[32]

A scholion confirms that ancient critics interpreted the bed's immobility as an expression of the immutability of marriage (*ad* 23.188). Homer himself playfully uses the bed's immovability as a reflection of the certainty with which Penelope finally recognizes her husband. Odysseus refers to the bed's 'particular feature' (23.188): it is steadfast in the literal sense of being 'the stump of the olive' (23.204) rooted in the ground. This in turn means constancy in the figurative sense and forms the 'clear proofs' (23.206) which Penelope needs to accept Odysseus. The bed's immovability therefore serves as a symbol both of his identity and of Penelope's fidelity.

Odysseus's bed provides a contrast to the one other significant bed which appears in the *Odyssey*, that of Hephaestus, which Demodocus sings of at the court of the Phaeacians. As previously shown, Odysseus resembles Hephaestus in several ways. He, too, is a skilled craftsman. Hephaestus is lame, and running the only athletic discipline in which Odysseus feels inferior to the Phaeacians. And finally, Hephaestus's triumph over Ares is reflected in Odysseus's superiority to the beautiful Euryalus, although the latter reviles him. But in Demodocus's song, it is not the bed that endures, but the bonds with which Hephaestus has tied the adulterers, Ares and Aphrodite, to the bed in order to expose them to the mockery of all the other gods (8.275). Homer not only emphasizes 'the difference between legitimate and illegitimate sexuality',[33] but also shows the gap between the divine and human worlds: Odysseus kills the

32. Starobinski (1975); Katz (1991): 180.
33. Zeitlin (1996): 34. For a differently weighted comparison of the two beds, see Newton (1987): 18 n. 22.

suitors for their mere desire to claim his wife in his absence, while Hephaestus releases Ares, who has just slept with his wife, and returns to Aphrodite. What is straightforward and an occasion for mirth among the gods weighs heavily on earth, and ends in a bloodbath.

In Penelope's anagnorisis scene, therefore, it is again not a matter of simple identification, but of identity, and this is even more clearly tailored to the recipient than is the case with Eurycleia scene. Penelope recognizes Odysseus once he proves that he really is her husband. The bed is the object with which Penelope puts him to the test, and his identity is ultimately proved by a narrative. He does not give a straightforward description of the bed, which would have sufficed to identify him, but explains how he had built it:

> There was the bole of an olive tree with long leaves growing
> strongly in the courtyard, and it was thick, like a column.
> I laid down my chamber around this, and built it, until I
> finished it, with close-set stones, and roofed it well over,
> and added the compacted doors, fitting closely together.
> then I cut away the foliage of the long-leaved olive,
> and trimmed the trunk from the roots up, planning it with a
>   brazen
> adze, well and expertly, and trued it straight to a chalkline,
> making a bed post of it, and bored all holes with an auger.
> I began with this and built my bed, until it was finished,
> and decorated it with gold and silver and ivory. (23.190–200)

As with the scar digression, Penelope's recognition underscores that narratives establish identities. Odysseus's role as her husband becomes apparent in experiences that have acquired narrative form in memory. When he relates how he had once built the bed, he looks back on the beginnings of their marriage and tells the story of an object that embodies their bond. The effect of Odysseus's speech reveals the significance of narrative in shaping identity: the story not only captures his status as husband, but also restores it.[34] By explaining in detail how he had built

34. Katz (1991): 182.

the marriage bed, Odysseus reconstructs the marriage itself; Penelope accepts him at this point, and their subsequent reunion is referred to as their second wedding night.[35]

Laertes

The son is the first to whom Odysseus reveals himself, the father the last.[36] Laertes in turn does not recognize Odysseus, and at the same time seems to be transformed or in disguise himself. Like Odysseus, he wears filthy clothes (13.434–35); his attire includes gloves and patched gaiters (24.227–30).[37] Odysseus notes that he resembles a king, but is neglected and subject to 'dismal old age' (24.249–53). But whereas Odysseus has been aged artificially and wrapped in rags by Athena, Laertes wears clothes that are suited to working in the garden, and his grief over the loss of his son has aged him in actuality. The difference between the two is also apparent from the fact that Odysseus has no difficulty recognizing Laertes as his father, while the latter does not recognize him. He introduces himself to his father as a man from Alybas who had entertained Odysseus five years previously. When Laertes faints at receiving news of his son, Odysseus breaks his incognito, yet Laertes still demands an 'unmistakable sign' (24.329).

The son makes use of two different signs to convince his father: he shows his scar, and lists the trees in the grove. Once more, identity is established through narrative. Both the scar and the trees enable recognition by evoking one of Odysseus's important roles, and both are embedded in short narratives. The scar narrative is much more concise than in the digression in the Eurycleia scene, but one detail is added— Odysseus mentions that it had been his father and mother who sent him to stay with Autolycus. This small change shows how the same story may be adapted for different recipients.

---

35. See, for instance, Segal (1994): 75.

36. On anagnorisis by Laertes, see Thornton (1970): 115–19; Heubeck (1981); Murnaghan (1987): 28–33.

37. On Laertes's disguise, see Murnaghan (1987): 28–30; on his resemblance to Odysseus, Falkner (1989): 51.

But just as the scar had not sufficed for Penelope, Odysseus seems to feel the need to add a more specific sign:

> Or come then, let me tell you of the trees in the well-worked
> orchard, which you gave me once. I asked you of each one,
> when I was a child, following you through the garden. We went
> among the trees, and you named them all and told me what
>   each one
> was, and you gave me thirteen pear trees, and ten apple trees,
> and forty fig trees; and so also you named the fifty
> vines you would give. Each of them bore regularly, for there were
> grapes at every stage upon them, whenever the seasons
> of Zeus came down from the sky upon them, to make them
>   heavy. (24.336–44)

The sign which he uses here is particularly vivid, since he and Laertes are standing among the same trees, the latter even being busy tending them. At the same time, the trees have a symbolic function. In the Homeric world, they symbolize the cycle of coming into being and passing away, which also determines human life.[38] In the famous analogy of the leaves in the *Iliad*, Homer compares people to leaves that grow in spring and are torn off by the wind later in the year (6.146–49). A boy or young man is referred to as a 'shoot' (*ernos*), and Eumaeus relates that the gods had made Telemachus grow up 'like a young tree' (14.175). And finally, the trees in Laertes's grove symbolize the most tangible part of the passing of generations and inheritance in Odysseus's family.[39] When Odysseus first addresses Laertes, he contrasts the latter's neglected figure with the well-kept state of the garden; the man and natural environment are here in opposition. When Odysseus lists the trees as a sign of his identity as well as a symbol for the generations of his family, he again introduces an analogy for the contrast between humans and nature.

It is remarkable that Homer not only introduces a sign, but links it to a narrative. Instead of simply listing the trees, Odysseus tells of a walk

38. See Grethlein (2006): 85–94.
39. Wender (1978): 61.

during which Laertes instructed him and gave the trees to him. It is a narrative that also reverses the father–son relationship. Odysseus tells how Laertes once helped him discover the world while he is now an old man who himself requires care. The walk through the garden shows Odysseus as son and heir and links this identification scene to a narrative that establishes another important aspect of Odysseus's identity. This time, too, it refers to the role that determines their relationship. In the anagnorisis scenes with Eurycleia and Penelope, Odysseus is shown as hero and husband respectively; now he is shown as the son. In the process, the recognition scenes acquire depth; Odysseus is not only identified, but recognized in terms of who he is to each respective counterpart. The signs used show how Odysseus re-enters his previous life step by step and role by role. Each anagnorisis and each sign enables him to reclaim another part of his identity.

The signs that aid recognition are not significant in themselves. They acquire potency from the narratives that are associated with them; it is these narratives that endow the signs with meaning. Conversely, the narratives are evoked by objects, whether this be a scar, an artefact or a landscape—they are things that invoke fundamental experiences through which Odysseus had once become what he is, and is in process of becoming once more. Other objects also harbour narratives in the Homeric epic.[40] Odysseus's bow, for instance, was a host gift from Iphitus and recalls that Heracles killed Iphitus and stole his horses before the latter could come to Ithaca and receive a gift in recompense (21.11–38). It is generally an important function of host gifts that they provide a reminder of hosts and their hospitality, and entire genealogies are sometimes developed from former owners of valuable objects. The boar's tusk helmet, for instance, which Odysseus receives from Meriones, represents the memory of five owners from three generations. The objects discussed in the *Odyssey*—the scar, the marriage bed and Laertes's grove—evoke histories that do not reach back quite as far, but which are fundamental to Odysseus's identity. The historicality of objects therefore acquires a prominent narrative role.

---

40. On material objects as memory carriers in the Homeric epic, see Grethlein (2008).

The Tall Tales

The narrative shape of identity not only becomes apparent in the anagnorisis scenes, but is also exploited by Odysseus when he invents biographies in five separate encounters on Ithaca in order to preserve his incognito. These tall tales demonstrate that narrative, when used to portray personal identity, can also be designed to deceive, and they will be the next focus, in order first to examine how they relate to each other; thereafter, the complex relationship of truth and falsehood as encompassed by these tales will be discussed. Odysseus's invented stories show that important aspects of what is narrated do not depend on their truthfulness, and raise the question of the extent to which the *Odyssey* is itself a 'deceptive thing looking like a genuine thing'.

The Tall Tales and Their Recipients

Immediately upon his arrival on Ithaca, Odysseus tells a tall tale to Athena, who is disguised as a young shepherd. He claims to be a Cretan who killed a son of Idomeneus after the latter had disputed his share of the booty from Troy. A Phoenician ship, by means of which he was trying to reach Pylos or Elis, was blown off course by the wind and forced to head for Ithaca. The Phoenicians had unloaded his possessions while he slept and had sailed off without him.

The yarn which Odysseus spins for Eumaeus is the most detailed of all his tall tales. Once more, he poses as a Cretan, this time appearing as the illegitimate son of a nobleman who had been drawn to foreign lands, where he acquired great wealth on nine expeditions before joining the march against Troy together with Idomeneus. A month after his return, he set out again, this time to go to Egypt. While his companions were thoughtlessly plundering the coast there, they were attacked and defeated by indigenous inhabitants. He himself had been lucky; the Egyptian king had compassion for him and took him under his wing so that he was able to gather riches in Egypt—until he accepted an invitation from a treacherous Phoenician, that is, whose real intention was to sell him as a slave. They were shipwrecked, however, and he had been the only one to survive. Stranded on the coast of Thesprotia, he had met the king's son, who gave him a friendly welcome and who saw the rich gifts Odysseus was storing there while himself seeking advice for his voyage home from the oracle of Dodona. The king of Thesprotia had given him an escort home, but the ship's crew in turn decided to sell him as a slave. When the ship docked at Ithaca, he had managed to escape. Later that evening, the beggar tells an anecdote from Troy in which he, the beggar, and Odysseus had been ambushed.

Odysseus tells one episode to Antinous to persuade him to give him alms—he, too, had been noble and rich, but Zeus had sent him to his doom in Egypt. This is followed by the narrative previously told to Eumaeus, of how plundering Egypt's coast had failed. But this time, the story ends with the Egyptians selling him on Cyprus, so that he set out for Ithaca from there.

The account Odysseus gives to his wife in the nineteenth book is more elaborate in turn. Once more, he introduces himself as a Cretan, this time purporting to be Idomeneus's younger brother and giving his name as Aithon. The brother had gone to Troy, while he stayed on Crete, where he had entertained Odysseus on the latter's journey to Troy. In tears, Penelope demands proof that he has seen and looked after her husband. The beggar describes Odysseus's coat with the brooch and names the herald who was accompanying him. When Penelope interrupts him to lament that her husband would not return, the beggar contradicts her—Odysseus's arrival was imminent. He had heard in the land of the Thesprotians that Odysseus was shipwrecked off Thrinacia and had lost his crew, but was saved when he reached the Phaeacians. He had acquired enormous riches and was in process of collecting further gifts. He was probably in Dodona at this point to consult the oracle about his return home.

The final tall tale is told to Laertes. The beggar pretends to have come from Alybas and to have given hospitality to Odysseus there. He had landed on Ithaca after being blown off course by unfavourable winds. When the old man asks how long ago he had seen Odysseus, he replies that it was five years.

The tall tales behind which Odysseus hides his real identity on Ithaca therefore share elements, yet each is distinct. For instance, the beggar tells both Eumaeus and Antinous of an Egyptian adventure. He even largely uses the same words, but while in one story the king takes care of him and he remains in Egypt for five years, in the other he is immediately sold on to Cyprus. In three of the narratives, Odysseus introduces himself as a Cretan. He uses Idomeneus, known from the *Iliad*, as an anchor to which to attach his false identity, but outlines a different relationship each time: first he has killed a son of Idomeneus, then taken part in the Trojan War alongside Idomeneus, and finally, he is Idomeneus's younger brother who had once been host to Odysseus on Crete.[41]

The content of each tall tale is tailored to the respective recipient. To the armed young shepherd, Odysseus presents himself as a father and warrior who would kill anyone who tried to rob him of his possessions and goods. To Eumaeus, who is the son of the ruler of Syra but who was kidnapped and sold into slavery as a child, Odysseus assumes the guise of the illegitimate son of a rich family who narrowly escaped enslavement twice. Like Eumaeus's master, he had fought at Troy and can even tell an anecdote from a night watch they had shared. When Odysseus asks for alms from Antinous, he confines himself to a single episode, a journey to Egypt designed to illustrate the fragility of human fortune, as he explains how he went from being a rich man to a beggar. To appeal to Penelope, the beggar invokes royal descent from the house of Minos and at length tells of her husband, to whom he offered hospitality. Similarly, he appears before Laertes as a foreign aristocrat who had once entertained Odysseus.[42] In all these cases, Odysseus creates characters who meet their counterpart on an equal footing and whose life stories are designed to arouse sympathy in their tailor-made specificity.

While each tall tale is suited to the situation at hand, a structure becomes apparent when they are considered together.[43] In the first deceptive speech, the beggar does not mention Odysseus at all. Thereafter, he tells Eumaeus that the king of Threspotia had shown him Odysseus's treasures and that he had taken part in an ambush with Odysseus at

---

41. Haft (1984).

42. On the descriptive names of this false biography, see Erbse (1972): 101.

43. Goldhill (1991): 45.

Troy. While Odysseus is again not mentioned in the short speech to Antinous, he inexorably moves to the foreground when the beggar talks with Penelope and Laertes, at which point the narrator focuses his accounts on Odysseus and claims to have entertained him as a guest. The intensifying presence of Odysseus in the tall tales parallels the gradual recovery of his identity in the anagnorisis scenes. Odysseus may still be concealed behind these tales, but the invented biographies increasingly allow his person to emerge.

The deceptive character of Odysseus's narratives is particularly apparent in the encounter with Eumaeus. Even before he relates his story as that of a Cretan and announces Odysseus's impending return, Eumaeus remarks,

> Old sir, there is none who could come here [*alalēmenos*],
>   bringing a report
> of him, and persuade his wife and his dear son; and yet
> there are vain and vagabond [*alētai*] men in need of sustenance
> who tell lies [*pseudont'*] and are unwilling to give a true story
>   [*alēthea*];
> and any vagrant [*alēteuōn*], who makes his way to the land of
>   Ithaca,
> goes to my mistress and babbles his lies to her. (14.122–27)

Homer here has Eumaeus play with the similar-sounding words for 'vagabond' (*aletēs*), 'roam' (*alēteuō*) and 'true' (*alēthes*).[44] The assonance and consonance, clearly audible in repetition, suggest a natural connection. Their very name insinuates that tramps do not tell the truth.

Odysseus protests resolutely, 'For as I detest the doorways of death I detest that man who / under constraint of poverty babbles beguiling falsehoods' (14.156–57). Both this affirmation and the oath the beggar swears relate to the claim that Odysseus will return, yet the vehemence with which he defends his narrative also highlights that his story is composed of lies. Even the narrative itself subtly reminds the audience of

---

44. Ibid.: 38.

this. The Phoenician who is 'well skilled in beguilements' (14.288), and who lures the stranger on board with 'lying advices' (14.296) in order to enslave him, also evokes the untruthfulness of the speech Odysseus is about to make.

Eumaeus, who raises the subject of dishonest speech, ironically confuses what is true and untrue.[45] He believes the beggar's fictitious biography, but doubts the return of Odysseus, which has already come to pass as they converse. While Eumaeus's scolding arises from a general scepticism about news concerning his master's survival, the beggar's life story convinces him due to its plausibility. According to Homer, Odysseus 'knew how to say many false things that were like true sayings' (19.203). As previously shown, he skilfully tailors these biographies to resonate with their respective recipients. Each story conforms closely enough to the listener's expectations of reality for Eumaeus, as well as the other listeners, to believe them.

Indeed, the tall tales are more realistic than Odysseus's actual adventures.[46] They do not contain the monsters and mythical creatures of the Apologoi and fit well within the turbulent world of the early Archaic period. At that time, the Mediterranean was full of adventurers trying their luck, as well as of merchants moving from one place to another. The various lives which Odysseus invents also reflect the temptation to acquire riches in foreign lands and the associated risk of losing one's status, possibly to end up as a slave. An inscription dating back to the beginning of the sixth century (*ML* no. 7),[47] for instance, testifies that such events were not uncommon. It is inscribed on the left leg of a colossal statue of Ramses II (r. 1279–1213 BCE) and records that the Egyptian king Psammetichos II (r. 595–589 BCE) made use of Greek mercenaries in an expedition to Ethiopia. Among the Greek mercenaries who accompanied the pharaoh to Egypt were 'Archon', son of Amoibichos and 'Peleqos', son of Eudamus, figures who might be termed the real counterparts of the characters Odysseus invented.

45. See, for instance, Fenik (1974): 70; Todorov (1977): 61.
46. Hölscher (1988): 313; Rutherford (1992): 71.
47. Meiggs and Lewis (1969).

Lies and Truth

The word 'lie' doesn't have particularly positive connotations. Yet our contemporary inclination to condemn telling of falsehoods cannot be applied to the Homeric world. Ethnologists have even claimed that in contemporary rural Greece, lying is considered a legitimate means of gaining an advantage when faced with an uncertain situation or adversaries.[48] In any case, in the Homeric world, telling untruths is judged more as a sign of cleverness than as a moral deficit. Athena praises her protégé Odysseus when he, not recognizing her, pretends to be a Cretan:

> It would be a sharp one, and a stealthy one, who would ever get
>> past you
> in any contriving; even if it were a god against you.
> You wretch, so devious, never weary of tricks, then you would
>> not
> even in your own country give over your ways of deceiving
> and your thievish tales. They are near to you in your very nature.
> But come, let us talk no more of this, for you and I both know
> sharp practice, since you are far the best of all mortal
> men for counsel and stories, and I among all the divinities
> am famous for wit and sharpness. (13.291–99)

The high value accorded to deception in the Homeric epic is also evident from the fame that Odysseus acquires for his cunning trick with the wooden horse at Troy.

The *Odyssey* also reveals the complexity of what tends simplistically to be referred to as a 'lie'. The verse 'He knew how to say many false things that were like true sayings' not only refers to the plausibility of Odysseus's tall tales, but also suggests that the line between fact and fiction may not always be clearly drawn.[49] His tales contain facts as well as inventions when it comes to persons, places and events. The Trojan War,

---

48. On lies in the Homeric epic, see especially Pratt (1983): 55–94; on modern ethnological parallels, Walcot (1977).

49. See Goldhill (1991): 46–47; Segal (1994): 177; Maronitis (1981): 126.

for instance, is mentioned several times, and when he speaks to Penelope, the beggar's account includes important stages of Odysseus's voyage: the sacrilege against the cattle of the sun god, Poseidon's and Zeus's wrath, which is unleashed in a storm that only Odysseus survives, and the Phaeacians' hospitality (19.273–82).

Odysseus's adventures also shine through his tall tales. His invented characters have not gone through as many travails as himself, yet his lament is reminiscent of his actual suffering. For example, the first deceptive speech includes the phrase 'my heart suffered many / pains: the wars of men; hard crossing of the big waters' (13.263–64), which repeats verbatim what is said about Odysseus himself and also alludes to the Proem (13.90–91; 1.4). Similarly, the description at the beginning of the *Odyssey* that 'many were they whose cities he saw, whose minds he learned of, / many the pains he suffered in his spirit on the wide sea' (1.3–4) is evoked when the beggar introduces himself to Penelope as someone who is 'wandering many cities of men and suffering hardships' (19.170). While it may be a case of varying or repeating formulae, parallels are nevertheless created which allow Odysseus's experiences to shine through.

Some of the invented experiences are deliberately modelled on adventures that Odysseus has previously experienced.[50] The life story he tells to the beggar Eumaeus includes plundering on the Egyptian coast, followed by a devastating counterattack by the local inhabitants, which recalls the Greeks' attack on the Cicones, who ultimately put the Greeks to flight (14.259–72; 9.39–66). While there are differences—the beggar says that the looting had taken place without his consent and that the locals' counterattack met with no significant resistance[51]—the shipwreck is described in the same terms as the storm following the departure from Thrinacia (14.303–15; 12.403–25). The king's son who meets the invented character on the beach in Thesprotia and leads him to the palace recycles the motif of Odysseus's meeting with Nausicaa (14.317–20; 6.127–315). Finally, the oracle of Dodona, which the fictitious Odysseus consults before his return home, fulfils the same function as Teiresias

50. Fenik (1974): 167–71.
51. Emlyn-Jones (1986): 5–6.

in the Apologoi (14.327–30; 11.100–137). In particular, the phrase that he will return home either 'in secret or openly' (14.330) evokes Teiresias's prediction that Odysseus will kill the suitors 'either by treachery, or openly with the sharp bronze' (11.120).

The inclusion of truthful elements and variations on Odysseus's adventures are not the only way in which fact and fiction are combined. Despite their mendacity, Odysseus's tales serve to convey a true message, along the lines that 'Odysseus returns! Take courage, Eumaeus and Penelope, and you, suitors, beware . . .'. The pragmatic dimension of a narrative evidently does not depend on whether it is true or not. This is particularly clear in the anecdote of Troy, in which the beggar does more than simply entertain Eumaeus by the fire. The night is advanced; it is raining and a cold west wind is blowing, and the beggar tells of a night he had spent in an ambush under the leadership of Odysseus and Menelaus. He had gone out without his cloak and was very cold; the ground was covered with snow. Then Odysseus obtained a cloak for him by trickery, by sending a messenger back to the Greek camp on a pretext, and in this way he was able to use the coat which the messenger left behind and survived the cold night.

Eumaeus immediately recognizes this as an *ainos*, a story with a message, and moves the beggar's bed closer to the fire, giving him sheepskins and goatskins as well as a coat. Whether the anecdote happened as told by the beggar is irrelevant. What matters is the message, a request for protection from the cold. Narratives, it is made clear, may not only reflect previous actions and events; they can also be a speech act, serving to persuade the listener to do something with or without an explicit request. Other stories told by Odysseus also influence the actions of his listeners, both implicitly and explicitly. One reason for introducing himself as a man of war to the armed shepherd is to warn him not to lay a hand on his treasures. The fate of Idomeneus's son, whom he says he slew, here serves as a cautionary tale. And the description of his own vicissitudes serves to persuade Antinous to give him alms. At the same time, his story is a warning to the suitors not to feel too safe, albeit they do not heed it.

As a speech act, the Troy anecdote draws attention to another level of truth that is present in the tall tales. As well as containing an appeal to give the beggar a cloak, it reveals Odysseus's nature. The story of the cloak tells of a ruse and sets a ruse in motion; the content of the speech is simultaneously its purpose. The beggar tells how Odysseus, using a ruse, succeeded in obtaining a coat—in order to obtain one. The fact that the narrative tells of and achieves what Odysseus has actually done indicates that the speaker is none other than he. The skill with which Odysseus is able repeatedly to invent life stories, always adapting them to the respective recipient to arouse their sympathy, reveals the nature of a shrewd and devious hero. His listeners are taken in by the false biographies, while the goddess Athena and the audience see Odysseus in the tall tales.

Like the anagnorisis scenes, Odysseus's tales demonstrate how identities are constructed in narratives. At the same time, stories have the potential to relate not only events that have actually happened, but also those that are imaginary, and to pass both off as true. They both determine identities and serve to enable Odysseus's deception. The tall tales show that, when it comes to storytelling, truth and lies are not simple opposites. The biographies are inventions that vary and include truthful elements. And notwithstanding the deception that serves to illustrate Odysseus's character, the message of his return is true throughout.

The 'Odyssey' Itself: A Tall Tale?

What is the extent of the reflexivity of the tall tales, especially when it comes to the characterization of lies as 'false things that were like true sayings'? This formula also appears in the proem of Hesiod's *Theogony*. Hesiod reports how the Muses showed themselves to him in a valley of Helikon. Before giving him a sceptre and breathing into him a divine voice, they say 'shepherds camping in the fields, base objects of reproach, mere bellies! We know how to say many false things that are like true [*etuma*] sayings, but we also know how, whenever we wish it, to proclaim things that are true [*alēthea*] (26–28).'[52] Many philologists,

---

52. Translation by Gregory Nagy (adapted to correspond to Lattimore's translation of *Od.* 19.203): see Nagy (n.d.). On this much-discussed passage of Hesiod, see the sources in Halliwell (2011): 13 n. 26.

probably the majority, assume that Hesiod is quoting from Homer in this programmatic passage, but it has also been variously claimed that the *Odyssey* is quoting from the *Theogony*, and that there is no direct correlation between the two passages.[53] An allusion to the *Odyssey* is likely, yet even without this, it is noteworthy that Hesiod uses the phrase 'false things that are like true sayings' to describe a category of narration. It does not really matter whether Hesiod is referring to Homeric poetry and denigrating it compared to his own work, which he holds up as committed to truth. His reflection on poems that 'are like true sayings' raises the question of whether such a characterization of Odysseus's tall tales might also apply to Homer's epic as a whole. Is the *Odyssey* ultimately a text that 'is like a true saying'?

The *Odyssey* itself suggests this, by comparing Odysseus, as the narrator of the tall tales, to a bard. Eumaeus praises his oratory to Penelope:

> But as when a man looks to a singer, who has been given
> from the gods the skill with which he sings for delight of mortals,
> and they are impassioned and strain to hear it when he sings
>   to them,
> so he enchanted me in the halls as he sat beside me. (17.518–21)

Other passages, too, describe Odysseus as being akin to a bard. On Scheria, Alcinous comments, 'you have / a grace upon your words, and there is sound sense within them, / and expertly, as a singer would do, you have told the story' (11.366–68). At a turning point in the plot, when Odysseus claims his bow, first to pass the test and then to commence the slaughter of the suitors, the narrator comments,

> as when a man, who well understands the lyre and singing,
> easily, holding it on either side, pulls the strongly twisted
> cord of sheep's gut, so as to slip it over a new peg,
> so, without any strain, Odysseus strung the great bow.
>   (21.406–9)

---

53. For quotation from Hesiod in the *Odyssey*, see West (1966): 27; against a necessary correlation between the two, see Rutherford ad *Od.* 19.203.

These comparisons seem to invite the audience to view Odysseus's speeches as a mirror for the epic itself.

Moreover, the tendency of ancient audiences to attribute the characters' words to the author should not be forgotten. Heraclitus, for example, criticizes Homer for wanting to banish strife from the world without noting that it is Achilles, not Homer, who curses strife (DK A22).[54] This is akin to a previously discussed comment on Homer, which seems to eliminate the difference between him and Odysseus. Pindar (as we saw in chapter 3) argues in the seventh Nemean ode that poets are capable of distorting events:

> Myself, I hold that what is said
> about Odysseus has turned out to exceed the things he suffered,
> thanks to Homer and his sweet speech,
> since on his lies, through soaring craftsmanship,
> there rests some quality of awe. Poetic skill
> deceives, leading astray with stories. (20–23)[55]

Who is the source of the lies here and whose is the 'soaring craftmanship'? Odysseus is famous both for being an orator and a trickster; at the same time, Pindar criticizes Homer for unduly magnifying his suffering. Due to the ambiguity, the accusation of deception is applied to both Odysseus and Homer;[56] the author is liable for his characters.

Hesiod's reflections on poetry, the Homeric comparison of Odysseus to a bard and the tendency of ancient audiences not to distinguish between characters and the author all seem to suggest that Homer is characterizing his own poetry when he says that Odysseus 'told many false things that were like true sayings'. Since uttering falsehoods was not necessarily considered a transgression, nothing seems to stand in the way of such an interpretation. And yet some important arguments do speak against this short-circuit between Odysseus and Homer.[57] First

---

54. Rösler (1980): 288.

55. Translation by Andrew M. Miller (with translator's lineation): see Miller (2019).

56. Most (1985):150–51.

57. On the differences between singers and narrators such as Odysseus, see Mackie (1997); Scodel (1998); Beck (2005).

of all, Odysseus is not a bard; he is only compared to one. The narrator, in fact, goes on to say that it is Odysseus who appears instead of a bard, and that singing is replaced by a bloodbath.

Further, the tall tales differ fundamentally from the bards' recitals in the *Odyssey*, as well as from the *Odyssey*'s narrative. For instance, in the context of the plot, Odysseus relates his tall tales to achieve a definite goal. The bards, on the other hand, sing of the deeds of others to enhance a festive occasion; their song may inform the plot, as seen with the songs of Demodocus, but they do not serve any utilitarian purpose within it. Most importantly, while it is made explicit that Odysseus's tales are untrue, the bards' song is inspired by the Muses. Although the Homeric epic is not described at any point as true (*alethes*), the juxtaposition of unconfirmed reports with the all-embracing knowledge of the Muses leaves no doubt that, unlike in Hesiod, the Homeric Muses vouch for the truth of the bard's song:

> For you, who are goddesses, are there, and you know all things,
> and we have heard only the rumour of it and know nothing.
>   (*Il.* 2.485–86)

The tall tales, therefore, are not simply a mirror for the *Odyssey*; the epic is not to be understood as 'the deceptive thing looking like the genuine thing'. And yet Odysseus's tales do shed light on important aspects of narrative, which are also not without significance for the *Odyssey*. First of all, it is important to note that these tales do not thematize fictionality, even though they are repeatedly used as testimony in the debate about when the Greeks invented fictionality.[58] This debate is subject to various, often tacitly assumed and opposing, concepts of fictionality. In order to avoid obfuscation, it is useful to define fictionality as 'the suspension of referential claims in the acts of narration and reception'.[59] Odysseus does not relate his invented biographies as fictitious, but as events that really happened. Moreover, Eumaeus, Antinous, Penelope

---

58. Pratt (1983): 63–93; Bowie (1993): 8–20; Maronitis (1981): 120. For a bibliographical survey of fictionality in antiquity, see Halliwell (2011): 10 n. 19.

59. For a comprehensive definition of fictionality, see Zipfel (2001).

and Laertes all believe they are looking at someone who has experienced what he narrates. The juxtaposition of truth and falsehood, regardless of whether the lie resembles reality or not, does not capture what is indispensable to fiction: the representation and reception of a plot as fictional.

Nevertheless, the tall tales offer profound reflections on storytelling. As has been shown, they demonstrate that truth and lies are not irreconcilable opposites and can include a variety of correspondences—whether this be that an invented story contains real events, conveys a true message, or reveals the character of the narrator. The Odyssean tall tales also demonstrate that important aspects of storytelling are independent of their referentiality. The characters' exhortations and affirmations that their reports are accurate and reliable do illustrate the value placed on the authenticity of narratives.[60] Yet the plausibility of narratives does not depend on their veracity. The invented biographies are composed in such a way that everyone except Athena believes in them implicitly.

Additionally, the effectiveness of narratives does not depend on their veracity, and can even serve to disguise their deceitfulness. Eumaeus says to the beggar that he has 'troubled the spirit within me' and 'enchanted me' (14.361; 17.521) and urges him to stop talking about Odysseus's return, as he should not 'try to please me nor spell me with lying / words' (14.387–88). He is wary of being so enchanted by the beggar's narrative power that he might end up believing what he feels cannot be true. The anagnorisis scenes show narrative to be an important means with which to construct and maintain identity. The tall tales demonstrate its ambivalence and the potential of narratives to manipulate. Since plausibility and effectiveness do not depend on veracity, narratives can be used to deceive.

And yet, the beggar's false biographies also show once more how narratives can help to process experiences. In the telling of them, Odysseus draws on a rich set of fixed elements, which he skilfully varies and reassembles. The plundering on the Egyptian coast, for instance, is modelled

60. Mackie (1997): 85–86.

on the adventure with the Cicones, and appears in two of the tall tales. The shipwreck which the Cretan suffers on the Phoenicians' ship is almost identical to Odysseus's shipwreck after Thrinacia. On the one hand, this reveals a Homeric compositional technique, which builds up the epic on the basis of formulae and typical scenes. On the other hand, the importance which patterns have for narrative emerges in a more general sense.[61] The Apologoi show that experiences are processed by giving them narrative form. For this, patterns, akin to scripts, are made use of to reduce complexity and engender meaning. While the tall tales are invented, their construction from existing patterns demonstrates the role of schemes in the narrative processing of experiences. The *Odyssey* has itself become such a scheme in Western culture. When someone is perceived as having been on an 'odyssey', Odysseus serves as the underlying symbol for a person who, waylaid by fate and exposed to ordeals, ultimately does manage to return home. The epilogue at the end of this study will examine a literary work whose author artfully uses the figure of Odysseus to deal with extreme and all but unspeakable experiences.

---

61. Murnaghan (1987): 167. Murnaghan's assertion, which levels the difference between tall tales and 'true' tales, is too radical: 'Their deliberate falsity represents simply a more apparent version of the distance from the experience recounted that characterizes every narrative.'

6

Ethics and Narrative

IN THE *Odyssey*'s Proem, Homer calls upon the Muse and asks her to speak to him of the man 'who was driven / far journeys, after he had sacked Troy's sacred citadel' (1.1–2). Odysseus is initially described in general terms as the narrator proclaims, 'many were they whose cities he saw, whose minds he learned of, / many the pains he suffered in his spirit on the wide sea, / struggling for his own life and the homecoming of his companions' (1.3–5) before going on to refer to a specific adventure:

> Even so he could not save his companions, hard though
> he strove to; they were destroyed by their own wild recklessness,
> fools, who devoured the oxen of Helios, the Sun God,
> and he took away the day of their homecoming. (1.6–9)

Other adventures seem more worthy of mention, such as the encounter with Polyphemus, which Odysseus recounts in detail in the Apologoi as well as mentioning it on Ithaca when he recalls the suffering his voyages had entailed, or the confrontation with Scylla, which Odysseus describes as 'the most pitiful scene that these eyes have looked on / in my sufferings as I explored the routes over the water' (12.258–59). In quantitative terms, the shipwreck off the coast of Thrinacia is also dwarfed by the battle with the Laestrygonians, in which Odysseus loses not one, but eleven ships including their crews. And yet, in the Proem, Homer refers only to the sacrilege against the cattle of the sun god.

The reason seems to be that the episode in Thrinacia allows Homer to present Odysseus in a favourable light.[1] Further, the audience is informed that the gods implacably punish acts of sacrilege, before the narrative has even properly begun. Anchored in the Proem, divine justice acquires a prominent place in the *Odyssey*. At the same time, Homer contrasts the sacrilegious companions with Odysseus, the hero of the epic, who was not punished and ultimately returned home. As noted in Byzantine bishop Eustathius's commentary on the *Odyssey*, Homer is 'philodysseus' (1878.47); he who is fond of his hero, and anxious to paint a favourable picture of him, is a friend to him.[2] From the outset, Homer introduces ethics as an important aspect of his narrative about Odysseus.

The theme of human iniquity and divine justice is further highlighted when, immediately after the Proem, Zeus complains,

> Oh for shame, how the mortals put the blame upon us
> gods, for they say evils come from us, but it is they, rather,
> who by their own sacrilege win sorrow beyond what is given,
> as now lately, beyond what was given, Aegisthus married
> the wife of Atreus's son, and murdered him on his homecoming,
> though he knew it was sheer destruction, for we ourselves had
>   told him,
> sending Hermes, the mighty watcher, Argeiphontes,
> not to kill the man, nor court the lady for marriage. (1. 32–39)

Homer has Zeus repeat the word *atasthalia* (sacrilege), which appears in the Proem, to establish a parallel between Odysseus's companions and Aegisthus: like them, the latter perishes through his own fault, having been punished for a wilful offence.

Athena's response to Zeus's speech alludes to those who are characterized by *atasthaliai* above all others in the *Odyssey*—the suitors. By voicing the wish that 'any other man who does thus [should] perish as

1. See Nagler (1990): 336–45; Cook (1995): 21–28. According to Rüter (1969): 50–51, the mention of Thrinacia serves to explain why Odysseus is alone. See also Friedrich (1987b): 394.
2. Strauss Clay (1983): 38.

[Aegisthus] did' (1.47), she turns the conversation to Odysseus, who has not yet returned home, since he is stuck on Ogygia. Upon his return home, which Athena was about to arrange, Odysseus would punish the suitors, whose *atasthaliai* are denounced eighteen times in this narrative. The fate of Agamemnon, who is killed in his own home by his wife and Aegisthus, repeatedly serves as a negative foil for the nostos of Odysseus. The latter finds his wife faithful and purges his palace of the intruders, and the sacrilege and punishment of Aegisthus becomes a mirror for the fate of the suitors in the process.

The ethical dimension of the beginning of the *Odyssey* has received much attention in Homeric studies. The honesty that distinguishes Odysseus from his companions has been cited as an important prerequisite for his nostos;[3] the hero earns his return home. The gods aid upright characters as much as they punish wrongdoers, especially if they demonstrate a capacity for suffering as Odysseus does. His nostos, therefore, appears as a display of divine justice.

Zeus's speech at the beginning of the *Odyssey* has been interpreted as the first theodicy in Western history. It is not the gods, but human beings themselves who are responsible for their suffering; the gods only punish offences against the divine order. According to several prominent scholars, the *Odyssey* represents an important step in the development of the ancient understanding of the gods.[4] In the *Iliad*, the gods are still capricious and human beings the hapless victims of their amoral intrigues. The gods of the *Odyssey*, by contrast, are advocates of justice and only make people suffer in retribution for their misdeeds. Even Hugh Lloyd-Jones, who fundamentally questions that ancient thought was subject to such a developmental process, maintains that there is a clear difference between the two epics.[5]

Widespread though this assumption is, a closer look at the *Odyssey* serves to cast doubt on it. While Odysseus does not contribute to the

3. See, for instance, Lloyd-Jones (1971): 29; Griffin (1980): 164–65; Kullmann (1985): 7; Cook (1995): 36.

4. See Reinhardt (1960): 6; Rüter (1969): 70; Rutherford (1986): 147–48; Schmidt (2010): 44–53. By contrast, cf. Allan (2006); Grethlein (2012): 25–32.

5. Lloyd-Jones (1971): 28–30.

slaughter of the sun god's cattle, he is involved in questionable actions elsewhere. Although Homer strives to portray his hero favourably, it becomes apparent that he is, in fact, culpable when it comes to his companions' fate. The killing of the suitors appears above all as a well-deserved punishment, yet an alternative, more critical view emerges of the slaughter of the hundred and eight young men in the context of attacks Odysseus is himself subjected to during his wanderings. The idea that the *Odyssey* offers a substantially different, more progressive, view of the gods and the world than the *Iliad* ultimately does not stand up to scrutiny. By referring to divine punishment of the wicked, the Proem does indeed highlight an important theme of the *Odyssey*, but this idea is not absent from the *Iliad*. Conversely, the *Odyssey* does not abolish the arbitrariness of the gods—its characters are also at the mercy of gods who are by no means bound by moral considerations. Rather than presenting a new way of thinking, the differences between the two texts arise from divergent plot forms.

The Justice of Odysseus?

Odysseus has many epithets—he is 'resourceful' (*polymēchanos*), 'cunning' (*polymētis*), 'steadfast' (*talasiphrōn*) and 'long-suffering' (*polytlas*). He is not, however, described as 'just' or 'virtuous' anywhere. 'Good' (*esthlos*) and 'blameless' (*amymōn*) are two adjectives that Homer ascribes to him as well as to other heroes, but these do not necessarily imply any moral virtue. It is commonly asserted in Homeric studies that the gods grant Odysseus his nostos because of his honesty, yet it is difficult to find any clear evidence for this. Athena, who advocates Odysseus's return, justifies her claim on Olympus:

> But the heart in me is torn for the sake of wise Odysseus,
> unhappy man, who still, far from his friends, is suffering
> griefs, on the sea-washed island, the navel of all the waters
> [. . .].
> But you, Olympian,
> the heart in you is heedless of him. Did not Odysseus

do you grace by the ships of the Argives, making sacrifice
in wide Troy? Why, Zeus, are you now so harsh with him?'
  (1.48–62)

Odysseus's suffering and generous sacrifices do not constitute any moral explanation for Athena's intercession; the decisive factor is the goddess's sympathy.

A previously quoted passage, which describes the meeting of Athena and Odysseus on the beach at Ithaca, shows the reason for her sympathy. The goddess responds to the tall tale which Odysseus tells in order to mislead her:

> It would be a sharp one, and a stealthy one, who would ever get
>   past you
> in any contriving; even if it were a god against you.
> You wretch, so devious, never weary of tricks, then you would not
> even in your own country give over your ways of deceiving
> and your thievish tales. They are near to you in your very nature.
> But come, let us talk no more of this, for you and I both know
> sharp practice, since you are far the best of all mortal
> men for counsel and stories, and I among all the divinities
> am famous for wit and sharpness. (13.291–99)

Athena and Odysseus share the ability to deceive and to derive pleasure from the deception. Lying is not necessarily condemned in the Homeric world, but nor does it constitute a moral virtue to justify her demand for Odysseus's return. What it does achieve is to ensure Athena's approval.

Additionally, while Zeus emphasizes that he and the gods ruthlessly pursue human transgressions, it does not follow that righteous behaviour will be rewarded. Homer presents the murder of the suitors as a fit punishment, but Odysseus's ultimate return is not granted as a reward for any virtue. Odysseus survives thanks to his capacity for suffering. This, however, is not the reason that the gods grant his nostos, either. Instead, a theme emerges which will be discussed in more detail later: like the *Iliad*, the *Odyssey* presents gods who act from moral as well as personal motives. The present focus, however, continues to be on Odysseus and his deeds. As has been shown, Odysseus is not an unreliable narrator in the Apologoi; however, he is adept at presenting his own skills and achievements to maximum effect. It is clear from the Proem that Homer is fond of his hero and strives to present Odysseus in the most favourable light. Nevertheless, there are hints in the *Odyssey* that the hero is responsible for the deaths of some of his companions, and that the murder of the suitors could be viewed from perspectives other than that of just retribution.

The Fate of Odysseus's Companions

Especially in the Polyphemus adventure, Odysseus bears some of the responsibility for his companions' downfall, and he admits this in the Apologoi:

> From the start my companions spoke to me and begged me
> to take some of the cheeses, come back again, and the next time
> to drive the lambs and kids from their pens, and get back quickly
> to the ship again, and go sailing off across the salt water;
> but I would not listen to them, it would have been better their way,
> not until I could see him, see if he would give me presents.
> (9.224–29)

It is both Odysseus's curiosity about the inhabitant of the cave and his heroic pride which cause him to insist on receiving honours and gifts that prove fatal to his companions. In the case of the Cicones, disaster strikes because Odysseus's comrades do not heed his warning; they go on celebrating their victory with a lengthy feast, which gives the invaded people's allies time to regroup (9.43–44). In the Polyphemus adventure, however, it is Odysseus who throws his companions' misgivings to the wind and conjures up the catastrophe. Remaining in the cave at his behest, six of the men are devoured by the cyclops.

If Odysseus's account is to be trusted, he had, in fact, foreseen the danger. He tells the Phaeacians that he deliberately took the wine with which he intoxicated Polyphemus: 'for my proud heart had an idea that presently / I would encounter a man who was endowed with great strength, / and wild, with no true knowledge of laws or any good customs' (9.213–15). If this premonition is not dismissed as an invention of the narrating Odysseus, who strives to appear more circumspect and cautious than he had really been, then it serves to heighten his irresponsibility and guilt in respect of his companions' death.

One of Polyphemus's victims is mentioned in the second book. The aged and wise Aegyptius is the first speaker in the Ithacan assembly of the people:

> His own dear son, Antiphus the spearman, had gone off
> with godlike Odysseus to Ilion, land of good horses,
> in the hollow ships, and now the wild cyclops had killed him
> deep in his cave, and this was the last man he had eaten. (2.17–20)

This is one of the passages in which the narrator refers to events told in the Apologoi, thereby vouching for Odysseus's account. The detail that Antiphus was the last to be devoured adds poignancy to the tragedy to his death.

Odysseus's guilt is also made explicit in a speech made by a companion. Eurylochus is the only member to return from the scouting party to Aeaea, where Circe has turned the other men into animals. When Odysseus wants to go to Circe's house with his remaining companions, Eurylochus resists:

> Ah, poor wretches! Where are we going? Why do you long for
> the evils of going down into Circe's palace, for she will
> transform the lot of us into pigs or wolves or lions,
> as so we shall guard her great house for her, under compulsion.
> So too it happened with the cyclops, when our companions
> went into his yard, and the bold Odysseus was of their
>   company;
> for it was by this man's sacrilege that these too perished.
>   (10.431–37)

In this scene, Eurylochus proves himself to be a coward, and later it is he who persuades the Greeks to land on Thrinacia and slaughter the cattle of the sun god against Odysseus's will. But his questionable role in the plot does not detract from the plausibility of his accusation that the companions whom Polyphemus devoured were on Odysseus's conscience. If anything, the accusation is made forceful by his diction: the 'sacrilege' of which Eurylochus accuses Odysseus is on a par not only with that of the companions who perish on Thrinacia, but also with the suitors, who are the embodiment of recklessness.

The severity of Eurylochus's reproach is evident from Odysseus's violent reaction:

> So he spoke, and I considered in my mind whether
> to draw out the long-edged sword from beside by big thigh,
> and cut off his head and throw it on the ground, even though
> he was nearly related to me by marriage; but my companions
> checked me, first one then another speaking, trying to soothe
>   me. (10.438–42)

Odysseus, who is generally self-possessed, here resembles the volatile Achilles at the beginning of the *Iliad*.[6] When Agamemnon insults Achilles and deprives him of the beautiful Briseis, daughter of the Trojan priest Brises and Achilles's personal captive (*Il.* 1.188–92), Achilles considers drawing his sword and slaying his opponent. But while Odysseus permits himself to be appeased, in the *Iliad* it takes Athena's intervention to stop Achilles from erupting into violence.

Odysseus's desire to meet Polyphemus not only affects the companions who perish, but indirectly impacts on the others as well. After they have escaped from the cave, he reviles Polyphemus from the safety of his ship and divulges his real name to him. In doing so, he puts himself and his companions in immediate danger once more. His action not only enables the blinded Polyphemus to hurl boulders towards the ship; the revelation of his real name also allows Polyphemus to curse Odysseus, as previously discussed:

---

6. On similarities between Odysseus in the Mnesterophony and Achilles in the *Iliad*, see Bakker (2013): 150–56. See also Grethlein (2017). On the *Odyssey*'s ethical ambiguities in general, see Loney (2019).

Hear me, Poseidon who circle the earth, dark-haired. If truly
I am your son, and you acknowledge yourself as my father,
grant that Odysseus, sacker of cities, son of Laertes,
who makes his home in Ithaca, may never reach that home;
but if it is decided that he shall see his own people,
and come home to his strong-founded house and to his own
    country,
let him come late, in bad case, with the loss of all his companions,
in someone else's ship, and find troubles in his household.
    (9.528–35)

It is not made explicit in the Apologoi how Poseidon delays and blights Odysseus's return. Poseidon's only direct intervention is reported by Odysseus as being the shipwreck off Scheria (5.279–387). Other than that, it is not clear how Poseidon directly harms Odysseus. This may be because in the Apologoi, Homer lets Odysseus narrate a large part of his adventures himself and meticulously keeps to the limits of personal knowledge, especially in respect of divine action.[7] Instead, both the narrator and speakers endowed with authority, such as Teiresias, repeatedly refer to the wrath of Poseidon as the cause of Odysseus's prolonged wandering.[8] Therefore, Odysseus is indirectly responsible for the fate of his companions who, like him, are driven across the seas by Poseidon, as well as for the downfall of those who seal their own fate on Thrinacia. His vanity and desire to tell the cyclops who has really managed to outwit him conjures up the curse that not only delays him for years but also costs his companions their lives.

Both Odysseus's guilt regarding the death of Polyphemus's victims and his general responsibility for his companions are explicitly mentioned in the *Odyssey*. After the murder of the suitors, their relatives gather to discuss what should be done. The first to speak is Eupeithes, father of Antinous: 'Friends, this man's will worked great evil upon the Achaians. / First he took many excellent men away in the vessels / with

---

7. See Murgatroyd (2015) on Poseidon's role, and Jörgensen (1904) on the limits of Odysseus's knowledge of the gods in general.

8. See *Od.* 1.20–21; 1.68–75; 6.330–31; 11.101–3; 13.341–43.

him, and lost the hollow ships, and lost all the people' (24.426–28). While Homer is *philodysseus* and grants his hero the right to narrate his own adventures, here he lets Eupeithes express openly what is left implicit in the plot: Odysseus's responsibility for the fate of his companions, who do not return home. This guilt is not elaborated on, but it is made visible. The surprising emphasis on the companions' outrages in the Proem is an attempt at exculpation. However, it simultaneously highlights what it tries to diminish: namely, Odysseus's culpability.

The Murder of the Suitors

Eupeithes names both the companions and the suitors as Odysseus's victims since he, upon 'returning killed the best of the Cephallonians' (24.429). This parallel between the companions and suitors is also suggested by Aegyptus, the wise old man whose speech opens the assembly of the Ithacan people in the second book. Aegyptus has three sons besides the one who is devoured by Polyphemus. Two of them are at home but one, significantly, is among the suitors (2.21–22). The suitors and companions all seem to belong to the same social group, and a large number of young aristocratic men die on the voyages and in the Mnesterophony. Eupeithes's accusation therefore raises the question of whether the murder of the suitors casts Odysseus in as an unfavourable light as does the demise of his companions. At first glance, the question may seem surprising, even absurd, since the suitors represent sacrilegious behaviour. But it is nonetheless worth asking. As shall be seen, while the *Odyssey* goes to considerable rhetorical lengths to present the murder of the suitors as justified, it also opens up alternative perspectives which interpret this murder as an excessive act of violence and a brutal decimation of the population.

Taking a step back from the *Odyssey*, one might ask what offences the suitors actually perpetrate.[9] They take up residence in Odysseus's house and party at his expense. They also court Penelope and plan to assassinate Telemachus. But Telemachus escapes them and Penelope remains faithful to her husband. The offences perpetrated are that they

9. On this point, see Halverson (1985): 142; Erbse (1972): 113–42.

devour Odysseus's cattle and drink his wine. Should the penalty be execution, and is the carnage Odysseus inflicts on them proportionate? Doubts about the appropriateness of the murder of the suitors increase when comparing this to the *Oresteia*. The story of Clytemnestra and her lover Aegisthus plotting and carrying out Agamemnon's murder, which his son Orestes later avenges, is repeatedly held up as a parallel to the plot of the *Odyssey*. The first mention of the *Oresteia* occurs in the initial speech by Zeus, as previously quoted: 'beyond what was given, Aegisthus married / the wife of Atreus' son, and murdered him on his homecoming' (1.35–36). Before Athena turns the conversation to Odysseus, she affirms that 'Aegisthus indeed has been struck down in a death well merited. / Let any other man who does thus perish as he did' (1.46–47). As has been shown, she implicitly compares the suitors to Aegisthus: like him, they have transgressed and must atone for it. Yet adultery and murder such as Aegisthus actually commits are only *planned* by the suitors. While Orestes follows the principle of talion when he kills Aegisthus, Odysseus answers a material loss with a mass execution. He is given the option of accepting physical compensation: after killing Antinous, Eurymachus claims that he has punished the main culprit and should stop:

> Afterward we will make public reparation
> for all that has been eaten and drunk in your halls, setting
> each upon himself an assessment of twenty oxen.
> We will pay it back in bronze and gold to you, until your heart
> is softened. (22.55–59)

Again, a parallel appears between Odysseus and Achilles. In the *Iliad*, Achilles rejects Agamemnon's lavish recompense. Odysseus replies to Eurymachus,

> Eurymachus, if you gave me all your father's possessions,
> all that you have now, and what you could add from elsewhere,
> even so, I would not stay my hands from the slaughter,
> until I have taken revenge for all the suitors' transgressions.
> (*Od.* 22.61–64)[10]

10. On the similarity of *Od.* 22.61–62 to *Il.* 9.379–80, see Schein (1999): 352–54.

The Mnesterophony, therefore, can be interpreted more as an act of boundless revenge than as a fitting punishment. The comparison to the *Oresteia* in particular makes clear that it is not a question of retribution in kind. Yet one should resist the temptation to transfer a moral condemnation of revenge that is rooted in the Christian dictum of loving one's neighbour to archaic Greece. Revenge was considered a legitimate and even required defence of honour, as well as a spontaneous expression of the need for aristocratic self-validation.[11] The code was basically to be good to one's friends and vicious to one's enemies, with the latter aspect not necessarily being limited to the principle of talion. Even in classical times, Xenophon thought it a virtue to 'outdo' enemies with malevolence and friends with beneficence (*Mem.* 2.6.35). In the context of ancient ethics, the murder of the suitors amounts to legitimate, if far-reaching retribution.

At the same time, it is important to note that the *Odyssey* does not portray the murder of the suitors only as revenge. The event is also morally charged and styled as a well-deserved punishment. The suitors are described as 'criminals' (*aleitai*) who 'go too far' (*hyperēnoreoi*), and who are 'vainglorious' (*hyperphialoi*), 'violent' (*hybristai*) and 'savage' (*agrioi*). They are accused of 'violence' (*hybris*), 'shamelessness' (*anaidēs*), 'shameful deeds' (*aischea*) and of 'transgressing the laws' (*hyperbasiē*). With such terms, found not only in the speeches of characters but also of the narrator, Homer positions the suitors as being beyond law and order and proclaims their deeds to be unwarranted and inexcusable. A comprehensive lexical arsenal of expressions denoting hubris serves to present their behaviours as a serious breach of law, rather than as youthful folly.

The suitors' offence is heightened by the fact that they disregard a series of warnings. Omina, the seers Halitherses, Theoclymenus and Leodes, as well as the beggar, tell the suitors to desist. In the second book, Halitherses sees a divine message in the fight of two eagles after Telemachus has spoken:

> But what I say will be mostly a warning to the suitors,
> for a great disaster is wheeling down on them. Surely Odysseus

11. See Gehrke (1987); Blundell (1989): 26–59.

will not be long away from his family, but now, already,
is somewhere close by, working out the death and destruction
of all these men, and it will be an evil for many others
of us who inhabit sunny Ithaca. So, well beforehand,
let us think how we can make them stop, or better let them
stop themselves. It will soon be better for them if they do so.
   (2.162–69)

Here as elsewhere, the suitors turn a deaf ear to the warning and there-
fore contribute to their own demise.

Homer also underlines their transgressions by depicting the pro-
longed feasting at Odysseus's court as a complex travesty.[12] When re-
ferring to feasts, he uses words with the *dai* root, which are normally
used for the division of bounty after war.[13] This emphasizes the unhe-
roic character of the suitors, who help themselves to the belongings of
an absent ruler without having waged war and without offering hospi-
tality in turn. The word *dardaptein*, meaning 'to tear' and used elsewhere
regarding jackals, twice describes the distribution of food among them-
selves.[14] Like scavengers, the suitors raid supplies which they have not
captured. In the process, they violate both human and divine law. They
largely neglect to perform the libations and sacrifices that are an integral
part of the Homeric meal, and when they do sacrifice they deviate sig-
nificantly from protocol.[15]

The suitors repeatedly consume Odysseus's 'substance' or 'livelihood'
(*biotos*).[16] This formula not only expresses the extent of their plunder-
ing at his court, but also insinuates that the suitors are destroying his
life. *Biotos* above all means 'life', and, derived from this, 'that which
keeps one alive'. While the suitors do not physically kill anyone, the
phrase to 'eat all your substance away' indicates that Odysseus is being
deprived of life nevertheless. This meaning becomes particularly clear

---

12. Saïd (1979); (2011): 64–69; Seaford (1994): 52–65.

13. *Od.* 3.316; 15.13.

14. *Od.* 14.92; 16.315. Regarding jackals, see *Il.* 11.479.

15. See Saïd (1979): 32–41.

16. *Od.* 1.160; 11.116; 13.396, 428; 14.377; 15.32; 18.280. On 'life' in its original sense, see, for
instance, 1.287; 2.218; also Bakker (2013): 45.

when *biotos* is determined by the adjective *nēpoinos*. *Nēpoinos*, which can be translated as 'without compensation', generally refers to murders for which no blood money (*poinē*) is due.[17] The suitors, therefore, consume Odysseus's substance without offering any recompense.

Telemachus's injunction to the suitors to leave his court again illustrates the equation between the suitors' feasting and killing:

> Go out of my palace and do your feasting elsewhere,
> eating up your own possessions, taking turns, household by
>   household.
> But if you decide it is more profitable and better
> to go on, eating up [*olesthai*] one man's livelihood [*bioton*],
>   without payment [*nēpoinon*],
> then spoil my house. I will cry out to the gods everlasting
> in the hope that Zeus might somehow grant a reversal of fortunes.
> Then you may perish [*oloisthe*] in this house, with no payment
>   given [*nēpoinoi*]. (1.374–80 = 2.139–45)

Nēpoinos first denotes the suitors' revelry, and thereafter their deaths, which Telemachus desires. The suitors do not pay for their revels any more than Telemachus (in his wishful thinking) pays for the murder of the suitors. Telemachus uses the same verb, *ollymi/ollymai*, 'to ruin/to be ruined' to denote the consumption of Odysseus's victuals and the demise of the suitors. By referring to the suitors' feasting with a term that is also used for murder, Homer makes it seem natural that the only viable response to the suitors' behaviour is their execution.

The *Odyssey* not only depicts the suitors' feasting in terms of deprivation of life; it also compares the murder of the suitors to a meal: 'but there could not be a meal that was more unpleasant than this one, /such was to be the attack that the powerful man and the goddess /would make on them' (20.392–94).[18] Before shooting the first suitor, Odysseus says to Telemachus, 'Now is the time for their dinner to be served the Achaians / in the daylight' (21.428–29). Similarly, feasting and killing

---

17. See Levy (1963): 152.
18. See Saïd (1979): 25; Bakker (2013): 47.

are equated when Odysseus and his bow are compared to a bard and his lyre, since 'these things come at the end of the feasting' (21.406–9; 430). Presenting the suitors' feasting as wanton destruction and using the feast as a metaphor for murder presents their execution as appropriate retribution. Two fundamentally different events are being equated here: metaphorical murder results in actual murder; an actual feast is followed by a figurative one.

Homer also subtly anchors the adultery that does not take place in the plot. Unlike Clytemnestra, Penelope remains faithful to her husband. The suitors court her, but none receives her favour. Instead, they amuse themselves with the servants of the house. Odysseus accuses the suitors of 'forcibly [taking] my serving women to sleep beside you, / and [seeking] to win my wife while I was still alive' (22.37–38). That the accusation of consorting with servants is regarded as a negligible offence is shown by the fact that it is the only charge to which Eurymachus makes no reply. Joint mention of Penelope and the servants, however, makes the narrative function clear: by consorting with the 'serving women', the suitors take sexual advantage of Odysseus's property. They may not have slept with his wife, but they had done so with his servants. Just as the phrase 'to eat away his substance' insinuates murder, which, unlike Aegisthus, the suitors don't actually commit, their consorting with servants insinuates the adultery they do not manage to get Penelope to consent to.

Compared to Aegisthus's physical actions, the suitors' offence may seem relatively slight. And yet, Homer makes every effort to present their execution as just retribution. He draws on an extensive vocabulary of transgressions to represent the suitors' behaviour as sacrilegious. He portrays their revelries not only as a perversion of heroic feasting, but also as figurative murder and adultery that are punishable by death. How convincing Homer is can be seen from interpreters who assert that Odysseus pays the suitors in 'equal coin'.[19] Nevertheless, other views of the Mnesterophony do shine through the overall stigmatization of the suitors. Comments made by characters, the depiction of the murder of the

19. See, for instance, Reece (1993): 178–81.

suitors and, not least, parallels with Odysseus's adventures invite a critical look at what the *Odyssey* primarily presents as legitimate punishment.

A series of statements highlights the significance of the murder of the suitors. The previously quoted speech by Eurymachus, in which he begs for mercy and offers compensation for the damage done includes the phrase that Odysseus should 'spare your own / people' (22.54–55)—he is not about to slaughter his enemies, but kinsfolk. Some of the suitors hail from Ithaca, others are from the neighbouring islands. Like Odysseus, they belong to the nobility and are linked by a close network beyond their own polis. Amphimedon, for instance, is a friend of Agamemnon (24.114). Odysseus had fought side by side with Ajax and Achilles at Troy and on his voyages he fought the Cicones and magical beings alongside his allies; but now, as Eurymachus's words make clear, he is about to exterminate his own kind.

After the suitors have been killed, Odysseus's own words to Telemachus make clear the magnitude of the act:[20]

> For when one has killed only one man in a community,
> and then there are not many avengers to follow, even
> so, he flees into exile, leaving kinsmen and country.
> But we have killed what held the city together, the finest
> young men in Ithaca. It is what I would have you consider.
>   (23.118–22)

That the killer of a single kinsman is usually forced to flee is also illustrated by Theoclymenus, who had to leave Argos (15.224), and by an Aitolian whom Eumaeus entertained (14.380). Exile after committing murder is so much the norm that Odysseus makes use of it when he narrates 'false things that are like true sayings' and when he initially pretends to Athena that he is a Cretan on the run after having slain a son of Idomeneus (13.259).[21]

Odysseus kills not just one man, but 'the finest young men in Ithaca' and with them, that which 'held the city together'. Even the shade of Agamemnon remarks, as the slain suitors arrive in the underworld,

20. See Nagler (1990): 351.

21. See also *Il.* 2.661–67; 13.694–97; 15.335–36; 15.430–32; 16.570–76; 23.85–90; 24.480–83.

Amphimedon, what befell you that you came under the dark earth,
all of you choice young men, of the same age, nor could one,
   gathering
the best men out of all a city have chosen otherwise.
Was it with the ships, and did Poseidon, rousing a stormblast
of battering winds and waves towering prove your undoing?
Or was it on the dry land, did men embattled destroy you
as you tried to cut out cattle and fleecy sheep from their holdings,
or fighting against them, for the sake of their city and women?
   (24.106–13)

While the *Odyssey* primarily portrays the Mnesterophony as just retribution, it also points out the gravity of extinguishing an entire generation of young nobles on Ithaca. The massacre and damage Odysseus inflicts on the city resemble a war or disastrous natural event.

Eurymachus says that in killing Antinous, Odysseus had removed the ringleader who was responsible for the suitors' actions, and that he should spare the others (22.48–55). Although Homer by no means portrays Antinous as the only culprit, Eurymachus's assertion seems to hint at distinctions between the suitors which the generalising statements about them do not reflect.[22] Two suitors in particular stand out. Amphinomus, first, argues against the planned assassination of Telemachus and is pleased when the attempt fails (16.351–57; 394–405; 20.244–46). He also talks kindly to the beggar and gives him food, standing protectively in front of him when Eurymachus hurls a stool at him (18.119–23; 412–21). Nevertheless, he is killed alongside the other suitors.

While Homer recounts the death of Amphinomus without much ado, he gives the seer Leodes a speech in which he begs Odysseus for mercy:

I am at your knees, Odysseus. Respect me, have mercy;
for I claim that never in your halls did I say or do anything
wrong to any of the women, but always was trying
to stop any one of the other suitors who acted in that way.
   (22.312–15)

22. Murnaghan (1987): 66–67. See also. Whitman (1958): 305; Allan (2006): 23–25.

Further, 'to him alone their excesses / were hateful, and he disapproved of all the suitors' (21.146–67). But this opposition helps Leodes no more than does his status as a seer; Odysseus kills him with his sword. Rejecting any supplication once more places Odysseus on a par with Achilles, the latter giving free rein to his rage over Patroclus's death and rejecting all pleas for mercy.[23] The killing of two suitors who had opposed their companions' actions does not fit with the idea of a just punishment. Given that the singer Phemius and the servant Medon are spared, the possibility of exempting individual men clearly exists. With the murder of Amphinomus and Leodes, however, the Mnesterophony presents an image of merciless revenge, rather than just retribution.[24]

The questions that arise from parallels between the killing of the suitors and the cyclops adventure are even more disturbing. Odysseus himself makes a comparison between the two episodes when he contrasts his experience as a beggar in his own palace with his encounter with Polyphemus (20.18–21). On the one hand, there are similarities between the suitors and Polyphemus—both are guilty of violating the law of hospitality, for instance. The suitors do not respect the beggar; Polyphemus even devours his guests. Significantly, on both occasions Odysseus takes revenge with the aid of a gift. He makes Polyphemus drunk with the wine of Maron and commences the murder of the suitors with a bow that had been a gift from Iphitus. In both cases, the means used to exact revenge correspond to the offence to be avenged.

Yet there are similarities between the suitors and Odysseus in the cyclops's cave that are also striking. Odysseus also invades someone's dwelling place and consumes the owner's food in his absence. This parallel does not reflect well on Odysseus: why should he accuse the cyclops of violating the laws of hospitality when he has himself intruded into his cave and gorged himself on his food?[25] To put it bluntly, Odysseus kills the suitors for a transgression he is himself guilty of, albeit in a mitigated form, in Polyphemus's cave.

23. On the parallels between the *Iliad* and the Leodes scene, see Pucci (1987): 128–38.
24. See Whitman (1958): 305–8.
25. See Newton (1987): 139–40.

While the situation of the suitors resembles that of Odysseus in Polyphemus's cave, there is also a similarity between Polyphemus and Odysseus when he turns to murdering.[26] The cyclops traps the intruders in his cave, and Odysseus locks the door to the megaron, turning it into an inescapable prison. The cyclops seals the entrance with a door stone 'like a man closing the lid on a quiver' (9.314). In the Mnesterophony, it is an actual quiver from which Odysseus draws his arrows. The imprisoned hero, who resorts to cunning to save his own life, becomes the active hero who imprisons and slaughters his opponents himself.

Some linguistic details highlight the change of roles as well as the parallels between Odysseus and Polyphemus. When Athena speaks to Odysseus about the impending battle with the suitors, she speaks of 'the time when we two go to this work, and I look for endless / ground to be spattered by the blood and brains of the suitors, / these men who are eating all your substance away' (13.394–96). This brutal wording has puzzled interpreters,[27] but above all, it draws attention to the parallel between the killing of the suitors and the Polyphemus adventure. The cyclops seizes two of the companions and strikes them on the ground, so that 'the brains ran all over the floor, soaking / the ground' (9.290–91); and after he has been blinded, Polyphemus wishes that the ram, to whose underside Odysseus, ironically, is clinging, could tell him where to find him, because 'then surely he would be smashed against the floor and his brain go / spattering all over the cave' (9.458–59). One difference emerges from the parallel: Athena realizes what Polyphemus can only wish for; unlike Polyphemus, Odysseus does not let his opponents escape.

Antinous is the first suitor whom Odysseus kills 'and through his nostrils there burst a thick jet / of mortal [*andromeos*] blood' (22.18–19). The adjective *andromeos* is very rare; it is used in just three other places in the *Odyssey*, and all occur in the cyclops episode. Polyphemus eats human flesh (9.297; 347) and vomits human remains (9.374). The repetition of this word in the Mnesterophony evokes the man-eating cyclops, inviting the audience to compare Odysseus to Polyphemus and

---

26. I am following the interpretation of Bakker (2013): 69–73 here.

27. See, for instance, Segal (1994): 222.

the murder of the suitors to the cyclops's dietary transgression. The comparison is fuelled by the previously described metaphor, which likens the murder to a meal.

The suitors fail to grasp their situation even after Antinous has been killed: 'poor fools, and they had not yet realized / how over all of them the terms of death [were fastened]' (22.32–33). Reference to hapless fools who are unaware of their real situation is a formula that appears five times in the *Odyssey*; here, however, it creates a subtle link with a particular passage. Homer's description of how the men escape Polyphemus's cave also uses a verb that signifies a fastening, this time literally, in the pluperfect passive form: 'but in his guilelessness [he] did not notice / how my men [had been] fastened under the breasts of his fleecy / sheep' (9.442–44). The suitors' misapprehension is here effectively contrasted with that of Polyphemus, who is physically unable to perceive that his captives are about to escape. The parallel shows Odysseus to be a more successful version of Polyphemus—literal shackles enable Polyphemus's captives to escape, while it is a metaphorical noose that seals Odysseus's captives' fate. While Polyphemus's captives manage to escape, Odysseus retains his prisoners and kills them.

But it is the lion analogy that probably provides the most disturbing parallel. After the suitors have been killed, Telemachus finds Odysseus

> among the slaughtered dead men,
> spattered over with gore and battle filth, like a lion
> who has been feeding on an ox of the fields, and goes off
> covered with blood, all his chest and his flanks on either
> side bloody, a terrible thing to look in the face; so
> now Odysseus' feet and the hands above them were spattered.
> (22. 401–6)[28]

Apart from allusions to the encounter with Polyphemus, this analogy paints an eerie picture of Odysseus. Epic heroes are frequently compared

---

28. The comparison is briefly taken up in 23.48, a verse which many editors reject, since papyri and several manuscripts do not contain it. For its authenticity, however, see Russo, Fernandez-Galiano and Heubeck (1992), ad loc.

to lions, and three preceding passages make that association in the *Odyssey*. Menelaus and Telemachus describe Odysseus as a lion who finds two calves in his camp, led there by the unwitting hind. In this context, the hind's carelessness and the calves' defencelessness is intended to illustrate the behaviour and situation of the suitors (4.333–40 = 17.124–31). Moreover, when Odysseus emerges from the thicket on the beach of Scheria and approaches Nausicaa, the narrator compares him to a hungry lion, to depict both Odysseus's plight and the Phaeacian girls' fear (6.130–36).

The analogy in Book 22, however, is different.[29] Rather than illustrating the hero's bravery or isolation, it emphasizes his animalistic aspect. Odysseus is covered in blood; not just his hands and feet, but his cheeks too are dripping with it, like those of a wild animal that has just devoured its prey. This likening of the killing to the arbitrary hunt of an animal does not cast a favourable light on Odysseus's revenge on the suitors. He is depicted as being merely *akin to* the lion, but the image emphasizes the bestial dimension of murder, nevertheless.

Odysseus once more appears disconcertingly similar to Achilles, who, after Patroclus's death, expresses the wish to eat Hector raw (*Il.* 22.346–47) and goes hunting like a wild lion. In a dispute with the other gods, Apollo says,

> No, you gods; your desire is to help this cursed Achilles
> within whose breast there are no feelings of justice, nor can
> his mind be bent, but his purposes are fierce, like a lion
> who when he has given way to his own great strength and
>   his haughty
> spirit, goes among the flocks of men, to devour them.
>   (*Il.* 24.39–43)[30]

In the *Iliad*, Achilles is likened to a hungry lion, while the *Odyssey* describes its hero as a sated lion. But as with Achilles, the simile suggests that Odysseus gives way to a bloodlust that is more bestial than human.

29. On comparisons to the lion and other animal comparisons in Homer, see Schnapp-Gourbeillon (1981); Lonsdale (1990).

30. On the bestial character of Achilles in the *Iliad*, see Grethlein (2005).

The lion analogy is all the more poignant because Polyphemus, too, is compared to a lion: 'He cut them up limb by limb and got supper ready, / and like a lion reared in the hills, without leaving anything, / ate them, entrails, flesh and the marrowy bones alike' (9.291–93). In the case of the cyclops, it is not just the killing, but the manner of devouring that corresponds to the lion. Polyphemus literally eats his opponents. The fact that a parallel exists between Polyphemus and Odysseus puts the latter in proximity to cannibalism, so that the comparison of the murder of the suitors adds a sinister hue to the narration and raises questions that are both disconcerting and far-reaching. How does Odysseus's revenge differ from Polyphemus's rage? How different is Odysseus from a one-eyed giant who negates the fundamental laws of civilization?

That said, it is an interpretation that should not be taken too far. After being compared to a lion, Odysseus is shown to exercise restraint when he forbids Eurycleia to rejoice over the suitors' death (22.412–16). Ultimately, the *Odyssey* goes to great rhetorical lengths to present the murder as just retribution. The suitors are portrayed as evil, sacrilegious men who ultimately get the punishment they deserve, and, as their antipode, Odysseus is an agent of justice. Yet there are undertones to this depiction that permit of a different reading. The sacrilegious actions of Odysseus's companions, as outlined in the Proem, do not disavow that Odysseus is to blame for their demise and, in a similar vein, the stigmatization of the suitors may be taken to suggest that their misdeeds are perhaps not so heinous. Unlike Aegisthus, they only commit figurative murder, and they seduce the servants rather than the mistress of the house. Further, the *Odyssey* emphasizes the gravity of killing kinsmen and the great loss suffered by Ithaca when Odysseus wipes out an entire generation of the local aristocracy. The killing of two suitors who were not guilty of committing transgressions and the parallels between Odysseus and Polyphemus both point to an act of excessive violence, while the resemblance of this episode to Achilles's rampage after Patroclus's death also raises the question whether Odysseus's revenge is appropriate.

Homer's interest in ethical questions is made evident in the Proem. Especially in this regard, the *Odyssey* proves to be a multilayered text that invites different—at times contradictory—perspectives on its plot.

This includes its hero. When Odysseus is compared to his companions or to the suitors, his integrity comes to the fore. Yet speeches and parallels between individual episodes invite a critical examination of Odysseus's dealings with his companions, as well as with the suitors. The *Odyssey*, therefore, demonstrates the ethical dimension that philosophy, theology and literary studies have begun to ascribe to narratives.[31] Proponents of a radical extension of 'narrative ethics' view narrative as an alternative to an ethics of principle, while more moderate representatives hold that the two complement and cross-fertilize each other. The value of narrative for the field of ethics appears to be based, at least in part, on the significance which it has for real life. Whether life is perceived as narrative or narrative is seen as a way of processing experience, we are always already 'enmeshed in narratives'.[32] As a form that embodies life, or at least shapes our reflections on it, narrative is characterized by a particular closeness to its subject, insofar as it deals with moral questions.

Even if Homer's moral standards are in many respects foreign to the contemporary reader, the *Odyssey* shows both the advantages and limitations of moral reflections in narrative form. What it lacks in abstraction, it makes up for in terms of tangibility. Ethics is concerned with questions of action, and narrative, in its depiction of actions, lends itself very well to this. Through its dynamics as well as its wealth and diversity of perspectives, the *Odyssey* prompts many questions about just action. Theoretical reflections are replaced by multifaceted discussions, which, however, are unlikely to provide any clear-cut answers or readily transferable patterns. It becomes apparent that the significance of narrative for ethics is probably found not so much in its ability to deliver answers as in its ability to facilitate a deeper understanding of ethical problems. Narratives make it possible to witness the forces that act on

31. The moral theologian Mieth seems to have coined the term 'narrative ethics' (1976). For other texts of importance, see Metz (1977): 181–94; Ritschl (1984): 39–54; most recently, Joisten (2007); Hofheinz, Mathwig and Zeindler (2009); Öhlschläger, Schäffer and Roser (2009); C. Grethlein (2016): 529–34.

32. The metaphor 'enmeshed in narratives' comes from Schapp (1953). On the narrative character of life, see MacIntyre (1981); Ricœur (1984–88 [1983–85]); Carr (1986).

and against each other, as well as to view conflicting interests from different angles and in their temporal dynamics. Simple messages can, of course, also be communicated, but these might find more appropriate expression in aphorisms and maxims.

The Justice of the Gods?

The ethical dimension which Homer reveals at the beginning of the *Odyssey* includes not just the heroes and their actions, but also the gods and their responses to misdeeds. In respect of divine justice and its limits, narrative once more proves to be a form that is able to deal with ethical questions in a manner that is differentiated and rich in perspectives, even if this means that clear-cut answers cannot be obtained. At the same time, the impact which this specific narrative and its plot has on the worldview expressed in the epic narrative becomes apparent. The idea that the *Odyssey* is based on a more progressive image of the gods and of the world than the *Iliad* enjoys great popularity, as has already been pointed out. While the Iliadic heroes suffer from the arbitrariness of the gods, the gods of the *Odyssey* are said to be committed to a moral code, and Zeus's speech in the council of the gods offers nothing less than the first theodicy in Western intellectual history.

However, this is an idea that is based on a misinterpretation of Zeus's words, and it robs the worldview that is presented in the *Odyssey* of its complexity. The retribution of injustice is indeed a central theme of the *Odyssey*, but at the same time, its characters emphasize the unpredictability of the gods in Iliadic fashion. Further, there are plot elements that are difficult to reconcile with a reduction of the gods to a moral authority. The interventions of Poseidon and Helios in particular do not fit well with the simple theodicy that is supposed to be the *Odyssey*'s spiritual achievement. Conversely, in the *Iliad*, the gods do not invariably act arbitrarily; rather, they pursue misdeeds in a way that the *Odyssey* is supposed to be alone in having developed. The differences that undoubtedly do exist between the *Iliad* and *Odyssey* are not suggestive of intellectual development, but primarily due to the different plot forms of these two epics.

Zeus's lament is the focus of most works that identify a theodicy in the *Odyssey*:

> Oh for shame, how the mortals put the blame upon us
> gods for they say evils come from us, but it is they, rather,
> who by their own recklessness win sorrow beyond what is given,
> as now lately, beyond what was given, Aegisthus married
> the wife of Atreus's son, and murdered him on his homecoming,
> though he knew it was sheer destruction, for we ourselves had
>   told him,
> sending Hermes, the mighty watcher, Argeiphontes,
> not to kill the man, nor court his lady for marriage. (1.32–39)

Is Zeus really claiming that the gods are not responsible—that humans alone are to blame for the suffering that afflicts them?

An ancient grammarian (Scholion ad 1.34 DHJM) comments on the contradiction between this speech and the plot of the *Odyssey*, in which the gods do inflict suffering on humanity. He offers two solutions, both of which are pertinent. First of all, it was Zeus and not the poet who was speaking at this point. Indeed, the fact that Zeus is partisan on the one hand and defensive on the other must not be disregarded. Above all, however, the scholiast points out that Zeus is not claiming that all suffering stems from the gods' actions. The decisive words here are *kai* (also) and *hyper moron* (beyond their part): humans contribute to their own pain, creating suffering beyond the lot which the gods have allotted to them. For example, Aegisthus, who kills Agamemnon even after he was warned not to, incurs divine retribution. The persecution of injustice, which Zeus refers to, does not preclude that the gods also bestow evil fates, or evil fates mixed with good, upon humans, regardless of their actions. Zeus's speech does not formulate a theodicy that repudiates the gods' responsibility for human suffering. He only states that the gods are not responsible for suffering that results from divine retribution for transgressions.[33]

---

33. See Strauss Clay (1983): 217–18; Allan (2006): 16–17.

The idea of divine retribution for human wrongdoing, of course, plays a major role in the plot of the *Odyssey*. As early as the Proem, Homer states that Odysseus's companions perish as a result of their own wilful actions. Aegisthus, whom Zeus uses as an example, is repeatedly enlisted as a foil for the suitors. The rhetorical effort Homer makes to portray the suitors as sacrilegious, and their murder as just punishment, has already been discussed. That Odysseus kills the suitors as an agent of divine justice is starkly formulated by Laertes, for whom the end of the suitors amounts to proof of the gods' existence: 'Father Zeus, there are gods indeed upon tall Olympus, / if truly the suitors have had to pay for their reckless violence' (24.351–52).

Despite the centrality of the theme of divine retribution in the *Odyssey*, Homer does not lose sight of divine arbitrariness, which is not bound by any morality. He repeatedly has characters emphasize that the gods followed entirely their own will when they promoted people or plunged them into disaster.[34] When Odysseus entreats Nausicaa for help, she replies,

> My friend, since you seem not like a thoughtless man, nor a
>   mean one,
> it is Zeus himself, the Olympian, who gives people good fortune,
> to each single man, to the good and the bad, just as he wishes;
> and since he must have given you yours, you must even endure
>   it. (6.187–90)

The deep-rooted assumption that divine intervention is arbitrary is also seen when Odysseus thanks Eumaeus for his friendly reception and the latter asks him to enjoy what he has been given, casually adding that 'the god will give you such, or will let it / be, as in his own mind he may wish. He can do anything' (14.444–45). Such statements show that in the *Odyssey*, divine action is ultimately thought to be free from moral concerns.[35]

---

34. Strauss Clay (1983): 221–29. Some of these reflections may be subject to a context of false assumptions, especially about the return of Odysseus, but this does not detract from their general significance, as Olson (1995): 214–15 suggests.

35. In addition to this example, see Helena at 4236–37, Odysseus at 17.424 and Philoetius at 20.201–3.

For the Homeric heroes, the gods' arbitrariness and divine justice do not contradict each other. Telemachus, for example, rebukes his mother for spoiling Phemius's song about heroes who return from the Trojan War:

> Why, my mother, do you begrudge this excellent singer
> his pleasing himself as the thought drives him? It is not the
>   singers
> who are to blame, it must be Zeus is to blame, who gives out
> to men who eat bread, to each and all, the way he wills it
>   (1.346–49)

Thereafter, Telemachus wishes that 'Zeus might somehow grant a reversal of fortunes. / Then you may perish in this house, with no payment given' (1.378–79). To his mother, Telemachus emphasizes the gods' arbitrariness, and to the suitors, he depicts divine retribution for crimes committed. Like the other Homeric heroes, Telemachus uses both models. Significantly, divine arbitrariness appears mostly in observations, while divine justice is referred to mainly in wishes and prayers, which are not formulated in the indicative but in the optative, as a hypothetical mode.[36]

Both conceptions of the gods appear when Odysseus urges the suitor Amphinomus to return home before it is too late:

> Of all creatures that breathe and walk on the earth there is
>   nothing
> more helpless than a man is, of all that the earth fosters;
> for he thinks that he will never suffer misfortune in future
> days, while the gods grant him courage, and his knees have spring
> in them. But when the blessed gods bring sad days upon him,
> against his will he must suffer it with enduring spirit.
> For the mind in men upon earth goes according to the fortunes
> the Father of Gods and Men, day by day, bestows upon them.
>   (18.130–37)

36. See Strauss Clay (1983): 226.

In this general reflection, Odysseus describes humans as being at the mercy of the gods. In the context of his own life, however, he emphasizes his own guilt: 'I myself once promised to be a man of prosperity, / but, giving way to force and violence, did many reckless / things, because I relied on my father and brothers' (18.138–40). The notion of personal responsibility is behind Odysseus's appeal to Amphinomus to stop his reprehensible actions before it is too late. In the epic, divine justice and arbitrariness go hand in hand.

When they refer to the unpredictability of the gods, the characters emphasize an idea that is central to the worldview of the *Iliad*. Odysseus's previously quoted words, for example, evoke a statement by Zeus: 'among all creatures that breathe on earth or crawl on it / there is not anywhere a thing more dismal than man is' (*Il.* 17.446–47). The repeated statements that the gods give men what they want are condensed in Achilles's analogy of the barrels, which captures the worldview of the *Iliad* in a concise image:

> There are two urns that stand on the door-sill of Zeus. They are
>> unlike
> for the gifts they bestow: an urn of evils, an urn of blessings.
> If Zeus who delights in thunder mingles these and bestows them
> on man, he shifts, and moves now in evil, again in good fortune.
> But when Zeus bestows from the urn of sorrows, he makes a
>> failure
> of man, and the evil hunger drives him over the shining
> Earth, and he wanders respected neither of gods nor mortals.
>> (*Il.* 24.527–33)

In the plot of the *Odyssey*, likewise, the gods prove to be both judge and capricious authority. Unlike in the *Iliad*, conflict between humans is not mirrored by dissent among the gods—on Olympus, no one is representing the cause of the suitors. But the example of Athena shows that, in addition to moral considerations, the gods are motivated by personal preferences. Athena's commitment to Odysseus is due to the fact that he resembles her, in terms of his skills, oratory and deceit, like no one else on earth. While a divine whim here amounts to the hero's protection, such a whim can easily take on sinister overtones. The vengeance of Poseidon and the wrath of Helios illustrate that in the *Odyssey*, the actions of the gods are certainly not limited by moral considerations; they include the randomness that is well known from the *Iliad*.

Poseidon directly intervenes in the action just once, in the Apologoi, when he sends Odysseus a storm off Scheria that lasts two days and two nights. Beyond this, however, Homer leaves no doubt that it is Poseidon who is behind Odysseus's wanderings. At the outset, immediately after the invocation of the Muses, he states that Poseidon 'remained relentlessly angry / with godlike Odysseus, until his return to his own country' (1.20–21). In the council of the gods that follows, Zeus gives the reason for Poseidon's resentment:

> It is the Earth Encircler Poseidon who, ever relentless,
> nurses a grudge because of the Cyclops, whose eye he blinded;
> for Polyphemus like a god, whose power is greatest
> over all the Cyclopes. (1.68–71)

As the audience learns in the course of the plot, Polyphemus is in fact the son of the sea god.

A number of Homer scholars have stressed that Poseidon's anger is not justified, or that, in any case, it is disproportionate—Polyphemus has eaten six of Odysseus's companions, and if Odysseus had not outwitted him, would have been devoured himself. The act that enrages Poseidon so much that he denies Odysseus a direct return home was merely one of self-defence, and the hero was not to blame: 'Poseidon's rage cannot be taken as an example of divine justice. Odysseus would be acquitted in any court of law for blinding the cyclops on the grounds of self-defence and extenuating circumstances.'[37]

One might object to such an acquittal on the grounds that in the Homeric universe, it is the deed rather than any mitigating circumstances

---

37. Ibid.: 229. See also Focke (1943): 168; Heubeck (1950): 84–85; Lloyd-Jones (1971): 29; Fenik (1974): 211–12. Conversely, Odysseus's guilt is emphasized by Reinhardt (1960): 69; Kullmann (1985): 6; Olson (1995): 209–10; Schmidt (2003): 32–33; Bakker (2013): 124–25. Friedrich (1991) stresses that although Poseidon's actions do not fit with the theodicy of the first book, they also do not diminish Zeus's claim to justice.

FIG. 18. Roman mosaic (detail), showing Poseidon, second century CE, Bardo National Museum, Tunis. Photo: akg-images/De Agostini Picture Library/G. Dagli Orti.

that counts. It does not matter how or why Odysseus acts; he has blinded the son of the sea god.[38] It has also been noted that Odysseus's crime is not so much the blinding itself. He is guilty of boasting of his deed to the cyclops. Having unheroically posed as a 'nobody', Odysseus subsequently indulges in hubris. And his hubris acquires religious overtones when Odysseus passes off his own deed as a punishment from Zeus and the gods (9.479), and claims that not even Poseidon will be able to heal Polyphemus's eye (9.525). In this, Odysseus claims divine legitimacy on the one hand, and denies the omnipotence of the gods on the other.[39]

These objections are not unjustified. It would be a mistake to apply our own contemporary understanding of morals and law to a world in which revenge amounts to a legitimate and even necessary aspect of self-validation. And yet, the wrath of Poseidon clearly differs from Aegisthus's punishment, meted out by Zeus to illustrate the principle of divine justice. Hermes, sent by the gods, urges Aegisthus neither to woo Clytemnestra nor kill Agamemnon. Odysseus does not receive any such warning. The fact that his companions ask him to leave the cyclops's cave without delay is not comparable to receiving and dismissing the warning of a divine authority.[40] Even though Eurylochus accuses Odysseus of sacrilege, where this warning is concerned, an important aspect of *atasthalia* is missing from the Polyphemus adventure.

Even those who prefer to disregard the circumstances and who focus on the actions themselves will not be able to refute that Polyphemus's blinding is a less serious crime than Aegisthus's adultery and murder. Above all, Poseidon, unlike Zeus, is not reacting to a general wrong as is the case with Aegisthus, but rather, responds to an act that concerns him personally. His son has been blinded, and he himself has been belittled since he is unable to heal him. Poseidon does not operate as an advocate of any moral system; he is incensed by an attack on his own honour and his anger therefore springs from a personal motive. The divine intervention that triggers the wanderings of the Apologoi is not

38. See Bakker (2013): 124–25.
39. Friedrich (1991): 17–21, who develops Reinhardt (1948): 85–86.
40. See Cook (1995): 115.

so much an attempt to punish a crime, as a defence of honour. At this point in the plot, a god appears whose actions are not in keeping with the idea of a consistent theodicy.

That Poseidon is far from being concerned with justice is also seen in his behaviour towards the Phaeacians. The Phaeacians are not culpable of any transgression;[41] on the contrary, they generously fulfil the laws of hospitality with their gifts and escort. Poseidon, however, is so enraged by their support of Odysseus that he wants to smash up the ship they use to convey him to Ithaca, and to place a mountain range around the Phaeacians' city (13.149–52). Dissuaded by Zeus, he turns the ship to stone instead. This retribution is obviously unjust. In his conversation with Zeus, it becomes clear that Poseidon is driven by his own honour: 'Father Zeus, no longer among the gods immortal / shall I be honoured, when there are mortals who do me no honour, / the Phaeacians, and yet these are of my own blood' (13.128–30). He is, in fact, so concerned with his own honour that he inflicts suffering on his own descendants in response to a blameless action and in the absence of any moral justification.

The Thrinacia episode shows another action of the gods that is aimed at defending their honour rather than at establishing justice, albeit less drastically than in the Polyphemus adventure. The *Odyssey*'s Proem establishes the companions' guilt: the reason for their downfall is the sacrilege against the cattle of the sun god. Nevertheless, scholars have questioned that guilt, saying that the companions had slaughtered the cattle after all their supplies had run out and hunger propelled them to do so: 'They are forced either to eat and commit a crime in the process, or else to perish, similarly to the choice they are presented with in Polyphemus' cave, to maim the cyclops or be devoured by him.'[42] According to this interpretation, the gods deliberately lead the Greeks to their doom. First Zeus sends a wind that makes it impossible for them to

---

41. Rutherford (1986): 148; Allan (2006): 18–19. On the relationship between Zeus and Poseidon in this scene, see Friedrich (1987b): 398–99.

42. Strauss Clay (1983): 230. See also Focke (1943): 247–54; Heubeck (1954): 72–78; Fenik (1974): 212. On the other hand, Kullmann (1985): 6, Friedrich (1987a), Olson (1995): 211–12, Danek (1998): 262–63 and Bakker (2013): 117–18 argue for a guilt of the companions. See also Cook (1995): 109–27.

leave the island, then they put Odysseus to sleep, giving his companions the opportunity to satisfy their hunger by committing sacrilege.

Although it is true that Odysseus's companions only eat Helios's cattle to assuage their hunger, this interpretation ignores some important differences between this episode and the Polyphemus adventure. First of all, the Greeks are not forced to land on Thrinacia; they do so against the advice of Odysseus, who recalls both Teiresias's and Circe's prophecies (12.271–76). Once on the island, Odysseus twice warns his men not to slaughter Helios's cattle, making them swear that 'no one of you in evil and reckless action / will slaughter any ox or sheep' (12.300–301). Whether the men are really forced to eat the cattle to avoid dying of starvation is difficult to say. The narrator refers to them being hungry (12.332), but Eurylochus may be exacerbating the sense of urgency when he claims that their choice was between starving to death and slaughtering the cattle (12.340–51). During the slaughter, the companions strive for ritual observance, but they deviate from sacrificial custom by substituting wine and barley for water and oak leaves, which underscores the perversity of the meal.[43]

The gods' responsibility for the companions' doom has also been questioned. One astute interpreter notes that it is Odysseus who depicts Zeus as the cause of the winds, and his sleep as induced by the gods.[44] In the Apologoi, Homer takes pains to have Odysseus tell only what he can have personal knowledge of. This becomes especially clear when Odysseus cites the conversation between Helios and Zeus on the grounds that Circe had told him about it (12.389–90). But perhaps it is too sophistical to distrust Odysseus's attribution of the wind and his sleep to the gods. He is generally a reliable, if wily, narrator and there are no other signs that he is manipulating his account at this point. In the epic, it is generally the gods who send the winds and who put heroes to sleep when something is to be done against their will. But even given such divine intervention, on Thrinacia, the companions are culpable in a different way from Odysseus in respect of Polyphemus: they disregard authoritative warnings and commit sacrilege knowingly.

43. Cook (1995): 118; Bakker (2013): 106.
44. Friedrich (1987b): 385–89.

At the same time, Helios's wrath, to which the companions fall victim, does not correspond to any divine effort to establish justice, such as Zeus refers to in the first book. While the gods punish Aegisthus for committing adultery and murder, the sun god is punishing an attack on himself, more than the crime. His motivation becomes clear from his complaint to Zeus and the other gods:

> Father Zeus, and you other everlasting and blessed
> Gods, punish the companions of Odysseus, son of Laertes;
> for they outrageously killed my cattle, in whom I always
> delighted, on my way up into the starry heaven,
> or when I turned back again from heaven toward earth. Unless
> these are made to give me just recompense for my cattle,
> I will go down to Hades' and give my light to the dead men.
>   (12.378–83)

Helios cites his personal loss rather than any violation of the general order, and adds force to his view by making a dire threat rather than presenting any ethical arguments. Like Poseidon, he is intent on avenging his own honour. In the *Odyssey*, too, therefore, the gods inflict suffering on humans for personal motives as well as in punishment for transgressions.

At the same time, Poseidon's and Helios's behaviour does not amount to a contradiction of Zeus's remarks about the injustice of men, as is often claimed. Divine retribution for misdeeds is a central motif in the *Odyssey*—like Aegisthus, both the suitors and the companions pay for their wrongdoing with their lives. But this does not preclude the gods ruthlessly pursuing their own interests. As in the *Iliad*, and not unlike the epic heroes, the gods of the *Odyssey* are concerned with their own honour. Helios holds the loss of his cattle against the companions; Poseidon takes revenge for the blinding of his son. Similarly, comments made by characters indicate that the Iliadic divine arbitrariness has not given way to a more moral image of divinity in the *Odyssey*.

Further, the moral aspect of the gods, which such a developmental perspective views as an achievement of the *Odyssey*, also appears in the *Iliad*. A simile presents the following image of Zeus:

As underneath the hurricane all the black earth is burdened
on an autumn day, when Zeus sends down the most violent
    waters
in deep rage against mortals after they stir him to anger
because in violent assembly they pass decrees that are crooked,
and drive righteousness from among them and care nothing for
    what the gods think. (*Il.* 16.384–88)

The idea of Zeus punishing human injustice is here so clearly expressed that proponents of the developmental hypothesis have been known to dismiss the passage as a retrospective interpolation, albeit without giving any philological reasons for this.[45]

The characters of the *Iliad* also refer to the justice of the gods. After slaying Peisander, for example, Menelaus urges the Trojans to leave the Greek ships, adding,

So, I think, shall you leave the ships of the fast-mounted
    Danaans,
you haughty Trojans, never to be glutted with the grim war
    noises,
nor go short of all that other shame and defilement
wherewith you defiled me, wretched dogs, and your hearts knew
    no fear
at all of the hard anger of Zeus loud-thundering,
the guest's god, who some day will utterly sack your steep
    city.
You who in vanity went away taking with you my wedded
wife, and many possessions, when she had received you in
    kindness. (*Il.* 13.620–27)

Menelaus's invective reflects his assumption that whoever commits an injustice must fear Zeus. He even views the imminent fall of Troy as a divine punishment for Paris's breach of hospitality. Even though Menelaus thereafter wonders how Zeus might be moved to bestow his favour on the Trojans, he presupposes divine justice.

45. Dodds (1951): 32; Munding (1961).

In the third book, Menelaus prays to Zeus before his duel with Paris:

Zeus, lord, grant me to punish the man who first did me injury,
brilliant Alexandros, and beat him down under my hands'
   strength
that any one of the men to come may shudder to think of
doing evil to a kindly host, who has given him friendship.
   (*Il.* 3.351–54)

Here, too, Zeus is the authority who would punish injustice among humans. It is the abduction of Helen, which triggers the Trojan War and gives the *Iliad* its subject matter, that is to be avenged. Mention of 'the men to come' gives Menelaus's entreaty a meta-poetic meaning; it is, after all, the contemporary reader who learns of the consequences of Helen's abduction from the *Iliad*. This epic is like a medium for moral instruction: by presenting the sufferings endured in the Trojan War as a punishment for Paris's outrage, Homer discourages his audiences from perpetrating comparable actions.

Such an interpretation of the Trojan War is found in Herodotus's discussion of the myth of Helen: 'The severity of a crime is matched by the severity of the ensuing punishment at the gods' hands' (2.120.5). In contemporary research, William Allan discusses the moral dimensions of the 'will of Zeus' in depth, pointing out that the *Iliad* contains constant reminders of the wrongs committed by the Trojans. According to Allan, Pandarus's attempt to shoot Menelaus despite a truce and Priam's refusal to hand Helen over after the duel reiterate the injustice committed by Paris, which Homer refers to only in flashbacks.[46] The idea of divine justice appears not only in individual passages, but is anchored in the overall structure of the *Iliad*.

The differences between the two great Homeric epics should, of course, not be minimized or denied. The *Iliad* emphasizes divine arbitrariness, while the *Odyssey* emphasizes that the gods pursue injustice. The differing emphases emerge not least from the use of the relevant terms: *atasthalia*, which appears nine times in the *Odyssey* to denote acts of injustice,

46. Allan (2006): 4–5.

is found only twice in the *Iliad*. Conversely, *atē*, denoting the arbitrariness with which the gods repeatedly strike men in the *Iliad* (mentioned fifteen times), only appears five times in the *Odyssey*. But the fact that both epics refer to both the arbitrariness and the justice of the gods argues against any fundamental change of attitude, let alone progress in terms of the worldview portrayed.

If anything, it is their plot types that constitute a real difference between the *Iliad* and *Odyssey*. The *Odyssey*—subject to the limitations that will be discussed in the next chapter—has a fortuitous ending. Its hero is taken to the ends of the earth and undergoes extreme dangers, but ultimately returns home to his wife and family. His return gains depth and meaning from being staged as a battle against evil usurpers and from the plot being morally charged. The *Odyssey*, therefore, presents the type of adventure story that lets a hero suffer, yet ultimately triumph over villainous adversaries. As noted in the first and second chapters, Homer creates a narrative pattern which, through the mediation of the novel of late antiquity, has had considerable influence on the development of the modern novel and which continues today, especially in popular literature, perhaps. The type of plot which the *Odyssey* presents does not exclude reflections on divine arbitrariness and human insecurity. At the same time, while the hero's ultimate success prevents the idea of human frailty from gaining the upper hand, the moral charge of the conflict supports an ethical worldview.

The *Iliad*, on the other hand, is a tragic epic that focuses on human frailty. On the battlefield before Troy, the heroes experience the insecurity of human life in its most urgent form—the *condicio heroica* as an intensified *condicio humana*. The *Iliad* emphasizes the mortality of its hero, not by narrating Achilles's death, but anticipating it in an increasingly dense network of signs and prophecies. Not even Achilles, the best of the Achaians, can escape it; indeed, he must die young if he is to avenge the death of his friend Patroclus, as his heroic status dictates. Fame comes at the price of *mors immatura*, premature death. There is room for divine justice in the *Iliad*, but it must recede into the background to let the frailty of the human condition emerge. The utter dependence of human beings is forcefully revealed when Achilles's life is ended without any regard for morality.

The image of the gods and the worldview are nuanced differently in the *Iliad* and *Odyssey*, and this accords with their respective plots. The fact that both epics refer both to divine arbitrariness and divine justice has always bothered Homer scholars. There have been efforts not only to banish the depiction of a retributive Zeus from the *Iliad* by claiming that this was a later addition, but also to weaken references to the arbitrariness of the gods in the *Odyssey*. Analysts have attributed these to an earlier poet whose work Homer drew on; oralists have regarded them as older elements of the oral tradition.[47] Many contemporary scholars find that it is neither meaningful nor possible to draw a sharp line between different layers of the epic. The criteria for analytically derived divisions have too often proved arbitrary, while apparent contradictions have been successfully made use of for interpretational purposes. Similarly, the reading presented here highlights that the gods can both act arbitrarily and be concerned with retributive justice.

A look at Herodotus's *Histories* helps to refute evolutionary hypotheses about the Greek worldview. The *Histories* not only demonstrate the continuity of Homeric ideas, but also illustrate how different worldviews and images of the gods can coexist in the same narrative.[48] As previously noted, Herodotus interprets the destruction of Troy as a divine punishment. In other places, too, he views events as divine retribution. The Cyrenian queen Pheretima, for example, is eaten from the inside by worms because she took excessive revenge on the inhabitants of Barca after a rebellion (4.205). Herodotus also attributes the death of two Spartan heralds in Athens to the fact that the Spartans had killed Persian messengers (7.133–37). As in the epic, the gods here appear as judges who ruthlessly punish offences against order.

The *Histories*, however, also present other perspectives to explain suffering and misfortune. The divine arbitrariness that is seen in Homer

47. For the analytical perspective, see Schadewaldt (1960); for an oralist point of view, Fenik (1974): 209–27.

48. Grethlein (2010b): 188–96.

takes on a sinister hue when it appears in the shape of envy. Herodotus suggests, for example, that the envy of the gods is at work in the fate of Polycrates. As tyrant of Samos, Polycrates is exceedingly rich and accustomed to success. He follows a friend's advice to sacrifice his most valued possession because 'the gods are jealous of success' (3.40.2). But the ring which Polycrates throws into the sea to reduce his own abundance returns to him in the belly of a fish delivered by fishermen. The powerful tyrant Polycrates suffers an abrupt decline of fortune and finally dies on the cross, suffering a death that, as Herodotus notes, 'was not worthy of him or his disposition' (3.125.2). Even the attempt to limit one's own bounty cannot appease the gods in their envy.

Both interpretative patterns are found in the Croesus story, which programmatically stands at the beginning of the *Histories*. While Solon warns Croesus of the envy of the gods (1.32.1), Croesus seems to see his fall as a punishment for his own hubris (1.86). Herodotus himself speaks of 'divine anger' (1.34.1). Later, Croesus adds another model of interpretation when he tells Cyrus that 'human affairs are on a wheel' (1.207.2). This idea also seems to have made sense to Herodotus, since he notes in the introduction that 'most of [the cities] which were important in the past have diminished in significance by now, and those which were great in my own time were small in times past.' (1.5.4) What is the ultimate paradigm: that the gods punish injustice; that they are envious; or that human experience is simply subject to cyclicity?

Here, too, analysts may be quick to argue that the various explanatory patterns are due to the sources on which Herodotus relies. But such a thesis would fail to recognize the artful composition of the *Histories*, which Herodotus did not randomly piece together from various sources, but rather carefully composed. The interpretative patterns show the ways in which the *Histories* and the epic reflect on human life. As narratives, they lack the sharpness and systematic approach of a theoretical treatise, offering neither coherent ethics nor a philosophy of history. Therefore, interpretations that expect any kind of unified system are bound to fail and must needs postulate different layers to make up for the inevitable inconsistencies. This shortcoming of narrative, however, is at the same time its great strength: the Homeric epic as well as the

Histories of Herodotus capture the diversity of human experience, which at times views suffering as just retribution, and at other times as unjust, or as an expression of human frailty. Real-world experience, which is rarely clear-cut, corresponds to the ambiguity we feel when we ask ourselves what was responsible for Croesus's downfall, or when we weigh the contribution of the gods against the guilt of the companions on Thrinacia.

The limits and possibilities of ethical and ideological reflection in narratives become visible both in Odysseus's actions and in the gods' interventions. Narratives lack the abstraction of theoretical explanations, but in depicting actions they offer greater proximity to the world of lived experience. Since narratives are not subject to any requirement for theoretical coherence, they can reflect the ambivalence that characterizes real life. While narrative is not suited to providing any clear-cut answers, it is suited to penetrating to the heart of problems. It is in no small part the ability to present temporal dynamics and to allow different perspectives and voices to collide that allows dilemmas to be presented in a multidimensional way. Homer exploits these possibilities. There are many reasons for the extensive reception of his epics, which served as the Greeks' education up to Imperial times. One important aspect, however, is bound to be the narrative confrontation with ethical questions, and hence the impetus for reflection, which, notwithstanding all the changes that the centuries have brought, has remained potent to this day.

7

Narrating the Ending

IN NARRATIVES, characters are driven by the desire to attain their goals, while the reader wants to understand the plot as a whole. The two tendencies coincide when, as is the case with the *Odyssey*, it is the hero's striving that moves the plot forward. Odysseus desires to return home and reclaim his ancestral position; the reader or listener wants to know how his nostos succeeds. The wish to know the outcome is a driving force for the reader and the tension created as the plot unfolds serves as fuel, as it were. As Peter Brooks notes, the anticipation of retrospection is a central element of the reading process.[1] The reader wonders how the story will end and reads on in order to be able to look back on the action. This lends the ending a special significance—it marks the point at which the narrative terminates and the plot usually concludes, meaning that it becomes visible to the reader in its entirety.[2]

Narrative, therefore, enables something that is not possible in real life. While life is also understood as a narrative, it is a story that must necessarily remain in flux. Death is the point from which a life story can be told in its entirety, yet also marks the point when the ability to narrate ceases. Narrative mimics the sequential structure of life, and like

1. See Brooks (1992): 23.

2. The concept of closure has been extensively discussed by literary scholars. Kermode (1967) and Herrnstein Smith (1968) can be considered fundamental, in philosophical and technical terms respectively. In classical philology, see, for instance, Fowler (1989) and the contributions in Roberts, Dunn and Fowler (1997).

life, involves the reader in a dialectic of experience and expectation. However, unlike life, it also enables the plot to be viewed as a whole.

The relationship between narrative and life—both their shared sequential structure of events, that is, and the difference between them: the conclusion which narrative can provide—may be an important reason why people have narrated stories at all times and in all cultures. Narrative enables reflection on the temporal structure of life. Such reflection is neither theoretical nor conceptual, but performative, and gains its depth from taking the same form as the object of reflection: narratives expose the reader to the same temporal tension as life, but, after revealing the tension between expectation and experience in relation to an unfamiliar object, they ultimately resolve it. As Walter Benjamin notes in his essay on the narrator, 'that which draws the reader to the novel is the hope of warming his shivering life on a death of which he reads'.[3]

Narratives can, of course, withhold the conclusion; the ending may remain inconclusive or be dissonant. And even where there is a rounded ending and everything seems to resolve satisfactorily, cracks can appear upon closer inspection. Nevertheless, readers generally expect the ending to resolve tension and conflict, and to answer any remaining questions. The most commonly used narrative tense, the past tense, is itself an indication that a story is told in retrospect, which implies the promise that it—unlike the real-life story—is complete. This goes hand in hand with the wish for a satisfying conclusion, which stories unfolding in real life rarely provide. Of course, it is this very expectation, nourished by long custom, that narrators can deliberately choose not to fulfil, perhaps in an effort to prevent the gap between narrative and life becoming too wide. Openings and closures are the two poles between which endings oscillate: some narratives provide a rounded ending; others raise questions rather than providing answers. Moreover, different reading strategies come into play, and where one reader perceives a harmonious ending, another may sense some unresolved dissonance.[4] The *Odyssey* can be used to examine how loose ends may remain even in a work that

---

3. Benjamin (1991 [1936]): 457. For an interpretation of this passage, see Grethlein (2017), ch. 2.
4. See Fowler (1997).

seems to weave all the threads together. The first task of this chapter will be to consider the means Homer uses to bring the plot to a conclusion. In terms of form and content, the *Odyssey* offers a rounded ending. Nevertheless, Homer also directs the audience's attention beyond that ending, indicating its contingency in the process. Additionally, beyond the ending itself, a variety of moments all contribute to the conclusion of the *Odyssey*. Even in antiquity, critics found the conclusion to the twenty-fourth book unsatisfactory and sought the telos of the plot in Book 23. The *Odyssey*'s conclusion is composed of several scenes, the significance of which varies depending on interpretation. For the interpretation offered here, the nocturnal conversation between Penelope and Odysseus, which begins after she has recognized him, is the culmination. It enables insights into narrative that can be pursued with other texts of world literature.

The *Odyssey*'s Conclusion

After the wrath of Poseidon has driven Odysseus across the seas and he sets foot on Ithaca once more, ultimately to murder the suitors, the plot of the *Odyssey* concludes in the twenty-third book. The ending above all emerges from the successful conclusion of the nostos, and it is useful briefly to recollect it here. As will be shown, the ending also gains depth from a summary that is embedded in the plot and from Odysseus's status being enhanced through implicit comparisons to other heroes, and, not least, from references being made to the beginning of the epic, which place a ring around the *Odyssey*, as it were.

The twenty-fourth book consists of three parts: the second Nekyia, the anagnorisis scene involving Laertes and, finally, the battle with the suitors' relatives. All these parts contribute to the conclusion of the plot. The second Nekyia describes the entry of the suitors' souls to the underworld, confirming their departure from the plot. In the twenty-third book, the servants carry the corpses out of the house and cleanse it with sulphur. Thereafter the souls, detached from their bodies, arrive in the underworld. It will become apparent how the conversations of the shades in the underworld also help to complete the *Odyssey*.

In Odysseus's meeting with Laertes, a long chain of anagnorisis scenes is concluded. Several references to Laertes prepare for the appearance of this character at the end of the *Odyssey*.[5] Although the point at which Penelope recognizes her husband undoubtedly represents the climax of the anagnorisis scenes, the encounter between father and son is also significant, even if it does not take place until after the suitors have been killed. In his neglected state, Laertes, like the dog Argos, represents Ithaca's decline. When Odysseus reminds Laertes of the fruit trees he had received from the latter as a boy, the anagnorisis scene with Laertes serves to reinstate Odysseus's role as heir and proprietor—his final significant role after claiming the role of father to Telemachus, master of the house to the servants, and husband to Penelope. The idea of genealogical continuity carries over into the quarrel with the Ithacans when Laertes rejoices that 'my son and my son's son are contending over their courage' (24.515).

The final scene of the *Odyssey*, the battle with the relatives of the slain suitors, is also carefully prepared. Odysseus repeatedly refers to the revenge that he and his faithful followers will have to face after murdering the suitors,[6] and after a people's assembly many Ithacans do indeed join to avenge the death of their sons and brothers. Odysseus confronts them together with Laertes, Telemachus and his servants. After talking with Zeus, Athena joins Odysseus's side and eventually interrupts the battle to prevent the Ithacans from being decimated. When Odysseus does not heed her call to end the battle, Zeus hurls a thunderbolt at Athena's feet, and she addresses Odysseus personally. Only then does he stop and Zeus's plan is realized:

> Now that noble Odysseus has punished the suitors, let them
> make their oaths of faith and friendship, and let him be king
> always; and let us make them forget the death of their brothers
> and sons, and let them be friends with each other, as in the
>> time past,
> and let them have prosperity and peace in abundance. (24.482–86)

5. *Od.* 1.188–93; 4.735–54; 11.187–96; 15.353–57; 16.137–53; 22.184–86.
6. *Od.* 20.41–43; 23.118–52; 362–63. See also Laertes in 24.353–55.

Although the murder of the suitors is presented as a just punishment, it sets in motion, as one interpreter puts it, 'a chain of revenge that [...] is the most dangerous source of disorder in pre-legal societies'.[7] It is only once the cycle of blow and counterblow is broken that the plot is complete and the *Odyssey* concludes. Forgetfulness of the killing, induced by Zeus, finally allows a return to order. The nostos is at once a personal, familial and political matter. Odysseus's homecoming gains in significance, and the conclusion of the *Odyssey* acquires gravitas when viewed from a political perspective, as a restoration of peace and order.

The ending of the *Odyssey* gains importance likewise from the fact that the ethical dimension of the suitors' murder is brought up once more. In the people's assembly, Eupeithes accuses Odysseus of having both his companions and the suitors on his conscience:

> all this
> shall be a disgrace, even for the men hereafter to hear of,
> if we do not take revenge on the murderers of our brothers
> and sons; for there would be no pleasure in my heart to go on
> living, but I would wish to die and be with the perished.
> (24.432–36)

As has already been shown, Eupeithes's speech is one of the passages that point to an alternative view of the plot. It does not go unchallenged: Medon warns the Ithacans that Odysseus killed the suitors with divine aid and was therefore acting in accordance with the will of the gods (24.443–49). Similarly, Halitherses reproaches the Ithacans, saying that it was their own fault for not heeding his own and Mentor's warnings (24.454–62). These two speeches quickly close the window on the alternative view introduced by Eupeithes's speech, and underline the dominant understanding of the Mnesterophony as a just punishment. The ethical charge of the nostos endows the ending with meaning beyond a mere resolution of conflict.

It is not only the plot coming to a satisfying conclusion that lends the *Odyssey* its rounded ending; the conversations held in the second

---

7. Nagler (1990): 232.

Nekyia add a further keystone to its conclusion. Amphimedon tells Agamemnon how Odysseus had tricked and killed him and his peers. In doing so, he provides an overview of the final third of the *Odyssey* that complements the summary provided when Odysseus tells Penelope of his adventures in the twenty-third book. Homer, therefore, integrates the kind of overview which the audience desires into the plot.

The next section of this chapter will deal in more depth with elements that undermine the *Odyssey*'s ending, but it is worth briefly noting at this point that Amphimedon's account introduces a rift. He deviates from Homer,[8] by claiming that Penelope had arranged the archery contest at Odysseus's behest, and assumes that Penelope knew the real identity of the beggar, and that she was involved in the conspiracy against the suitors. Analysts see this as a relic of an earlier version of the *Odyssey*, in which Odysseus and Penelope may have conspired together. However, such a surmise about the genesis of this epic, plausible or otherwise, cannot replace an interpretation. Amphimedon misunderstands the situation and wrongly assumes that Penelope had been privy to the revenge plan. This gives a final example of the suitors' inability to recognize their own situation. Despite repeated warnings, they refuse to believe that Odysseus will return, and, as Amphimedon's speech demonstrates, they fail fully to understand the course of events, even in retrospect.[9]

Yet while Amphimedon is in error about Penelope's role, his surmise demonstrates the fundamental importance of perspective: the same events may be perceived very differently. This is also shown in Amphimedon's overall account. Rather than acknowledging the suitors' culpability, he justifies their prolonged stay at Odysseus's court by pointing to the cunning of the latter's wife, which serves as a seamless transition to their murder: Penelope had strung the young men along for years until they were ultimately outwitted and murdered by Odysseus. By giving such a summary of the Mnesterophony, Amphimedon's narrative adds another

---

8. See Page (1955): 120; Kirk (1962): 244–45 against the assertion that Amphimedon minimizes the time that lies between the discovery of Penelope's subterfuge and Odysseus's return; also Goldhill (1988): 1–3.

9. Goldhill (1988): 5–8.

facet to the *Odyssey*'s ending and undermines its conclusion by confronting the audience with an alternative view of the plot.

In addition to the summaries of the Mnesterophony, the shades' appraisal of Odysseus's fate also contributes to the conclusion. First, Achilles laments Agamemnon's ignominious death:

How I wish that, enjoying that high place of your power,
you could have met death and destiny in the land of the Trojans.
So all the Achaians would have made a mound to cover you,
and you would have won great glory for your son hereafter.
In truth you were ordained to die by a death most pitiful.
　(24.30–34)

Agamemnon responds by praising Achilles for the glory he achieved through his death on the battlefield. He describes in detail the sumptuous funeral, attended not only by his divine mother but also by the Muses, and refers to the tomb on the Hellespont, which is laid out 'so that it can be seen afar from out on the water / by men now alive and those to be born in the future' (24.83–84). While Agamemnon laments his own inglorious death, he attests to Achilles, 'even now you have died, you have not lost your name, but always / in the sight of all mankind your fame shall be great, Achilles' (24.93–94).

The comparison of heroic fates is further developed when Agamemnon, responding to Amphimedon's report of the Mnesterophony, praises Odysseus for having a wife who, unlike Clytemnestra, remains virtuous and faithful to her husband. Time and again, Homer uses the story of Atreus's house as a foil for the *Odyssey*, and here he contrasts Agamemnon's fate with that of Odysseus for one last time. Further, Agamemnon also implicitly compares Odysseus to Achilles. While speaking to Amphimedon, he mentions Odysseus by slightly varying a formula that he previously used for Achilles: 'O happy son of Peleus, Achilles, like the immortals'; 'O fortunate son of Laertes, Odysseus of many devices' (24.36; 192).

Odysseus's fate is contrasted not only with that of Agamemnon, but also with that of Achilles: unlike Agamemnon, Achilles achieves glory, but sacrifices his nostos in the process. Odysseus, however, achieves glory as well as returning home, or, more precisely, he acquires fame on account of his nostos. The comparison with Agamemnon and Achilles pays homage to Odysseus, which amounts to a commentary on the plot at the conclusion of the *Odyssey*.

By referring to Odysseus's renown, the epic also indirectly reflects on itself, since it is the medium of that renown. It is tempting to view the comparison of Odysseus and Achilles as a competition between the *Odyssey* with the *Iliad*, the Homeric epic that heralds the glory of Achilles. Such an interpretation might claim the fact that Agamemnon explicitly mentions use of the song. But Agamemnon speaks of a song that proclaims Penelope's virtue and Clytemnestra's disgrace (24.196–202); in other words, a song that cannot be identified with either the *Iliad* or the *Odyssey*. At the same time, it is not far-fetched to view the comparison of Odysseus with Achilles as a comparison of the *Odyssey* with the *Iliad*, since the former is dedicated to Odysseus's adventures and the latter to Achilles and his wrath.[10]

Homer, however, suggests a comparison with another medium that serves *kleos*. Rather than citing the epic, Agamemnon above all refers to the burial mound, which would continue to commemorate Achilles into the future as a guarantee for his lasting fame. In the *Iliad*, Hector depicts the function of burial mounds when he speculates on the fate of the man who will face him in duel:

> But his corpse I will give back among the strong-benched vessels
> so that the flowing-haired Achaians may give him due burial
> and heap up a mound upon him beside the broad passage of
>   Helle.
> And some day one of the men to come will say, as he sees it,
> one who in his benched ship sails on the wine-blue water:
> 'This is the mound of a man who died long ago in battle,
> who was one of the bravest, and glorious Hector killed him.'
> So will he speak some day, and my glory will not be forgotten.
>   (*Il.* 7.84–91)

10. Kullmann (1992): 297–98 goes even further and compares the *Odyssey* with the *Iliad*, the nostos poems and the *Aethiopica*.

There is irony in the fact that in Hector's imagination, the burial mound of his fallen opponent would ultimately reflect Hector's own glory. But apart from this, his speech demonstrates the idea that burial mounds preserved the memory of heroes and their deeds, not least through the inscription-like words of the *anonymus*. Like the epics, graves bestowed glory, yet their function cannot compete with that of poetry. An epic circulates freely; many bards can recite it in different places at the same time, while a grave, even if visible from afar, is spatially fixed. Only those who passed the Hellespont learned of Achilles's glory, while the *Odyssey* 'goes up to the heavens' (*Od.* 9.20).

Another passage in the *Iliad* also raises doubts on the capacity of tombs to commemorate a hero permanently. When Nestor gives his son Antilochus instructions for the chariot race, he describes the turning mark for him:

> I will give you a clear mark and you cannot fail to notice it.
> There is a dry stump standing up from the ground about six feet,
> oak it may be, or pine, and not rotted away by rain-water,
> and two white stones are leaned against it, one on either side,
> at the joining place of the ways, and there is smooth driving
>> around it.
> Either it is the grave-mark of someone who died long ago,
> or was set as a racing goal by men who lived before our time.
>> (*Il.* 23.326–32)

Nestor's uncertainty as to whether the stones and piece of wood are a burial mound shows that such monuments could easily lose their commemorative function. The fame conferred by graves is limited in space and time, and, being bound to a specific place, cannot endure like the epic. The *Odyssey* not only juxtaposes its hero with Achilles, but also compares itself to an inferior medium of fame. Homer strives to show his own work as well as his hero to best advantage, and by making the audience reflect on the *Odyssey* as a whole reinforces the sense that the plot has reached a conclusion.

The conclusion of the *Odyssey*, further, is reinforced by a double ring structure. The people's assembly which deliberates on revenge against Odysseus mirrors the people's assembly held by the Ithacans at the beginning of the second book (24.420–71; 2.1–259).[11] The second assembly, although shorter, has obvious parallels to the first. Whereas in the one, Antinous defends the suitors and blames Penelope for their continued presence at Odysseus's court, in the other, it is his father Eupeithes who denounces Odysseus for the death of both his companions and the suitors. Eupeithes resembles the first speaker of the first people's assembly, the aged Aegyptus: both are mourning the loss of a son—Eupeithes has lost Antinous, the suitor who is the first to die, while Aegyptus has lost Antiphus, a companion of Odysseus who, as the narrator adds, was the last to be devoured by Polyphemus. On both occasions, Halitherses takes Odysseus's side, even recalling his first speech in the course of his second (24.456–60), and both assemblies feature a second speaker who also opposes the suitors—Mentor in the first, and Medon in the second.

Two conversations among the gods form another ring. Before Athena joins Odysseus, she consults with Zeus about what to do (24.472–88). Their exchange takes the audience back to the beginning of the plot, where there is another conversation between them (1.22–95). While at the beginning of the first book Zeus and Athena decide to bring Odysseus home, at the end of the final book they deliberate on how he should break the Ithacans' resistance and remove the last obstacle. Zeus explicitly mentions Athena's advice to grant Odysseus's revenge on the suitors and thereby implicitly brings to mind his initial statement that people incurred divine punishment through their own misdeeds. The people's assemblies and the conversations between the gods form a double ring structure. Like other ring structures that are popular in oral poetry, this gives the audience a sense that a circle is closing and the plot is reaching a natural end. The plot's conclusion, therefore, is emphasized by the structure of the *Odyssey*.

Opening Up the Ending

The open ending of the *Iliad*—Hector is buried but Achilles remains alive and Troy still stands—has been contrasted with the closed ending of the *Odyssey*.[12] Indeed, as has been shown, both the structure and

---

11. See Heubeck (1954): 39 on the literal correspondences.

12. See, for instance, de Jong (2001): 566.

content of the *Odyssey* provide a rounded conclusion. Yet even this conclusion is subject to cracks that point to the difficulty of understanding life through narration. A fine tear appears in the fabric of the ending when Amphimedon gives his alternative account of the action. Another such tear appears at the very point when, in the eyes of many interpreters, the ending is rounded off. It has repeatedly been claimed that the ending of the *Odyssey* constitutes a new political order.[13] A blood feud that potentially sets in motion an endless exchange of blows, and therefore calls into question the future of the community, is said to be replaced by a new legal system. In this respect, the *Odyssey* supposedly resembles the Aeschylean *Oresteia*, in which Athena installs a constitutional authority, the Areopagus, to end the conflict between the Erinyes and Orestes, who is threatening Athens.[14]

The very thesis that Aeschylus brings the birth of the rule of law to the stage is questionable.[15] The court proceedings in the *Eumenides* are far removed from our standards of the rule of law. Apollo tries to bribe the judges of the Areopagus, and the Furies issue savage threats that have little to do with the concerns of the trial. Above all, it is not the judges' verdict which ends the conflict: after the acquittal, the enraged Furies threaten Athens. Only Athena's decision to offer them an officially recognized home in Athens and to grant them a new task there reconciles them. Far from representing the birth of the constitutional state, the *Eumenides* testifies to an understanding of government that is well described by Carl Schmitt,[16] who, rather than defining politics in terms of content, refers to varying degrees of association or dissociation, or, simply put, whether someone is considered friend or foe. In the *Eumenides*, it is not the court judgement, but the integration of the Furies into the polis and their transformation from foe to friend which restores the peace. The source of the aggression, which threatens the polis, is incorporated and redirected against its enemies.

13. See, for instance, Erbse (1972): 140; Hommel (1976): 11–13; Kullmann (1992): 303–4; Russo, Fernandez-Galiano and Heubeck (1992), ad 24.413–548; ad 24.482–85.

14. Hommel (1974): 17–19; 1976: 13.

15. See Grethlein (2003): 234–47; (2004).

16. Meier (1980) applies Schmitt's concept of politics to classical Athens.

And the rule-of-law interpretation applies even less to the *Odyssey*. In the *Eumenides*, a new authority is, at any rate, established in the form of the Areopagus, but at the end of the *Odyssey*, there is divine intervention. Akin to a *deus ex machina*, Zeus and Athena intervene to bring the escalating events back on track and to bring about the expected ending. This divine intervention is by no means arbitrary. Zeus fulfils his claim to punish human injustice, but does not establish a new legal order. Rather, he renews the old one: 'let them be friends with each other, as in the time past' (24.485). At the end of the *Odyssey*, conflict is resolved, yet there is no new order that can be said to endow the conclusion with its significance.

The idea that a new legal order is established at the end of the *Odyssey* has been so popular in part because it displaces a certain unease created by Homer bringing the gods into play to bring about the ending. Divine intervention is integrated into the plot insofar as Zeus enforces the ethical programme he proclaims at the outset, and yet there is something unsatisfactory about the ending. The divine intervention doesn't seem to develop organically, but is born of necessity. After Odysseus has rid himself of his adversaries, the action seems to get out of hand once more. The hero of the epic is unable to reinstate the peace himself; indeed, order has to be re-established against his resistance. And rather than devising a solution to the new conflict, Homer cuts it short with a *deus ex machina*.

Ancient audiences are bound to have perceived divine interventions in dramas and stories differently than modern readers do.[17] The gods, who seem strange to us, were firmly anchored in the understanding of ancient audiences, not just as figures in literature, but as realities, especially, but not only, in cult. For ancient audiences, the divine intervention at the end of the *Odyssey* would have seemed less like the poet 'selling out' than a sanctioning of the ending by the highest authority. When Athena and Zeus end the quarrel between Odysseus and the

---

17. Antiphanes *fr.* 189: 13–17 PCG, however, illustrates that even in antiquity, the use of a *deus ex machina* in theatre was considered a capitulation on the part of the poet. Dunn (1996): 26–44 elaborates on the complexity of the *deus ex machina*, using Euripides as an example.

suitors' relatives, they lend the divine seal of approval to the ending, adding special significance.

Yet even when viewed in this way, there seems to be a gap in the conclusion. The oaths which Athena imposes on the disputants in the last four verses ritually confirm the reconciliation; however, Homer fails to realize the divine plan. In his conversation with Athena, Zeus announces,

> Now that noble Odysseus has punished the suitors, let them
> make their oaths of faith and friendship, and let him be king
> always; and let us make them forget the death of their brothers
> and sons, and let them be friends with each other, as in the time
>> past,
> and let them have prosperity and peace in abundance.
>   (24.482–86)

The *Odyssey* ends abruptly with an oath sworn by Odysseus and the Ithacans; the audience learns nothing more of the friendship they enjoy henceforth or of the wealth and peace that will hold sway.[18] One might object that Homer wanted to avoid repeating himself and therefore made do with Zeus's words. Such an argument, however, ignores an important point of the oral epic, which frequently narrates the realization of predictions, often using the same words again. Homer has Zeus promise the fruits of the renewal but does not go on to outline how this manifests itself, even in a formulaic way. Peace and wealth remain an unfulfilled promise.

While Zeus's promise merely causes a subtle tear in the fabric of the *Odyssey* and its conclusion, a larger hole appears as a result of Teiresias's instruction to Odysseus in the underworld, which he communicates to Penelope in the twenty-third book:

> since he told me to go among many cities
> of men, taking my well-shaped oar in my hands and bearing it,
> until I come where there are men living who know nothing
> of the sea, and who eat food that is not mixed with salt, who never

18. The language is generally very condensed at the end. See Stössel (1975): 132.

have known ships whose cheeks are painted purple, who never
have known well-shaped oars, which act for ships as wings do.
And then he told me a very clear proof. I will not conceal it.
When, as I walk, some other wayfarer happens to meet me,
and says I carry a winnow fan on my bright shoulder,
then I must plant my well-shaped oar in the ground, and render
ceremonious sacrifice to the lord Poseidon,
one ram and one bull, and a mounter of sows, a boar pig,
and make my way home again, and render holy hecatombs
to the immortal gods who hold the wide heaven, all
of them in order. Death will come to me from the sea, in
some altogether unwarlike way, and it will end me
in the ebbing time of a sleek old age. My people
about me will prosper. All this he told me would be
   accomplished. (23.267–84)

This oracular instruction by Teiresias has been linked with other epics,
which recount Odysseus's fortunes beyond his return home to Ithaca
and which have survived only as fragments. While analytical and neo-
analytical scholars have tried to show that the *Odyssey* alludes to older
oral traditions that found their way into post-Homeric epics, propo-
nents of oralist theories posit a more sophisticated exchange: since epics
developed over a long period of time and circulated in parallel with each
other, they also alluded to each other.[19] Prominent among such sup-
positions is the case of the *Telegony* attributed to Eugammon. Its plot is
known above all from a summary in Proclus. According to this, Odys-
seus goes to Elis after his return to Ithaca. From Elis, he seeks out Ithaca
once more to perform the sacrifices prescribed by Teiresias. Thereafter,
he sets out again and travels to Thesprotia, where he marries the queen.
When he ultimately returns to Ithaca once more, Telegonus, a son born
to him by Circe, kills him. The difference between the demise of Odysseus
in the *Telegony* and the 'altogether unwarlike' death predicted by

---

19. For an oralist perspective on reciprocal allusions, see Ballabriga (1989): 297–304; Tsagalis
(2007): 68–90. For the analytical perspective, see, for instance, Merkelbach (1969): 142–55 and
the literature in Tsagalis (2007): 76 n. 42.

Teiresias indicates the complexity of the relationship between the different epic traditions. The individual poems do not fit together seamlessly to form one grand epic, but offer partly complementary, partly antagonistic and competing stories.

Comparativists have shown that the prophecy of Teiresias is based on a folktale motif which has been documented by various cultures, from the Middle Ages to the present day: the story of a seafarer who travels inland.[20] Stories like that of Saint Elijah, a sailor who renounces his sinful life and goes inland with an oar on his shoulder until people no longer recognize it as such are widespread in Greece. There, on a mountain, Saint Elijah settles down. An American version of the motif was published as a news item in the *New York Times* of 21 December 1982:

> Whitehorse, Yukon Territory. Some of the boys in a saloon here the other night were talking about a local woman who had won $1800 in a lottery. The consensus was that her decision to put the money in the bank showed a sorry lack of ambition. 'What I'd do,' said one, 'is tie a snow shovel to the hood of my car and drive south until nobody had the faintest idea what the damn thing was.'

This anecdote does not refer to an oar, which symbolizes familiarity with the sea, but to a snow shovel, which is only familiar in regions where snow falls. Arriving in a place where either oar or snow shovel are mistaken for something else denotes successful escape from a point of origin. While the *Odyssey* draws on this motif, it modifies it in two respects. Odysseus not only flees from something, but his voyage itself represents hardship. Further, he does not remain where the oar is no longer recognized, but returns home.[21]

When it comes to interpreting the significance of Teiresias's prophecy, the first thing to note is that the seer is looking far beyond the *Odyssey*'s conclusion. The extent to which his prophecy disrupts the ending of the *Odyssey* is illustrated by the subtle difference between Teiresias's words and Odysseus's repetition of them. It is only Odysseus who says,

---

20. Hansen (1977); (1990). See also Segal (1994): 187–94.
21. Carrière (1992): 36.

'he told me to go among many cities of men'. By having him quote the Proem, Homer underlines that his hero's voyaging has not yet reached its end. If in the Nekyia, Teiresias's prediction seems almost pleasant against a backdrop of lamentations by the dead, in the twenty-third book, it is a bitter pill that mixes with the joy of Odysseus and Penelope's reunion: 'Dear wife, we have not yet come to the limit of all our / trials. There is unmeasured labour left for the future, / both difficult and great, and all of it I must accomplish (23.248–50).[22]

Teiresias's prediction not only indicates that Odysseus's voyaging is far from complete; it also undermines the *Odyssey*'s conclusion by showing that Poseidon has not yet been reconciled. Since Eustathius, Odysseus's homage to Poseidon has been interpreted as part of a mission, or even as a kind of colonization: Odysseus was to spread the cult of Poseidon far beyond the god's natural sphere of influence, the sea.[23] Conversely, it has also been claimed that Odysseus could only break away from Poseidon's power where the latter could not reach and was unknown.[24] Whichever way the act of homage is interpreted, the fact of it obviously refers to the penance which Odysseus still owes to Poseidon. The god's anger, which had kept Odysseus away from home and set most of the plot in motion, has not been appeased at the end of the *Odyssey*, and a decisive conflict therefore remains unresolved. As rounded as the ending of the *Odyssey* may seem, Teiresias's prophecy briefly yet potently hints that the plot has not reached its final end.

Teiresias's prophecy not only transcends the temporal framework of the *Odyssey*, but also points to a world that lies beyond it.[25] The sea represents the spatial element of Odysseus's wanderings. While he ultimately manages to escape its dangers, his destination, Ithaca, is itself surrounded by the sea.[26] Teiresias, however, tells Odysseus to go far inland, where salt and ships are unknown. Not only does this point to a

22. See Peradotto (1990): 88. But see also the appeasing words of Penelope in 23.286–87.

23. Eustathius 1675, 30–35. See also Benardete (1997): 93–94; Dougherty (2001): 172–74.

24. Hartog (1996): 43–44.

25. Tsagalis (2007): 72–75; Purves (2010): 70–73.

26. See Segal (1994): 189–90 on the thesis that the plot of the *Odyssey* is framed as an escape from the sea.

world radically different from the world of the *Odyssey*, but in that unknown world the Homeric epic, which deals extensively with the sea and navigation, must itself be unknown. The idea that Odysseus will enter a space untouched by the epic is echoed in the phrase 'unmeasured labour' (*ametrētos ponos*), which Odysseus ascribes to the voyage foretold by Teiresias. *Metron* refers not only to geographical distance, but also to the poetic metre.[27] Immeasurability here means not only the extent and duration of the voyaging, but implies that it cannot be captured in metric verse. Suffering may be a central theme of epic poetry, but this effort to come, the long journey into the interior, lies beyond even its scope.

Teiresias also mentions an adventure of Odysseus that does not appear in the *Odyssey*. This adventure circumvents any simple conclusion and points to a very different, non-epic world. Teiresias's prophecy expresses awareness of the limits of epic narrative. It implies that there is a space beyond the epic; indeed, a central conflict of the *Odyssey*, Poseidon's wrath, is resolved in that non-epic world and moreover, this resolution is projected into an indefinite future. Such a temporal opening makes the artificiality of narrative conclusions visible. Narratives must end, and can bring actions to a satisfactory conclusion, yet time moves on regardless. The *Odyssey* grants the audience the satisfaction of a rounded conclusion, yet also signals its provisionality.

The Telos of the *Odyssey*

Two of the most important Homer exegetes of antiquity, Aristophanes and Aristarchus, both directors of the library of Alexandria, seem to have reflected on the aptness of the *Odyssey*'s ending. Two almost identical scholia show that the two Alexandrian scholars considered verse 23.296 to be the conclusion (*telos/peras*) of the *Odyssey*. It marks the point when Odysseus and Penelope 'gladly went together to bed, and their old ritual' (23.296). Analytical scholars have used Aristophanes's

---

27. A similar play on the double meaning of *metron* seems to appear in Hesiod's *Nautilia* (erg. 648–49). See Rosen (1990).

and Aristarchus's commentaries to search for linguistic and contextual problems in the remaining text to show that the *Odyssey* originally ended with verse 23.296 and that the rest is a spurious addition of an interpolator. As in other such cases, such assertions are difficult to prove, and the arguments that the remaining part is a later addition to the original poem do not really convince.[28]

Telos and *peras*, which according to the two scholia Aristophanes and Aristarchus saw in this verse, can denote completion in the sense of a climax as well as the ending per se, just as we refer to the telos of a narrative today. The Byzantine bishop Eustathius suspected that the two Alexandrians viewed the nocturnal reunion of Odysseus and Penelope as the narrative's climax rather than its ending (1948,49–1949,2). Two arguments speak for such an interpretation of the scholia. For one thing, the supposedly final sentence cannot have occurred at the end, since it is introduced by the particle *men* (although), which must be answered by the particle *de* (however) in a subsequent sentence. One might retort that the unknown interpolator may have edited the original verses and added the particle *men*, but there is another argument that is not so easy to refute. Other scholia testify that Aristarchus declared verses 23.310–43 and 24.1–204 to be inauthentic. Why would he discard specific verses in a passage that he had previously deleted? Nowhere else does he delete sections of a text that had already been removed. It is far more likely that Aristophanes and Aristarchus considered the couple's nocturnal reunion to be the climax, rather than the end, of the action.[29]

The Alexandrian scholars' commentaries show that there are a number of scenes in the *Odyssey* that close arcs of tension and prepare for the ultimate ending.[30] The murder of the suitors and the reunion of Odysseus and Penelope are among these. What constitutes the main climax depends on how the *Odyssey* is read—as a revenge narrative, the

28. See the literature in Russo, Fernandez-Galiano and Heubeck (1992), ad 23.297, who reject the athetesis for good reasons. See also the detailed study by Erbse (1972): 166–244.

29. See Erbse (1972): 166–77. Aristophanes's and Aristarchus's commentaries, however, do not need to be understood as an application of Aristotelian poetics, as Erbse thinks.

30. See Peradotto (1990): 60.

story of a couple, or the return of the king. While different readings are possible, the political reconciliation gains significance from the fact that Homer placed it at the end.

It has often been claimed that Aristophanes and Aristarchus' emphasis arose from a typically Hellenistic perspective that was still foreign to Homer.[31] It was only in Hellenism that greater attention was paid to love, and that romance consequently emerged as a plot type. However, lyrical fragments from the Archaic period disprove such a developmental perspective. Above all, Sappho's reflections on the joys and sorrows of love, jealousy and longing demonstrate a decided inclination towards romantic love.[32] The *Odyssey*'s conclusion with the reconciliation of the polis rather than with Odysseus and Penelope's reunion is due to the epic genre, rather than being the expression of an intellectual epoch. Apollonius Rhodius's great Hellenistic epic the *Argonautica* also mentions public events (the foundation of a circuit race and founding of a city) just before making concluding references to the heroes (4.1755–81). Public events are particularly appropriate to the ending of a heroic epic, whether it be archaic or Hellenistic.

According to the interpretation offered here, it is the section that follows on from the telos identified by Aristophanes and Aristarchus that represents the climax.[33] First Odysseus and Penelope 'enjoy their lovemaking', then revel in telling each other of their respective experiences while they were parted. It has already been shown how this amounts to a summary of a part of the plot, which contributes to the sense that the epic is reaching its end. We will now focus on how the scene reflects on narrative itself. Homer gives Penelope's account in just four verses, while that of Odysseus takes up forty-one. But the dual form *terpesthēn*

31. See, for instance, Stanford (1965): 16; de Jong (2001): 561–62, ad 23.296. It is significant that Seaford claims that Penelope and Odysseus's reunion marked the original ending, and that it was the strengthening of the polis that subsequently led to the addition of Book 24: (1994): 38–42.

32. See, for instance, Sappho *fr.* 1; 2; 16; 23; 26; 31.

33. While the analytical arguments concerning the actual ending of the *Odyssey* are not convincing, it should be added that Focke (1943): 372 and Schadewaldt (1960): 70; 74 shift the athetesis from 23.296 to 23.343 to 'save' Odysseus's and Penelope's stories.

FIG. 19. Bonaventura Genelli (1798–1868), *Odysseus and Penelope*, 1844, outline engraving. Photo: akg-images.

mythoisi (both feasted on the words)—a separate, rarely used number, alongside the singular and plural, that is reserved for the actions of a pair of subjects—underlines the reciprocity of the communication: both are simultaneously narrator and recipient, and both experience pleasure and satisfaction in listening as well as in telling.

The delight (*terpsis*) which Penelope and Odysseus derive from their memories contrasts sharply with the tears they had previously shed when hearing their own experiences being recounted. In the first book, Penelope begs Phemius not to sing of the return of the Trojan fighters (1.336–44). While Homer does not specify whether Phemius specifically sings of Odysseus's fate, he does explicitly state that the song recalls her husband's memory of Penelope. And Odysseus becomes tearful when he hears stories proclaiming his fame. He weeps at the court of the Phaeacians when Demodocus recites Odysseus's quarrel with Achilles and the capture of Troy (8.83–92; 521–31).

A remark by Eumaeus, which has been discussed above in the second and third chapters, holds the key to the transformation. While Eumaeus is entertaining the beggar at his modest homestead he says, 'For afterwards a man who has suffered / much and wandered much has pleasure in his sorrows' (15.400–401). It is only in retrospect that pleasure can be derived from bitter experiences. But Phemius sings about what is still causing Penelope pain. Similarly, although Demodocus proclaims Odysseus's successes, the narrated events refer to contexts in which Odysseus is still involved. Odysseus is safe with the Phaeacians for the time being but has yet to return home from Troy. However great his deeds may have been there, it is not yet certain whether Agamemnon's fate will befall him, too, to destroy his fame.

By the twenty-third book, on the other hand, Odysseus has arrived home, cleared his adversaries out of the way and taken his rightful place at his wife's side. Teiresias's prophecy hints at further hardships to come, but for the moment, the joy of his successful nostos prevails. While he is with the Phaeacians, Odysseus narrates some of his experiences to conceptualize and come to terms with them, but once reunited with his wife, he is able to look back on his wanderings and the suitors' invasion of his property as bygone acts. The satisfaction which narration can provide may well be increased when very difficult experiences are being recounted. What was hard on the narrator, and perhaps even threatened his existence, has been overcome. By telling the story, the narrator takes possession of the crises and places them within the meaningful context of a story.

It is not only the joy that Odysseus and Penelope derive from viewing their suffering in retrospect that is remarkable. In this scene, Homer lifts the narrative out of the flow of time in a literal way. He has Athena stop the dawn and prolong the night to give the couple time for their exchange. Penelope had interrupted her conversation with the beggar in the nineteenth book, saying that she would listen to his stories with pleasure and without succumbing to sleep, but it was divine law that people needed their sleep (19.589–93). Now, however, Athena gives Odysseus and Penelope the opportunity to do both, talk to their hearts' content and get the rest they need. Odysseus goes on narrating until 'the sweet sleep / came to relax his limbs and slip the cares from his spirit' (23.342–43).

Athena's intervention creates a grandiose scene that deserves closer attention:

> Now Dawn of the rosy fingers would have dawned on their
>   weeping,
> had not the grey-eyed goddess Athena planned it otherwise.
> She held the long night back at the outward edge, she detained
> Dawn of the gold throne by the Ocean, and would not let her
> harness her fast-footed horses who bring the daylight to people:
> Lampos and Phaethon, the Dawn's horses, who carry her.
>   (23.241–46)

Homer here modifies a counterfactual statement that is found in two other anagnorisis scenes. In the sixteenth book, the beggar reveals himself to Telemachus: 'And now the light of the sun would have set on their crying, / had not Telemachus spoken a quick word to his father' (16.220–21). Later, when Odysseus reveals his identity to the herdsman and the swineherd, 'the sun would have gone down while they were still thus clamouring, / had not Odysseus stayed them from it and said a word to them' (21.226–27).

The variation of this type of counterfactual statement emphasizes the miraculous nature of the scene. It is Odysseus's words that prevent Telemachus and the shepherds from lamenting long into the night. In the twenty-third book, however, the dawn is delayed by the divine intervention of a goddess. It is no longer human action, lamentation from which joy can ultimately be derived, but the end of the night that is the subject of the counterfactual statement. Time itself is being halted. Changing the substance of the counterfactual statement here emphasizes that the encounter with Penelope eclipses all the other scenes of recognition.

When time stands still, opening up the space for Odysseus and Penelope to share their experiences, the idea that storytelling transcends the experience of the passing of time is expressed. The feeling that time stands still while immersed in an exciting narrative is familiar to many readers. Proust describes this sense aptly in an inconspicuous scene in *Swann's Way*. The narrator tells of the strenuous pursuit of the hero through the pages of my book. And as each hour struck, it would seem to me that a few moments only had passed since the hour before; the latest would inscribe itself close to its predecessor on the sky's surface, and I was unable to believe that sixty minutes could have been squeezed into the tiny arc of blue which was comprised between their two golden figures. Sometimes it would even happen that this precocious hour would sound two strokes more than the last; there must then have been an hour which I had not heard strike; something that had taken place had not taken place for me; the fascination of my book, a magic as potent as the deepest slumber, that deceived my enchanted ears and had obliterated the sound of that golden bell from the azure surface of the enveloping silence.[34]

When Athena delays the dawn, the sense that time passes more slowly while reading is captured in the striking image of Eos's chariot being stopped.

Narratives can not only induce obliviousness to the passing of time; there can also be an altered experience of time, since narratives, told in time, unfold narrated time. While attending to the *Odyssey*, the audience follows Odysseus's adventures. Expectations that would otherwise be focused on the recipient's own life are diverted to the narrative action. Similar to real-life expectations being formed as a result of earlier experiences, that which has previously been heard or read of a narrative creates expectations about the further development of the plot. The term 'reading experience' is apt. Yet while it resembles real-life experience in its dynamics, it is also unique. It does not affect the recipient directly, since it is an indirect experience of what the characters of a narrative are subjected to. As has previously been shown, reading experience takes place within an 'as if' framework. No matter how great the immersion in a narrative world, a subliminal sense remains that it is, after all, a story. Narratives, therefore, offer an opportunity to feel the temporal dynamics of life—the dialectic of expectation and experience—liberated from the pressures of life.[35]

34. Proust (2005 [1913]): 103.
35. See Grethlein (2010c); (2017).

In his introduction to Enno Littmann's German translation of the *One Thousand and One Nights*, Hugo von Hofmannsthal remarks that this volume contains moments that make 'Homer appear pale [. . .] by comparison.'[36] And yet, the reflection on time and narrative in the twenty-third book of the *Odyssey* can be fruitfully compared to the framework of *One Thousand and One Nights*. After the sultan Shahriyar has seen his wife being unfaithful to him and his sister-in-law being unfaithful to his brother, he swears that he will only ever marry for one night and kill his wife on the following morning. When there are hardly any virgins left in the kingdom, the vizier's daughter, Scheherazade, comes forward to marry the sultan. On their wedding night, she tells him a story which she does not finish, interrupting it at the climax. Eager to know the ending, the Sultan spares her life and waits for the next night. Scheherazade pursues the same strategy for a total of a thousand and one nights, until the sultan pardons her.

Scheherazade's stories enable her to postpone her seemingly inevitable execution night after night: narration transcends time by stalling death, that most radical experience of human temporality. In the *Odyssey*, too, narrative transcends time, albeit in a different way. Time is not only suspended for an individual who thereby escapes death, but on a cosmic level, with the night itself standing still. The oriental fairy tale and Greek epic use different images to illustrate how narration can suspend the experience of time and engender an experience of time that is liberated from the constraints of real life.

Both texts link narration with erotic desire, thereby elaborating on its temporal structure. In *One Thousand and One Nights*, the desire to hear how the story ends replaces the wish to sleep with a new virgin every night, and Scheherazade's ability to tell stories ultimately cures the sultan of his perverse wish—he pardons and lives with her.[37] Homer juxtaposes the pleasure of storytelling with that of sexual intercourse: 'When Penelope and Odysseus had [taken their pleasure in] lovemaking, / they took their pleasure in talking, each one telling his

36. Hofmannsthal (1954): 8.
37. See Brooks (1984): 60–61.

story' (23.300–301). The same verb, both times used as a dual, describes both the pleasure of narration and that of physical union.

The parallel that both the *Odyssey* and *One Thousand and One Nights* draw between erotic desire and the wish to be immersed in narrative points to the intensity of the reading experience. Narratives can arouse eagerness as strong as erotic desire; the reader or listener can experience a craving similar to that of a lover. The parallel may be rooted in a structural similarity. Both the reader's and lover's desire are teleological in nature; both strive towards a climax where tension is released—the end of the plot or union with the beloved. The climax brings satisfaction, and, for the time being at least, release from desire. In love as well as in narrative, this gives rise to a logic of postponement: desire is increased when the ending is delayed.

The parallel between love and narrative as suggested in the *Odyssey* is spelled out in the Imperial-era novel mentioned previously, Heliodorus's *Aethiopica*, which narrates the story of Theagenes and Chariclea. As in the *Odyssey*, parts of the story are told by a narrator who is embedded in the novel, the Greek priest Calasiris. In place of the Phaeacians, a Greek named Cnemon appears as the recipient. When Cnemon interrupts Calasiris and asks what the heroic couple encounters next, Calasiris scolds him for being insatiable: the night was already advanced and Cnemon still wanted to hear more. Cnemon defends himself by saying,

> I cannot agree with Homer, Father, when he says that there is satiety of all things, including love.[38] In my estimation one can never have a surfeit of love, whether one is engaged in its pleasures or listening to tales of it. And if of the tale being told is the love of Theagenes and Chariclea, who could be so insensitive, so steely-hearted, that he would not be spellbound by the tale, even if it lasted a whole year? (4.4.3)[39]

While Cnemon criticizes Homer for his observation that satiety was the outcome of fulfilled desire, his rhetorical question not only echoes,

---

38. Cnemon refers to *Il.* 13.636–37.

39. Translation by J. R. Morgan: see 'Heliodorus: An Ethiopian Story', in Reardon (1989): 426.

but surpasses, Alcinous's claim when the latter was willing to listen to Odysseus's account until sunrise (*Od.* 11.375–76). Above all, Cnemon's justification highlights the parallel between physical love and immersion in narrative, which emerges when Odysseus and Penelope feel *terpsis* equally about their lovemaking and sharing their experiences. By declaring insatiable the desire that both love and narrative engender, Cnemon levels the gap between them: it did not matter whether one loved or read about love. Cnemon's assertion is obviously an exaggeration. There can be satisfaction for lovers as well as for the recipients of narrative—or at least, Heliodorus seems to think so. There is a considerable difference between experiencing love as a lover or in the context of a narrative. And yet, the intensity of feeling that can be derived from reading is well expressed in the exaggeration. The power of narratives to captivate readers is rooted at least partly in their temporal dynamics: that is, in the reader's desire to know the outcome, a desire that can be repeatedly stoked, and, after numerous obstacles and delays, finally satisfied.

In contemporary literary studies, Peter Brooks has made the similarity between love and narrative fruitful for a theory of reading. He understands plot as

> an activity, a structuring operation elicited in the reader trying to make sense of those meanings that develop only through textual and temporal succession. [. . .] We can, then, conceive of the reading of plot as a form of desire that carries us forward, onward, through the text. Narratives both tell of desire—typically present some story of desire—and arouse and make use of desire as dynamic of signification.[40]

The modern novel seems to suggest that the ending must remain unknown in order to ignite the reader's desire. But even ancient audiences must have been familiar with the *Odyssey*'s satisfying conclusion, which, moreover, Homer repeatedly anticipates. In the *Aethiopica*, too, genre conventions and references lead the reader confidently to expect the outcome. Yet even when the ending is known, suspense remains regarding the anticipated conclusion. Above all, both Homer and Heliodorus create

---

40. Brooks (1984): 37.

suspense about *how* the expected conclusion will be reached. The ending is the point from which the whole plot can be appreciated.

The *Odyssey* also shows that the process of reception is not only intellectual and centred on the search for meaning as postulated by Brooks. Odysseus's tears when hearing Demodocus' song, for example, illustrate the emotional and physical response that narratives can elicit. Odysseus is seized by the bard's recitation like a wife watching her husband's death throes at first hand. In the Sirens, the appeal of narratives acquires an uncanny form. The aesthetic experience not only equals the intensity of the real-life experience but surpasses it.

The motionless chariot of Eos is the Homeric image for how narratives can transcend time. Odysseus and Penelope recount both their own experiences and the story that Homer tells. The suspension of time, which creates space for storytelling, also reflects the spell that Homer has cast on audiences from antiquity to the present day. The waiting horses of the dawn appear at the end of the *Odyssey*, when a great narrative arc is rounded off in Odysseus and Penelope's union. The transcendence of time denotes not only the suspense with which narrated time can displace lived time, but also the closure which narrative, unlike life, can grant. At the same time, Teiresias's prophecy opens up the ending and prevents the gap between life and narrative from becoming too great.

8

Epilogue: Reflexivity
and Experience

IN THIS STUDY of the *Odyssey*, multiple forms of storytelling have been encountered. Bards sing of the deeds of men and gods on the isles of Scheria and Ithaca. But it is not only the bards who narrate in the *Odyssey*: at the beginning of the epic, Telemachus sets out in search of news of his missing father, and, at the courts of Nestor and Menelaus, listens to stories about the Trojan War and the Greek heroes' difficult homecoming. On Scheria, Odysseus tells the Phaeacians of his adventures after the fall of Troy. He describes monsters such as the one-eyed giant Polyphemus, who wanted to devour him, and beguiling nymphs who had wanted him for their husband. Upon his return to Ithaca, Odysseus tells tall tales to conceal his identity, while stories from his past play a role in the anagnorisis scenes, in which he reveals his real identity to relatives and friends.

The stories embedded in the *Odyssey* demonstrate the means and functions of narrative, its possibilities and limitations; indeed, when taken together, they amount to a reflection on narrative and narration that is as comprehensive as it is profound. As Demodocus's songs and Odysseus's tales show, narrators can captivate their listeners to such an extent that, enraptured and detached from their present, they experience what is being narrated as though at first hand. That said, the effectiveness of stories depends not only on the narrator's skill, but also on the audience's relationship to the material. The more closely a recipient identifies with the characters, the more intensely a story is experienced. At the same time, the narrative must not be too close to the recipient's own situation, since this compromises the necessary aesthetic distance.

In the *Odyssey*, narratives prove fundamental to human identity. Odysseus is generally recognized by his stories, rather than by his physical features. His identity as hero, husband, father and son is shaped by narratives. At the same time, his tall tales show that narratives can be manipulated. Plausibility can be detached from truthfulness; a convincing story does not have to be true, while a true story may not be convincing. In fact, truth is only an aspect of narratives. The Homeric heroes pursue goals with their stories; they want to convince their listeners of something or present themselves in a specific light. And the pragmatic dimension of narratives, too, is unaffected by whether something has happened in the same way it is being narrated.

The *Odyssey* places particular emphasis on the fact that narratives can help to process experiences. Before Odysseus returns to Ithaca, he tells the Phaeacians of his traumatic experiences. The Apologoi are not just a trick which Homer uses to integrate the back story into the epic; rather, they form an important part of the plot—it is only by narrating the horrors of his wanderings that Odysseus is able to overcome them and to turn from being nobody to a hero again. At the climax of the plot, both he and Penelope look back on their respective trials, he on his voyaging, she on her experiences on Ithaca. The retrospective view lends the narrator a sense of control that is absent during the experience. Contingency is replaced by an awareness of the outcome. When grasped as patterns and linked to causal chains, adversities that had appeared random become comprehensible and form part of a meaningful whole. The monsters that had threatened to overwhelm Odysseus are overcome in the retrospective view; they form part of his story.

But the *Odyssey*, of course, not only contains narratives; it is itself a narrative. It has been shown that it deals with ethical problems through narrative. It does not provide any simple or clear-cut answers when it comes to which actions are just, or what role the gods play, but it does illuminate these questions with a depth of focus that a philosophical treatise would hardly be able to achieve. To what extent, however, do the stories embedded in the *Odyssey* reflect the *Odyssey* itself? Above all, can the meaning-making function ascribed to the characters' narratives also be claimed for the *Odyssey*? Our reading of this epic concludes with a discussion of this question, which is, in turn, an invitation to consider the reflexivity of literature in general.

The internal narratives of the *Odyssey* hold up a distorted mirror, as it were. The difference between the recitation of an epic comprising over twelve thousand hexameters and a narrative told around the hearth or campfire, or indeed the short songs of Demodocus, should not be overlooked. The most significant aspect concerning the present discussion is probably the discrepancy in content. When the Homeric heroes tell their stories, they are dealing either with their own experiences or with events that happened to others, but which also have an impact on themselves, such as the fate of a brother or husband. The *Odyssey*, however, deals with a myth from which the ancient public was already separated by an unbridgeable gulf of time. The epic may reflect occurrences such as the Greeks' expansion into the Mediterranean, but it does not process experiences as though they were an autobiographical account.

Nevertheless—and to this day—the *Odyssey* does help to form meaning and to cope with contingency. It has been shown how narratives not only deal with experiences retrospectively, but in a certain sense also precede them.[1] Actions follow numerous schemata that have become established in the individual consciousness as a result of earlier experiences, or by social mediation. Personal experience is already narratively pre-structured. Literature can likewise form patterns through which reality is understood. The very concept of an 'odyssey' makes this process clear: it has come to refer not only to Homer's epic, but in general terms denotes a long sojourn with an ultimately fortuitous ending. An identifiable pattern borrowed from literature is being used here, named after a text that had originally invented the word: we make use of Homer's scheme whenever we perceive events as an odyssey, without ever thinking of him.

---

1. See p. 108.

The enormous reception history of the Homeric texts shows that ancient readers saw Odysseus as representative of the essence of a human being. Two aspects dominate, and both are inherent in the epithet *polytropos*. This refers to someone who has been lost; it alludes to the voyaging which Odysseus is forced to undergo, and the sufferings to which he is subjected. At the same time, *polytropos* denotes someone who knows many turns of phrase; that is, someone who is resourceful and knows how to help himself, someone who in Italian would be called *furbo*.[2] Odysseus is both *polytlas*—long-suffering—and *polymētis*—quick-witted; he embodies a being who on the one hand is a plaything of fate, and on the other an active and eloquent participant in his own destiny.

Odysseus's many characteristics appear between the poles of suffering and cunning, as is reflected in the manifold reception.[3] For Pindar, he is a liar; for Sophocles, an unscrupulous sophist, and in the Stoic tradition, he is a model of self-control. Christian authors have linked the mast of the ship to which Odysseus allows himself to be tied to avoid succumbing to the temptations of the Sirens with Christ's cross, and seen in Odysseus the patient sufferer who, resisting sensual temptations, strives for salvation. Dante's Odysseus is driven to his doom by his own curiosity and the urge to make discoveries beyond the natural limits set for man. Early modern texts that served to instruct princes show Odysseus as uniting strength and prudence in an exemplary way.

Rather than continuing with a list that may prove inexhaustible, it is useful to focus on an example of modern reception that highlights both the potential for meaning and the limits of the figure of Odysseus. Primo Levi is among the best-known authors who have described their first-hand experiences of concentration camps. In poems, stories and interviews, he describes life and death in the *universe concentrationnaire*. Time and again, Levi refers to Odysseus, both explicitly and implicitly.[4] Odysseus is subjected to severe trials; he is shipwrecked several times,

2. This aspect of Odysseus was most recently emphasized by Sloterdijk in 2018.

3. For an overview of the reception of Odysseus, see Stanford (1963); Boitani (1994); Hall (2008).

4. See, for instance, Druker (2009): 8, who declares the *Odyssey* together with Dante's *Divine Comedy* as the most important literary reference points in Levi's work.

threatened by monsters and even has to descend into the underworld. But ultimately, after years of wandering, he returns home and, once he has taken revenge on the suitors, resumes his place as Penelope's husband and king of Ithaca. For Levi the Shoah survivor, Odysseus symbolizes the hope of surviving even the most severe suffering and injustice, and to preserve his human dignity under the most adverse circumstances. He embodies the integrity of personality, which has been stripped from the so-called *Muselmänner*: prisoners who are only able to cower apathetically on the floor.

Levi's first narrative, *If This Is a Man*, published in 1947, describes how, on his way from work back to the camp, he sees a train with an Italian carriage. He imagines himself getting on and riding along until the train stops:

> I would feel the warm air and the smell of hay and would go out into the sun; then I would lie down on the ground to kiss the earth, as you read in books, with my face in the grass. And a woman would pass, and she would ask me 'Who are you?' in Italian and I would tell her my story in Italian, and she would understand, and she would give me food and shelter. And she would not believe the things I tell her, and I would show her the number on my arm, and then she would believe.[5]

Despite the differences, and without explicit references to it, the *Odyssey* stands out as a foil—Odysseus is escorted to Ithaca by the Phaeacians; the train takes Levi to Italy. There he meets a woman who, like Penelope, initially neither knows nor believes him. Only the number on his arm convinces her, not unlike the scar by which Eurycleia recognizes Odysseus. But if Odysseus's homecoming remains a fantasy for the prisoner, it becomes the model for Levi's own homecoming after liberation from the concentration camp, as narrated in his second book, *The Truce*. It is only after Levi has travelled through Ukraine, Belarus, Romania, Hungary, Austria and Germany that he finally returns to his home city of Turin. He explicitly refers to the *Odyssey* when he describes a transit

5. Levi (1987 [1947/1963]): 48.

camp run by the Red Army: 'They were cheerful, sad and tired, and took pleasure in food and wine, like Ulysses' companions after the ships had been pulled ashore.'[6]

The relevance of the *Odyssey* to Levi's literary work is also seen in *La Ricerca delle radici* (*The Search for Roots*), an anthology he edited in 1981.[7] Asked to trace the literary roots of his work, Levi chose as the second text, after a passage from the Book of Job, a passage from the ninth book of the *Odyssey*, when Odysseus proudly shouts out his real name to Polyphemus after having blinded him and reached his ship. The persona of a nobody, which Odysseus assumes to outwit Polyphemus, mirrors the fate of the concentration camp prisoner whose identity is erased through being reduced to a number; Odysseus's triumph over the cyclops confirms his own survival.

Levi sees more in Odysseus than a long-suffering man struggling to survive, however.[8] To him, he is also a primordial narrator. In an interview, Levi explains,

> If you ask me why I wanted to tell the stories, I couldn't answer. Probably it was part of an understandable instinct: I wanted to free myself from them. But often I have thought of Odysseus when he arrives at the Phaeacian court. Tired as he is, he spends the night telling the story of his adventures.[9]

While the suffering hero Odysseus serves as a mythical model for the inmate of a death camp, the Odysseus who recounts his experiences serves as a mirror for the author Levi. Like the ancient hero, he narrates in order to process his traumatic experiences.

It is not only in various aspects of the Homeric hero that Levi recognizes himself; the relationship between his own experience and the epic pattern is also complex. A degree of tension is already apparent when it

6. Ibid.: 251.

7. Levi (2001 [1981]).

8. Cohen (2012) attempts to show the variety of guises in which Odysseus is relevant to Levi (44): 'in him Levi finds not only a voice, a possibility of speech, but also a poetic way of unifying man, perpetrator, survivor, poet, and witness'.

9. Levi (2001): 129, see also 130.

comes to Odysseus's triumph over Polyphemus. The character of the cannibal Polyphemus is very different from the industrialized machinery of destruction initiated by the Third Reich. Literary patterns can both give form to experiences and make them more conscious by contrast. It is by no means inappropriate to relate the barbaric nature of the cyclops to the civilizational breakdown of the concentration camp, but Polyphemus acts as an individual rather than as a collective system—and his very primitiveness also presents a contrast to the technical rationality of the camp. The framework within which one's own experiences may be understood contains both similarities to and divergences from the literary pattern.

The ambivalence of Levi's references to Odysseus is illustrated in the chapter that is often referred to as the crux of *If This Is a Man*.[10] In 'The Canto of Ulysses', Levi recounts how he went to fetch food with Jean, the messenger clerk of the *Kommando*. His attempt to teach Jean a little Italian on the way turns into a lesson on Dante. Levi quotes verses from the twenty-sixth canto of the *Inferno* and translates them into French. He tells Jean how Dante and Virgil see the flames that envelop Odysseus and Diomedes in the eighth circle of hell. Questioned by Virgil, Odysseus relates how he had perished on the high seas. The further Levi progresses with his rendition, the more painfully he realizes that he can no longer remember all of the text and that he has forgotten lines and whole verses. Nevertheless, by the time they reach the kitchen, he quotes the final verse: 'And over our heads the hollow seas closed up.'[11]

The chapter 'The Canto of Ulysses' superimposes several layers of dialogue, some of which overlap and some of which clash. The narrator Levi tells the reader of *If This Is a Man* how the character Levi tells Jean about the canto of Odysseus in the *Divine Comedy*. In this canto, Odysseus describes the final shipwreck to Dante and his guide Virgil, including the speech he had used to persuade his companions to join the expedition. These convolutions call into question the success of communication. In

10. For interpretations of this chapter, see especially Jagendorf (1993); Druker (2004); Cohen (2012): 53–59.

11. Levi (1987 [1947/1963]): 128.

Dante, Odysseus is akin to a flame that speaks 'as if it were a plaything of the wind'. The character Levi struggles not only with his memory but also with the translation: 'Disastrous—poor Dante and poor French!'[12] He doubts that Jean is able to understand him. The jeopardized communication also casts doubt on the communication between Levi and his reader: can he successfully reproduce this walk with Jean and the conditions of life in the concentration camp? Is a representation of the Shoah possible?

In spite of the hermeneutical difficulties, however, the recitation of the Dante verses amounts to an act of resistance; it invokes the humanist tradition and pitches its image of a human being against the barbarity of the concentration camp. Levi himself comments on this function of recitation when, in a later text, he recalls the walk with Jean again:

> Culture was useful to me; not always, at times perhaps by subterranean and unforeseen paths, but it served me well and perhaps it saved me. [...] Then and there they [the recollections of the Dante verses] had great value. They made it possible for me to re-establish a link with the past, saving it from oblivion and reinforcing my identity.[13]

Indeed, as he also describes it in *If This Is a Man*, he would 'give today's soup to know how to connect "the like on any day" to the last lines'.[14]

It is not only the tradition which Dante embodies, however. More specifically, it is the figure of Odysseus that becomes a bulwark against the concentration camp for Levi. He cannot quite remember the verses in which Odysseus reproaches himself for not having been able to restrain his desire to explore the world as well as the virtues and sins of mankind, even while thinking of his family. Odysseus's heroic assertion, however, is remembered without any hint of uncertainty: 'So on the open sea I set forth.' Odysseus's daring speaks directly to him: 'it is a chain which has been broken, it is a throwing oneself over to the other side of a barrier, we know the impulse well'.[15]

12. Ibid.: 125.
13. Levi (2013 [1986]): 155–56.
14. Levi (1987 [1947/1963]): 127.
15. Ibid.: 125.

Levi is particularly moved by Odysseus's address to his companions:

Here, listen Pikolo, open your ears and your mind, you have to understand, for my sake: 'Think of your breed; for brutish ignorance / your mettle was not made; you were made men, / to follow after knowledge and excellence.' As if I also was hearing it for the first time; like the blast of a trumpet, like the voice of God. For a moment I forget who I am and where I am.[16]

Odysseus the Enlightenment philosopher, for whom ethics and science distinguish the human being from animals, here becomes a model for Levi, the chemist with a humanistic education who defies the dehumanizing conditions of the concentration camp.

The differences between Levi's situation and the literary pattern undermine Odysseus's function as a model capable of engendering meaning, however. To what extent can Odysseus, who perishes after having lured his companions to their deaths, serve as a model for Levi's struggle to survive? Further, Odysseus crosses borders of his own volition, while Levi is forcefully deported to the concentration camp. The difference between Odysseus's expedition, which leads him to the Pillars of Heracles, and Levi and Jean's one-hour walk is also impossible to overlook. At the end of the chapter, Levi quotes Odysseus's heroic downfall and contrasts it sharply with the banality of life in the camp: 'The official announcement is made that the soup today is cabbage and turnips: "Choux et navets. Kaposzta és répak." "And above our heads the hollow seas closed up."'[17] Does the human being really stand above the animal as the bearer of virtue and knowledge, as Odysseus claims? In this scene of *If This Is a Man*, food is the issue, pointing to needs which humans and animals share.

The ideological gap between Levi and Dante is even more disconcerting. In *If This Is a Man*, there is no sign of the God who rules in the *Divine Comedy*. Odysseus is in hell because he had defied boundaries and committed sacrilege during the Trojan War. The suffering endured

16. Ibid.: 126.
17. Ibid.: 128.

in the hell of a concentration camp lacks any such justification; it is senseless. In place of a theodicy, Levi can only make a limp analogy to a schema; his fate is not part of a divine cosmos. His halting recitation, the forgetting of entire verses shows that the framework and rules of Dante's world are fragile and have no validity in the concentration camp.

The image of a human being, as expressed in Odysseus's speech, is itself ambivalent. The origin, literally 'the seed', or 'semen' (*semenza*), to which Odysseus refers, actually fits well with the biologistic racial doctrine of the National Socialists that places the 'Aryan man' above Jewish and other 'sub-humans': 'The pressing question, which in its very formulation reveals scepticism about the manipulation of the word "human" in Western civilization, is whether Odysseus' words might not have been more useful to the Nazis and Italian fascists than to the prisoners of the death camps.'[18] The question of the relationship between the Shoah and the Enlightenment is here raised in an exemplary way. Levi uses Odysseus to pitch the Enlightenment against the barbarism of the concentration camps, but it must not be forgotten that the mass extermination was based on a highly rational system and on the products of technical progress. In the *Dialektik der Aufklärung* (*Dialectic of Enlightenment*), Horkheimer and Adorno describe how National Socialism takes rational reason to extremes. If, as critical theory claims, the Enlightenment culminates in the concentration camp, it can offer no protection from its horrors.

Levi's chapter on Odysseus illustrates how literary patterns help to process reality. Experience is not simply pressed into a schema, but rather acquires form in a space containing both similarities and differences. Levi sees his life as a concentration camp prisoner against the horizon of Odysseus's fate. Both the hero's daring and the enlightened image of a human being serve him as a model. At the same time, the differences from Dante's *Inferno* show that the concentration camp knows no divine justice. The Shoah represents the ultimate touchstone for the possibilities and limits of narrative representation. No other

18. Druker (2004): 154.

event makes the choice of perspective more crucial; no other dead elicit a greater sense of obligation, and no other experience eludes representation to the same extent. Primo Levi's use of Odysseus, whether in Homer or in Dante, underlines his importance as a model both in and beyond literature as a figure of a human being whose existence is called into question but who ultimately prevails. Even for experiences for which any attempts to create meaning must fail, the *Odyssey* offers a foil that enables, if not processing, then at least confrontation. The *Odyssey* may differ in many respects from its own internal narratives, yet both have the power to manage reality. Even though Homer creates a world that is alien to us, and speaks a language that is difficult to access, he has constructed a framework that enables even contemporary readers to grasp, contemplate and better understand their experiences.

Through its internal narratives, the *Odyssey* acquires reflexivity; the narratives of the various characters mirror the Homeric narrative, if at times in a distorted way. This mirror not only shows the functions of narration but can also open up a new perspective on the reflexivity of literature. The idea that literature implicitly or explicitly thematizes itself is a concept that post-structuralism placed at the centre of literary studies. Authors such as Jacques Derrida and Paul de Man have celebrated this reflexivity of literature, paying particular attention to texts that become their own subject, while emphasizing that every text ultimately refers back to itself. Indeed, post-structuralists play off the self-referentiality of literature against its relation to reality: texts, they argue, only refer to themselves; they have no relation to an extralinguistic reality.

Over the past two decades, post-structuralism has increasingly lost its lustre. New concepts of presence, experience and materiality testify to a broad scepticism in the humanities and cultural studies in respect of the notion of being locked in a windowless prison of language.[19] A wave of 'New Romantics' is driven by a longing for a reality from which post-structuralists have cut off language. In philosophy, too, a 'New

19. See, for instance, Pickering (1997; Ankersmit (2005); Gumbrecht (2010).

Realism' is challenging constructivism and striving to rehabilitate objectivism.[20] It may in no small part be due to the general impression of an increasing virtualization of our life-worlds, whether correct or otherwise, that the desire for authenticity and directness is displacing the fetish of irony in the humanities and cultural studies.

The emergence of the 'New Romantics' and 'New Realists' goes hand in hand with a turning away from narrative. It seems as though to them, narrative, as a form of representation, cannot satisfy the need for presence. Yet the *Odyssey* demonstrates that narrative is more than representation.[21] The Homeric epic counters the postmodern isolation of language from life by showing that narratives, whether literary fiction or non-fiction, deal with experience. In various episodes, Homer shows how characters give form to experience, and by narrating, endow events with meaning, even if they were traumatic. And the reception history of the *Odyssey* in turn illustrates that literary patterns can help to illuminate new experiences. Experience and narrative are closely interwoven; not only are experiences processed through narrative, they also happen against a horizon of already existing narrative patterns. Similarly, narratives depend on experience, but also enable readers to have experiences through reading. The significance that the Homeric epic assigns to narrative goes beyond the dichotomy of presence and representation, to which both post-structuralists and their critics adhere.

Finally, Homer shows that reflexivity need not be bloodless. Instead of wrapping up the narrative like some isolated 'glass bead game', as pictured in Hermann Hesse's eponymous novel *Das Glasperlenspiel*, the reflections of the *Odyssey* revolve around its place in life. It is not without irony that reflection, which poststructuralism contrasts with reference and which 'New Romantics' stigmatize as being hostile to presence, brings the close relationship of narrative and experience to

20. See, for instance, Ferraris (2014); Dreyfus and Taylor (2015).

21. In his assessment of the history of theory, Latour (2004) shows how the rejection of reference to reality ('matters of fact') has obscured the view of the significance of linguistic and other constructions in reality ('matters of concern'). The same applies, *mutatis mutandis*, to narrative: the focus on representation obscures the lifeworld function of narrative.

the fore. Just as experience and narrative interweave, life and reflection also permeate each other. On the one hand, relation to life gives meaning to reflection: self-referentiality is not exhausted in *l'art pour l'art,* but exposes the rootedness of narrative in life. On the other hand, the confrontation with experience gains depth through reflection. The *Odyssey* not only narrates as we narrate in everyday life to process experiences; it makes this function of narrative its subject. Homer tells of narrating by making us experience Odysseus's encounters.

BIBLIOGRAPHY

Note: publication dates given in square brackets for translated works refer to first publication in the original language.

Ahl, F. (1989). 'Homer, Vergil, and complex narrative structures in Latin Epic: An essay'. *Illinois Classical Studies* 14(1/2): 1–31

Alden, M. J. (1992). 'Ψεύδεα πολλὰ ἐτύμοισιν ὁμοῖα', in *Homer 1987: Papers of the Third Greenbank Colloquium, April 1987* (Liverpool Classical Papers, 2), ed. by J. Pinsent and H. V. Hurt. Liverpool, 9–14

Alden, M. J. (1997). 'The resonances of the song of Ares and Aphrodite'. *Mnemosyne* 50(5): 513–29

Allan, W. (2006). 'Divine justice and cosmic order in early Greek epic'. *Journal of Hellenic Studies* 126: 1–35

Allione, L. (1963). *Telemaco e Penelope nell''Odissea'*. Turin

Ameling, W. (1988). 'Alexander und Achilleus: Eine Bestandsaufnahme', in *Zu Alexander d[em] Gr[oßen]*, vol. 2, ed. by W.W. Heinrichs and J. Heinrichs. Amsterdam, 657–92

Amory, A. (1963). 'The reunion of Odysseus and Penelope', in *Essays on the Odyssey: Selected Modern Criticism*, ed. by C. H. Taylor. Bloomington, IN, 100–121

Andersen, Ø. (1977). 'Odysseus and the wooden horse'. *Symbolae Osloenses* 52(1): 5–18

Anderson, B.R.O. (1983). *Imagined Communities: Reflections on the Origin and Spread of Nationalism*. London

Ankersmit, F. R. (2005). *Sublime Historical Experience*. Stanford, CA

Arend, W. (1933). *Die typischen Scenen bei Homer*. Berlin

Auerbach, E. (2003 [1946]). *Mimesis: The Representation of Reality in Western Thought*, trans by Willard R. Trask. Princeton, NJ

Austin, N. (1969). 'Telemachos polymechanos'. *California Studies in Classical Antiquity* 2: 45–63

Austin, N. (1972) 'Name magic in the *Odyssey*'. *California Studies in Classical Antiquity* 5: 1–19

Austin, N. (1975). *Archery at the Dark of the Moon: Poetic Problems in Homer's 'Odyssey'*. Berkeley, CA

Austin, N. (1983). 'Odysseus and the Cyclops: Who is who?', in *Approaches to Homer*, ed. by C. A. Rubino and C. W. Shelmerdine. Austin, TX, 3–37

Austin, N. (1991). 'The wedding text in Homer's *Odyssey*'. *Arion*, third series, 1(2): 227–43

Bakhtin, M. M. (1981). *The Dialogic Imagination: Four Essays*, ed. by M. Holquist. Austin, TX

Bakker, E. J. (2005). *Pointing at the Past: From Formula to Performance in Homeric Poetics*. Washington, DC

Bakker, E. J. (2009). 'Homer, Odysseus, and the narratology of performance', in *Narratology and Interpretation: The Content of the Form in Ancient Literature*, ed. by J. Grethlein and A. Rengakos. Berlin, 117–36

Bakker, E. J. (2013). *The Meaning of Meat and the Structure of the Odyssey*. Cambridge

Ballabriga, A. (1989). 'La prophétie de Tirésias'. *Mètis* 4(2): 291–304

Beck, D. (2005). 'Odysseus. Narrator, storyteller, poet?'. *Classical Philology* 100(3): 213–27

Benardete, S. (1997). *The Bow and the Lyre: A Platonic Reading of the 'Odyssey'*. Lanham, MD

Benjamin, W. (1991 [1936]). 'Der Erzähler', in Benjamin, *Gesammelte Schriften*, ed. by R. Tiedemann and H. Schweppenhäuser, 2.2. Frankfurt am Main, 438–65

Bergren, A.L.T. (1981). 'Helen's "good drug": *Odyssey* IV 1–305', in *Contemporary Literary Hermeneutics and Interpretation of Classical Texts*, ed. by S. Kresic. Ottawa, 201–14

Berktold, P. (2007). *Ithaka und Homer*. Munich

Biles, Z. (2003). 'Perils of song in Homer's *Odyssey*'. *Phoenix* 57(3/4): 191–208

Bittlestone, R. (2005). *Odysseus Unbound: The Search for Homer's Ithaca*. Cambridge

Blundell, M. W. (1989). *Helping Friends and Harming Enemies: A Study in Sophocles and Greek Ethics*. Cambridge

Boardman, J. (1980). *The Greeks Overseas: Their Early Colonies and Trade* trans. by K.-E. Felten and G. Felten. London

Boedeker, D. (1998). 'Presenting the past in fifth-century Athens', in *Democracy, Empire, and the Arts in Fifth-Century Athens*, ed. by D. Boedeker and K. Raaflaub. Cambridge, MA, 185–202

Boitani, P. (1994) *The Shadow of Ulysses: Figures of a Myth*, trans. by A. Weston. Oxford

Bömer, F. (1982). *P. Ovidius Naso, 'Metamorphosen': Kommentar, Buch XII–XIII*. Heidelberg

Bowie, E. L. (1993). 'Lies, fiction and slander in early Greek poetry', in *Lies and Fiction in the Ancient Greek World*, ed. by C. Gill. Exeter, 1–37

Braswell, B. K. (1982). 'The song of Ares and Aphrodite: Theme and relevance to *Odyssey* 8'. *Hermes* 110(2): 129–37

Bremer, D. (1976). *Licht und Dunkel in der frühgriechischen Dichtung: Interpretationen zur Vorgeschichte der Lichtmetaphysik*. Bonn

Bremmer, J. N. (2002). 'Odysseus versus the Cyclops', in *Papers from the First International Symposium on Symbolism at the University of Tromsø, June 4–7, 1998*, ed. by S. Des Bouvrie. Athens, 135–52

Brockmeier, J. and D. Carbaugh (eds) (2001). *Narrative and Identity: Studies in Autobiography, Self and Culture*. Amsterdam

Brooks, P. (1984). *Reading for the Plot: Design and Intention in Narrative*. Oxford

Brooks, P. (1992). *Reading for the Plot: Design and Intention in Narrative*. Cambridge, MA

Bruner, J. S. (1986). *Actual Minds, Possible Worlds*. Cambridge, MA

Bruner, J. S. (1990). *Acts of Meaning*. Cambridge, MA

Burgess, J. S. (2001). *The Tradition of the Trojan War in Homer and the Epic Cycle*. Baltimore

Burkert, W. (1960). 'Das Lied von Ares und Aphrodite: Zum Verhältnis von *Odyssee* und *Ilias*'. *Rheinisches Museum fur Philologie* 103(2): 130–44

Burkert, W. (1979). *Structure and History in Greek Mythology and Ritual*. Berkeley, CA

Cairns, D. (2003). 'Ethics, ethology, terminology: Iliadic anger and the cross-cultural study of emtion' *Yale Classical Studies* 32: 11–49

Caracciolo, M. (2014). *The Experientiality of Narrative: An Enactive Approach*. Berlin

Carr, D. (1986). *Time, Narrative, and History. Studies in Phenomenology and Existential Philosophy*. Bloomington, IN

Carrière, J.-C. (1992). 'La réponse de Tirésias: Le dernier voyage et la mort d'Ulysse selon l'Odyssée', in *Mélanges Pierre Lévêque*, vol. 6: *Religion*, ed. by M.-M. Mactoux. Paris, 17–44

Cave, T. (2016). *Thinking with Literature: Towards a Cognitive Criticism*. Oxford

Clarke, H. W. (1963). 'Telemachus and the Telemacheia'. *American Journal of Philology* 84(2): 129–45

Cobet, J. (1971). *Herodots Exkurse und die Frage der Einheit seines Werkes*. Wiesbaden

Cohen, U. (2012). 'Consider if this is a man: Primo Levi and the figure of Ulysses'. *Jewish Social Studies* 18(2): 40–69

Coldstream, J. N. (1993). 'Mixed marriages at the frontiers of the early Greek world'. *Oxford Journal of Archaeology* 12(1): 89–107

Cook, E. F. (1995). *The Odyssey in Athens: Myths of Cultural Origins*. Ithaca, NY

Cook, E. F. (1999). '"Active" and "passive" heroics in the *Odyssey*'. *Classical World* 93(2): 149–67

Crielaard, J. P. (ed.) (1995). *Homeric Questions: Essays in Philology, Ancient History and Archaeology; Including the Papers of a Conference Organized by the Netherlands Institute at Athens (15 May 1993)*. Amsterdam

Crotty, K. (1994). *The Poetics of Supplication: Homer's Iliad and Odyssey*. Ithaca, NY

Danek, G. (1998). *Epos und Zitat: Studien zu den Quellen der Odyssee*. Vienna

D'Arms, E. F. and K. K. Hulley (1946). 'The Oresteia-story in the *Odyssey*'. *Transactions and Proceedings of the American Philological Association* 77: 207–13

De Jong, I.J.F. (1985). 'Eurykleia and Odysseus' Scar: *Odyssey* 19.393–466'. *Classical Quarterly* 35(2): 517–18

De Jong, I.J.F. (1992). 'The subjective style in Odysseus' wanderings'. *Classical Quarterly* 42(1): 1–11

De Jong, I.J.F. (1999). 'Auerbach and Homer', in *Euphrosyne: Studies in Ancient Epic and Its Legacy in Honor of Dimitris N. Maronitis*, ed. by J. N. Kazazis. Stuttgart, 154–64

De Jong, I.J.F. (2001). *A Narratological Commentary on the 'Odyssey'*. Cambridge

Dench, E. (1995). *From Barbarians to New Men: Greek, Roman, and Modern Perceptions of Peoples of the Central Apennines*. Oxford

De Temmermann, K. (2014). *Crafting Characters: Heroes and Heroines in the Ancient Greek Novel*. Oxford

Dimock, G. (1970). 'Crime and punishment in the *Odyssey*'. *Yale Review* 60(2): 199–214

Dirlmeier, F. (1966). *Die Giftpfeile des Odysseus (zu Odyssee 1, 252–266)*. Heidelberg

Dodds, E. R. (1951). *The Greeks and the Irrational*. Berkeley, CA

Doherty, L. E. (1995). *Siren Songs: Gender, Audiences, and Narrators in the 'Odyssey'*. Ann Arbor, MI

Doody, M. A. (1996). *The True Story of the Novel*. New Brunswick, NJ

Dougherty, C. (1993). *The Poetics of Colonization: From City to Text in Archaic Greece*. Oxford

Dougherty, C. (2001). *The Raft of Odysseus: The Ethnographic Imagination of Homer's Odyssey*. Oxford

Dougherty, C. (2003) 'The Aristonothos Krater: Competing stories of conflict and collaboration', in *The Cultures within Ancient Greek Culture: Contact, Conflict, Collaboration*, ed. by C. Dougherty and L. Kurke. Cambridge, 35–56

Dreyfus, H. L. and C. Taylor (2015). *Retrieving Realism*. Cambridge, MA

Droysen, J. G. (1977 [1868]) *Historik* (Historisch-kritische Ausgabe, 1), ed. by P. Leyh and H. W. Blanke. Stuttgart

Druker, J. (2004) 'The shadowed violence of culture: Fascism and the figure of Ulysses in Primo Levi's survival in Auschwitz'. *Clio* 33(2): 143–61

Druker, J. (2009). *Primo Levi and Humanism after Auschwitz: Posthumanist Reflections*. Basingstoke.

DuBois, P. (1988). *Sowing the Body: Psychoanalysis and Ancient Representations of Women*. Chicago

Dunn, F. M. (1996). *Tragedy's End: Closure and Innovation in Euripidean Drama*. Oxford

Edwards, M. W. (1986). 'Homer and oral tradition: The formula, Part I'. *Oral Tradition* 1(2): 171–230

Edwards, M. W. (1988). 'Homer and oral tradition: The formula, Part II'. *Oral Tradition* 3(1): 11–60

Edwards, M. W. (1992). 'Homer and oral tradition: The type-scene'. *Oral Tradition* 7(2): 284–330

Elsner, J. (2007). *Roman Eyes: Visuality and Subjectivity in Art and Text*. Princeton, NJ

Emlyn-Jones, C. (1986). 'True and lying tales in the *Odyssey*'. *Greece and Rome* 33(1): 1–10

Erbse, H. (1972). *Beiträge zum Verständnis der Odyssee*. Berlin

Erbse, H. (1980). 'Homerische Götter in Vogelgestalt'. *Hermes* 108(3): 259–74

Falkner, T. M. (1989). 'The wrath of Alcmene: Gender, authority and old age in Euripides', in *Old Age in Greek and Latin Literature*, ed. by T. M. Falkner. Albany, NY, 114–31

Felson-Rubin, N. (1994). *Regarding Penelope: From Character to Poetics*. Princeton, NJ

Fenik, B. (1974). *Studies in the 'Odyssey'*. Wiesbaden

Ferrari, G. (1986). 'Eye-Cup'. *Revue archéologique* n.s. 1: 5–20

Ferraris, M. (2014). *Manifest des neuen Realismus*, trans. By M. Osterloh. Frankfurt a. M.

Finkelberg, M. (1990). 'Homer's view of the epic narrative: Some formulaic evidence'. *Classical Philology* 82(2): 135–38

Fleming, I. (2006 [1953]). *Casino Royale*. London

Fludernik, M. (1996). *Towards a 'Natural' Narratology*. London

Focke, F. (1943). *Die Odyssee*. Stuttgart

Foley, J. M. (1991). *Immanent Art: From Structure to Meaning in Traditional Oral Epic*. Bloomington, IN

Fontane, T. (2013 [1888]). *On Tangled Paths*, trans. P. J. Bowman. London

Ford, A. (1992). *Homer: The Poetry of the Past*. Ithaca, NY

Fowler, D. (1989). 'First thoughts on closure: Problems and prospects'. *Materiali e discussioni per l'analisi dei testi classici* 22: 75–122

Fowler, D. (1997). 'Second thoughts on closure', in *Classical Closure: Reading the End in Greek and Latin Literature*, ed. by D. H. Roberts, F. M. Dunn and D. P. Fowler. Princeton, NJ, 3–22

Fränkel, H. (1993). *Dichtung und Philosophie des frühen Griechentums: Eine Geschichte der griechischen Epik, Lyrik und Prosa bis zur Mitte des fünften Jahrhunderts*, 4th edn. Munich

Fried, M. (1980). *Absorption and Theatricality: Painting and Beholder in the Age of Diderot*. Chicago

Friedrich, R. (1987a). 'Heroic man and *polymetis*: Odysseus in the Cyclopeia'. *Greek, Roman, and Byzantine Studies* 28(2): 121–33

Friedrich, R. (1987b). 'Thrinakia and Zeus' ways to men in the *Odyssey*'. *Greek, Roman, and Byzantine Studies* 28: 375–400

Friedrich, R. (1991). 'The hybris of Odysseus'. *Journal of Hellenic Studies* 111: 16–28

Fritz, K. von (1967). *Die griechische Geschichtsschreibung*. Berlin

Garvie, A. F. (1994). *Homer, 'Odyssey': Books VI–VIII*. Cambridge

Gehrke, H.-J. (1987). 'Die Griechen und die Rache: Ein Versuch in historischer Psychologie'. *Saeculum* 38: 121–49

Germain, G. (1954). *Genèse de l'Odyssée: Le fantastique et le sacré*. Paris

Gierth, L. (1971). *Griechische Gründungsgeschichten als Zeugnisse historischen Denkens vor dem Einsetzen der Geschichtsschreibung*. Clausthal-Zellerfeld

Gill, C. (1990). 'The character-personality distinction', in *Characterization and Individuality in Greek Literature*, ed. by C. Pelling. Oxford, 1–31

Gill, C. (1996). *Personality in Greek Epic, Tragedy, and Philosophy: The Self in Dialogue*. Oxford

Gill, C. (2006). *The Structured Self in Hellenistic and Roman Thought*. Oxford

Giuliani, L. (2003). *Bild und Mythos: Geschichte der Bilderzählung in der griechischen Kunst*. Munich

Glenn, J. (1971). 'The Polyphemus folktale and Homer's *kyklôpeia*'. *Transactions and Proceedings of the American Philological Association* 102: 133–81

Goldhill, S. (1988). 'Reading differences: The *Odyssey* and juxtaposition'. *Ramus* 17: 1–31

Goldhill, S. (1991). *The Poet's Voice: Essays on Poetics and Greek Literature*. Cambridge

Graham, A. J. (1984). 'Religion, women and Greek colonization', in *Religione e città nel mondo antico: Atti del convegno internazionale. Bressanone (Brixen) 1981, 24–27 ottobre*. Rome, 293–314

Graziosi, B. (2002). *Inventing Homer: The Early Reception of Epic*. Cambridge

Grethlein, C. (2016). *Praktische Theologie*. Berlin

Grethlein, J. (2003). 'Die poetologische Bedeutung des aristotelischen Mitleidbegriffs: Überlegungen zu Nähe und Distanz in der griechischen Tragödie'. *Poetica* 35: 41–67

Grethlein, J. (2004). 'Aeschylus' *Eumenides* and Legal Anthropology', in *Nomos: Direito e sociedade na Antiguidade Clássica*, ed. by D. Leao. Madrid, 113–25

Grethlein, J. (2005). 'Die anthropologische Dimension des Essensstreites im 19. Buch der *Ilias*: Odysseus Erntemetapher (19.221–224) und die Transgressivität Achills'. *Hermes* 133: 257–279

Grethlein, J. (2006). *Das Geschichtsbild der 'Ilias': Eine Untersuchung aus phänomenologischer und narratologischer Perspektive*. Göttingen

Grethlein, J. (2007). 'The poetics of the bath in the *Iliad*'. *Harvard Studies in Classical Philology* 103: 25–49

Grethlein, J. (2008). 'Memory and material objects in the *Iliad* and the *Odyssey*'. *Journal of Hellenic Studies* 128: 27–51

Grethlein, J. (2010a). 'From imperishable glory to history: The *Iliad* and the Trojan War', in *Epic and History*, ed. by K. Raaflaub and D. Konstan. London, 122–44

Grethlein, J. (2010b). *The Greeks and Their Past: Poetry, Oratory and History in the Fifth-Century BCE*. Cambridge

Grethlein, J. (2010c). 'The narrative reconfiguration of time beyond Ricoeur'. *Poetics Today* 31(2): 313–29

Grethlein, J. (2012). 'Die Griechen–Barbaren Dichotomie im Horizont der *conditio humana*'. *Heidelberger Jahrbuch* 54: 135–47

Grethlein, J. (2015a). 'Social minds and narrative time: Collective experience in Thucydides and Heliodorus'. *Narrative* 23(2): 123–39

Grethlein, J. (2015b). 'Is narrative "the description of fictional mental functioning"? Heliodorus against Palmer, Zunshine & Co'. *Style* 49(3): 257–84

Grethlein, J. (2015c). 'Vision and reflexivity in the *Odyssey* and early vase-painting'. *Word & Image* 31(3): 197–212

Grethlein, J. (2015d). 'Aesthetic experiences, ancient and modern'. *New Literary History* 46(2): 309–33

Grethlein, J. (2016). 'Sight and reflexivity: Theorising vision in Greek vase-painting', in *Sight and the Ancient Senses*, ed. by M. Squire (The Senses in Antiquity, 4). Durham, NC, 85–106

Grethlein, J. (2017). *Aesthetic Experiences and Classical Antiquity*. Cambridge

Grethlein, J. (2018). 'Homeric motivation and modern narratology: The case of Penelope'. *The Cambridge Classical Journal* 64: 70–90

Grethlein, J. and L. Huitink (2017). 'Homer's vividness: An enactive approach'. *Journal of Hellenic Studies* 137: 67–91

Griffin, J. (1980). *Homer on Life and Death*. Oxford

Grimm, W. (1887 [1858]). 'Die Sage von Polyphem', in *Kleinere Schriften*, vol. 4, ed. by G. Hinrichs. Gütersloh, 428–62

Gumbrecht, H. U. (2010). *Diesseits der Hermeneutik: Über die Produktion von Präsenz*. Frankfurt a. M.

Hackmann, O. (1904). *Die Polyphemsage in der Volksüberlieferung: Akademische Abhandlung*. Helsinki

Haft, A. J. (1984). 'Odysseus, Idomeneus and Meriones: The Cretan lies of *Odyssey* 13–19'. *The Classical Journal* 79(4): 289–306

Hainsworth, J. B. (1993). *The Iliad: A Commentary, III. Books 9–12*. Cambridge

Hall, E. (2008). *The Return of Ulysses: A Cultural History of Homer's 'Odyssey'*. Baltimore

Hall, J. M. (1997). *Ethnic Identity in Greek Antiquity*. Cambridge

Hall, J. M. (2002). *Hellenicity: Between Ethnicity and Culture*. Chicago

Halliwell, S. (2011). *Between Ecstasy and Truth: Interpretations of Greek Poetics from Homer to Longinus*. Oxford

Halverson, J. (1985). 'Social order in the *Odyssey*'. *Hermes* 113(2): 129–45

Hansen, W. F. (1977). 'Odysseus' last journey'. *Quaderni urbinati di cultura classica* 24: 27–48

Harsh, P. W. (1950). 'Penelope and Odysseus in *Odyssey* XIX'. *American Journal of Philology* 71: 1–21

Harmon, A. M. (trans.) (1913). 'A True Story (*Verae Historiae*)', in *The Works of Lucian*, vol. 1. London, 247–357

Hartog, F. (1996). *Mémoire d'Ulysse: Récits sur la frontière en Grèce ancienne*. Paris

Haug, A. (2015). 'Das Auge und der Blick: Zum Auftreten von Zuschauern in der griechischen Bilderwelt', in *The Public in the Picture: Involving the Beholder in Antique, Islamic, Byzantine and Western Medieval and Renaissance Art*, ed. by B. Fricke and U. Krass. Zürich, 23–56

Herrnstein Smith, B. (1968). *Poetic Closure: A Study of How Poems End*. Chicago

Heubeck, A. (1950). 'Die homerische Göttersprache'. *Würzburger Jahrbücher für die Altertumswissenschaft* 4: 197–218

Heubeck, A. (1954). *Der Odyssee-Dichter und die Ilias*. Erlangen

Heubeck, A. (1981). 'Zwei homerische πεῖραι. ω 205 ff. und â 53 ff.' *Živa Antika* 31: 73–83

Hofheinz, M., M. Mathwig and M. Zeindler (eds) (2009). *Ethik und Erzählung: Theologische und philosophische Beiträge zur narrativen Ethik*. Zurich

Hofmannsthal, H. von (1954) 'Einleitung' (Introduction), in E. Littmann (trans.), *Erzählungen aus den Tausendundein Nächten*. Wiesbaden

Holoka, J. P. (1983). '"Looking darkly" (ΥΠΟΔΡΑ ΙΔΩΝ): Reflections on status and decorum in Homer'. *Transactions of the American Philological Association* 113: 1–16

Hölscher, T. (1998). *Aus der Frühzeit der Griechen: Räume—Körper—Mythen*. Leipzig

Hölscher, T. (1999). 'Immagini mitologiche e valori sociali nella Grecia arcaica', in *Im Spiegel des Mythos: Bilderwelt und Lebenswelt*, ed. by F. De Angelis and S. Muth. Wiesbaden, 11–30.

Hölscher, U. (1965). 'Selbstgespräch über den Humanismus', in *Die Chance des Unbehagens: Drei Essais zur Situation der klassischen Studien*. Göttingen, 53–86

Hölscher, U. (1967a) 'Die Atridensage in der *Odyssee*', in *Festschrift für Richard Alewyn*, ed. by H. Singer and B. von Wiese. Cologne, 1–16

Hölscher, U. (1967b) 'Penelope vor den Freiern', in *Lebende Antike: Symposion für Rudolf Sühnel*, ed. by H. Meller, R. Sühnel and H.-J. Zimmermann. Berlin, 27–33

Hölscher, U. (1988). *Die Odyssee: Epos zwischen Märchen und Roman*. Munich

Hommel, H. (1974). 'Aischylos' Orestie: Mythischer Stoff, geistige Voraussetzungen, historischer Rahmen'. *Antike und Abendland* 20(1): 14–24

Hommel, H. (1976). 'Aigisthos und die Freier: Zum poetischen Plan und zum geschichtlichen Ort der *Odyssee*', in *Symbola: Kleine Schriften zur Literatur- und Kulturgeschichte der Antike*, ed. by H. Hommel. Hildesheim, 1–17

Hopman, M. (2012a). 'Narrative and rhetoric in Odysseus' tales to the Phaeacians'. *American Journal of Philology* 133: 1–30

Hopman, M. (2012b). *Scylla. Myth, Metaphor, Paradox*. Cambridge

Horkheimer, M. and T. W. Adorno (1969 [1947]). *Dialectic of Enlightenment: Philosophical Fragments*, ed. by G. Schmid Noerr, trans. by E. Jephcott. Stanford, CA

Hulme, P. (1986). *Colonial Encounters: Europe and the Native Caribbean, 1492–1797*. London

Hurwit, J. M. (1977). 'Image and frame in Greek art'. *American Journal of Archaeology* 81(1): 1–30

Immerwahr, H. R. (1966). *Form and Thought in Herodotus*. Cleveland, OH

Jacoby, F. (1913). 'Herodotos', in *Pauly-Wissowa Real-Encyclopädie*, vol. 8, supplement 2: 205–520

Jagendorf, Z. (1993). 'Primo Levi goes for soup and remembers Dante'. *Raritan* 12(4): 31–51

Joisten, K. (2007). *Narrative Ethik: Das Gute und das Böse erzählen*. Berlin

Jonas, H. (1994). '*Homo pictor*: Von der Freiheit des Bildens', in *Was ist ein Bild?*, ed. by G. Boehm. Munich, 105–24

Jörgensen, O. (1904). 'Das Auftreten der Götter in den Büchern ι-μ der *Odyssee*'. *Hermes* 39: 357–82

Kannicht, R. (1982). 'Poetry and art: Homer and the monuments afresh'. *Classical Antiquity* 13: 70–86

Katz, M. A. (1991). *Penelope's Renown: Meaning and Indeterminacy in the Odyssey.* Princeton, NJ

Kermode, F. (1967). *The Sense of an Ending: Studies in the Theory of Fiction.* New York

Kim, L. (2010). *Homer between History and Fiction in Imperial Greek Literature.* Cambridge

Kingsley, P. (2016). *The New Odyssey: The Story of the European Refugee Crisis.* London

Kirchhoff, A. (1879). *Die homerische Odyssee,* 2nd edn. Berlin

Kirk, G. S. (1962). *The Songs of Homer.* Cambridge

Klingner, F. (1964). *Studien zur griechischen und römischen Literatur.* Zurich

Köhnken, A. (1976). 'Die Narbe des Odysseus: Ein Beitrag zur homerisch-epischen Erzähltechnik'. *Antike und Abendland* 22: 101–14

Koschorke, A. (2012). *Wahrheit und Erfindung: Grundzüge einer allgemeinen Erzähltheorie.* Frankfurt a. M.

Krischer, T. (1988). 'Odysseus und Telemach'. *Hermes* 116: 1–12

Kullman, W. (1985). 'Gods and Men in the *Iliad* and the *Odyssey*'. *Harvard Studies in Classical Philology* 89: 1–23

Kullmann, W. (1992). *Homerische Motive: Beiträge zur Entstehung, Eigenart und Wirkung von Ilias und Odyssee.* Stuttgart

Kunisch, N. (1990). 'Die Augen der Augenschalen'. *Antike Kunst* 33: 20–27

Laird, A. (2008). 'Approaching style and rhetoric', in *The Cambridge Companion to the Greek and Roman Novel,* ed. by T. Whitmarsh. Cambridge, 201–17

Lamberton, R. (1986). *Homer, the Theologian: Neoplatonist Allegorical Reading and the Growth of the Epic Tradition.* Berkeley, CA

Lateiner, D. (1992). 'Heroic proxemics: Social space and distance in the *Odyssey*'. *Transactions of the American Philological Association* 122: 133–63

Latour, B. (2004). 'Why has critique run out of steam? From matters of fact to matters of concern'. *Critical Inquiry* 30: 225–48

Lattimore, R. (trans.) (1961 [1951]). *The Iliad of Homer.* Chicago

Lattimore, R. (trans.) (1975). *The Odyssey of Homer.* New York

Ledbetter, G. M. (2003). *Poetics before Plato: Interpretation and Authority in Early Greek Theories of Poetry.* Princeton, NJ

Leumann, M. (1950). *Homerische Wörter.* Basel

Levi, P. (1987 [1947/1963]). *If This Is a Man/The Truce,* trans. by S. Woolf. London

Levi, P. (2001) (with G. Grassano). 'A conversation with Primo Levi (1979)', in *The Voice of Memory: Primo Levi, Interviews 1961–1987,* ed. by M. Belpoliti and R. Gordon, trans. by R. Gordon. New York, 121–35

Levi, P. (2001 [1981]). *The Search for Roots: A Personal Anthology,* trans. by P. Forbes. London

Levi, P. (2013 [1986]). *The Drowned and the Saved,* trans. by R. Rosenthal. London

Levy, H. L. (1963). 'The Odyssean Suitors and the Host–Guest Relationship'. *Transactions and Proceedings of the American Philological Association* 94: 145–53

Lloyd, M. (1987). 'Homer on Poetry: Two passages in the *Odyssey*'. *Eranos* 85: 85–90

Lloyd-Jones, H. (1971). *The Justice of Zeus.* Berkeley, CA

Loney, A. S. (2019). *The Ethics of Revenge and the Meaning of the Odyssey.* Oxford

Lonsdale, S. H. (1990). *Creatures of Speech: Lion, Herding, and Hunting Similes in the 'Iliad'.* Stuttgart.

Lorimer, H. L. (1950). *Homer and the Monuments.* London

Lowe, E. J. (2002). *A Survey of Metaphysics*. Oxford

Lukács, G. (1971 [1916]). *The Theory of the Novel*, trans. by Anna Bostock. Cambridge, MA

Lynn-George, M. (1988). *Epos: Word, Narrative and the 'Iliad'*. London

MacIntyre, A. (1981). *After Virtue: A Study in Moral Theory*. London

Mack, R. (2002). 'Facing down Medusa (an aetiology of the gaze)'. *Art History* 25(5): 571–604

Mackie, H. (1997). 'Song and storytelling: An Odyssean perspective'. *Transactions of the American Philological Association* 127: 77–95

Macleod, C. W. (1983). 'Homer on poetry and the poetry of Homer', in Macleod, *Collected Essays*. Oxford, 1–15

Malkin, I. (1998). *The Returns of Odysseus: Colonization and Ethnicity*. Berkeley, CA

Malkin, I. (2004). 'Postcolonial concepts and ancient Greek colonization'. *Modern Language Quarterly* 65(3): 341–64

Malkin, I. (2009). 'Foundations', in *A Companion to Archaic Greece*, ed. by K. A. Raaflaub and H. van Wees. Malden, MA, 373–94

Marg, W. (1957). *Homer über die Dichtung*. Münster

Maronitis, D. N. (1981). 'Die erste Trugrede des Odysseus in der *Odyssee*: Vorbild und ariationen', in *Gnomosyne: Menschliches Denken und Handeln in der frühgriechischen Literatur; Festschrift für Walter Marg zum 70. Geburtstag*, ed. by G. Kurz. Munich, 117–34

Martens, D. (1992). *Une esthétique de la transgression: Le vase grec de la fin de l'époque géométrique au début de l'époque classique*. Brussels

Meiggs, R. and D. Lewis (1969). *A Selection of Greek Historical Inscriptions to the End of the Fifth Century BC*. Oxford

Meier, C. (1980). *Die Entstehung des Politischen bei den Griechen*. Frankfurt a. M.

Merkelbach, R. (1969). *Untersuchungen zur Odyssee: Mit einem Anhang; Die pisistratische Redaktion der homerischen Gedichte*. Munich

Merrill, R. (trans.) (2011). 'The Homeric Hymn to Apollo', in *A Californian Hymn to Homer*, ed. by T. Pepper. Washington, DC, ch. 8. Available at https://chs.harvard.edu/chapter/8-the-homeric-hymn-to-apollo-translated-by-rodney-merrill/ (accessed 5 December 2023)

Mertens, D. (2006). *Städte und Bauten der Westgriechen von der Kolonisationszeit bis zur Krise um 400 vor Christus*. Munich

Metz, J. B. (1977). *Glaube in Geschichte und Theologie: Kurze Darstellung der Zusammenhänge theologischer Grundgedanken*. Munich

Mieth, D. (1976). *Dichtung, Glaube und Moral: Studien zur Begründung einer narrativen Ethik; mit einer Interpretation zum Tristanroman Gottfrieds von Strassburg*. Mainz

Millar, C.M.H. and J.W.S. Carmichael (1954). 'The growth of Telemachus'. *Greece & Rome* n.s. 1(2): 58–64

Miller, A. M. (trans.) (2019). *Pindar: The Odes*. Oakland, CA

Miller, T. (1997). *Die griechische Kolonisation im Spiegel literarischer Zeugnisse*. Tübingen

Moggi, M. (1983). 'L'elemento indigeno nella tradizione letteraria sulle ktiseis', in *Modes de contacts et processus de transformation dans les sociétés anciennes: Actes du colloque de Cortone (24–30 mai 1981)*. Pisa, 979–1004

Mondi, R. (1983). 'The Homeric Cyclopes: Folktale, tradition, and theme'. *Transactions of the American Philological Association* 113: 17–38

Montiglio, S. (2005). *Wandering in Ancient Greek Culture*. Chicago

Morales, H. (2004). *Vision and Narrative in Achilles Tatius' Leucippe and Clitophon*. Cambridge

Moreau, A. (1992). 'Odyssée, XXI, 101–139: L'examen de passage de Télémaque', in *L'initiation: Actes du colloque international de Montpellier, 11–14 avril 1991*, vol. 1, ed. by A. Moreau. Montpellier, 93–104.

Moser von Filseck, K. (1996). *Blickende Bilder: Versuch zu einer hermeneutischen Archäologie*. n.p.

Most, G. W. (1985). *The Measures of Praise: Structure and Function in Pindar's Second Pythian and Seventh Nemean Odes*. Göttingen

Most, G. W. (1989). 'The structure and function of Odysseus' Apologoi'. *Transactions of the American Philological Association* 119: 15–30

Munding, H. (1961). 'Die Bewertung der Rechtsidee in der Ilias'. *Philologus* 105(1/2): 161–77

Murgatroyd, P. (2015). 'The wrath of Poseidon'. *Classical Quarterly* 65(2): 444–48

Murnaghan, S. (1987). *Disguise and Recognition in the Odyssey*. Princeton, NJ

Mylonas, G. E. (1957). *Ho prōtoattikos amphoreus tēs Eleusinos*. Athens

Nagler, M. N. (1990). 'Ethical anxiety and artistic inconsistency: The case of oral epic', in *Cabinet of the Muses: Essays on Classical and Comparative Literature in Honor of Thomas G. Rosenmeyer*, ed. by M. Griffith. Atlanta, GA, 225–40

Nagy, G. (1976). 'Formula and meter', in *Oral literature and the Formula*, ed. by B. A. Stolz. Ann Arbor, MI, 239–60

Nagy, G. (1979) *The Best of the Achaeans: Concepts of the Hero in Archaic Greek Poetry*. Baltimore

Nagy, G. (trans., with J. Banks) (n.d.). *Hesiod: Theogony*. Available at https://chs.harvard.edu/primary-source/hesiod-theogony-sb/ (accessed 5 December 2023)

Newton, R. M. (1983). 'Poor Polyphemus: Emotional ambivalence in *Odyssey* 9 and 17'. *Classical World* 76(3): 137–42

Newton, R. M. (1987). 'Odysseus and Hephaestus in the *Odyssey*'. *The Classical Journal* 83(1): 12–20

Niles, J. D. (1978). 'Patterning in the Wanderings of Odysseus'. *Ramus* 7(1): 46–60

Öhlschläger, C., B. Schäffer and C. Roser (eds) (2009). *Narration und Ethik*. Paderborn

Olson, S. D. (1989a). '*Odyssey* 8: Guile, force and the subversive poetics of desire'. *Arethusa* 22(2): 135–45

Olson, S. D. (1989b). 'The stories of Helen and Menelaus (*Odyssey* 4.240–89) and the return of Odysseus'. *American Journal of Philology* 110(3): 387–94.

Olson, S. D. (1995). *Blood and Iron: Stories and Storytelling in Homer's Odyssey*. Leiden

Osborne, R. G. (1988). 'Death revisited; death revised: The death of the artist in archaic and classical Greece'. *Art History* 11(1): 1–16

Osborne, R. G. (1998). 'Early Greek colonization? The nature of Greek settlement in the west', in *Archaic Greece: New Approaches and New Evidence*, ed. by N. Fisher and H. van Wees. London, 251–70

O'Sullivan, J. N. (1987). 'Observations on the Kyklopeia'. *Symbolae Osloenses* 62: 5–24

Page, D. L. (1955). *The Homeric Odyssey: The Mary Flexner Lectures delivered at Bryn Mawr College, Pennsylvania*. Oxford

Parry, H. (1994). 'The *apologos* of Odysseus: Lies, all lies?'. *Phoenix* 48(1): 1–20

Parry, M. (1971). *The Making of Homeric Verse: The Collected Papers of Milman Parry*. Oxford.

Pavel, T. G. (2003). *La Pensée du roman*. Paris

Pelling, C. (1997). 'East is east and west is west—or are they? National stereotypes in Herodotus'. *Histos* 1: 50–65

Penella, R. J. (trans. and ed.) (2007). *Man and the Word: The Orations of Himerius*. Oakland, CA

Peponi, A.-E. (2012). *Frontiers of Pleasure: Models of Aesthetic Response in Archaic and Classical Greek Thought*. Oxford

Peradotto, J. J. (1990). *Man in the Middle Voice: Name and Narration in the 'Odyssey'*. Princeton, NJ

Pickering, M. (1997). *History, Experience and Cultural Studies*. Basingstoke

Podlecki, A. J. (1961). 'Guest-gifts and nobodies in *Odyssey* 9'. *Phoenix* 15(3): 125–33

Podlecki, A. J. (1971). 'Some Odyssean similes'. *Greece and Rome* 18(1): 81–90

Pratt, L. H. (1983). *Lying and Poetry from Homer to Pindar: Falsehood and Deception in Archaic Greek Poetics*. Ann Arbor, MI

Prier, R. A. (1980). 'That gaze of the hound: *Odyssey* 19.228–231'. *Rheinisches Museum für Philologie* 123: 178–80

Proust, M. (2005 [1913]). *Swann's Way*, trans. by C. K. Scott Moncrieff and T. Kilmartin. London

Pucci, P. (1987). *Odysseus Polutropos: Intertextual Readings in the 'Odyssey' and the 'Iliad'*. Ithaca, NY

Purves, A. (2010). *Space and Time in Ancient Greek Narrative*. Cambridge

Radke-Uhlmann, G. (2009). 'Über eine vergessene Form der Anschaulichkeit in der griechischen Dichtung'. *Antike und Abendland* 55: 1–22

Rahner, H. (1984). *Griechische Mythen in christlicher Deutung*. Basel

Rank, L. P. (1951). *Etymologiseering en verwante verschijnselen bij Homerus* (doctoral dissertation, University of Utrecht). Assen

Reardon, B. P. (ed.) (1989). *Collected Ancient Greek Novels*. Berkeley, CA

Redfield, J. M. (1983). 'The economic man', in *Approaches to Homer*, ed. by C. A. Rubino and C. W. Shelmerdine. Austin, TX, 218–47

Reece, S. (1993). *The Stranger's Welcome: Oral Theory and the Aesthetics of the Homeric Hospitality Scene*. Ann Arbor, MI

Regenbogen, O. (1930). 'Herodot und sein Werk'. *Antike* 6: 202–48

Reinhardt, K. (1948). *Von Werken und Formen: Vorträge und Aufsätze*. Godesberg

Reinhardt, K. (1960). *Tradition und Geist: Gesammelte Essays zur Dichtung*, ed. by C. Bekker. Göttingen

Richardson, N. J. (1983). 'Recognition scenes in the *Odyssey* and ancient literary criticism'. *Papers of the Liverpool Latin Seminar* 4: 219–36

Richardson, S. (1996) 'Truth in the tales of the *Odyssey*'. *Mnemosyne* 49(4): 393–402

Ricœur, P. (1984–88 [1983–85]). *Time and Narrative*, 3 vols, trans. by K. McLaughlin and D. Pellauer (vols 1–2); K. Blamey and D. Pellauer (vol. 3). Chicago

Rinon, Y. (2006). '*Mise en abyme* and tragic signification in the *Odyssey*: The three songs of Demodocus'. *Mnemosyne* 59(2): 208–25

Rinon, Y. (2008). *Homer and the Dual Model of the Tragic*. Ann Arbor, MI

Ritschl, D. (1984). *Zur Logik der Theologie: Kurze Darstellung der Zusammenhänge theologischer Grundgedanken*. Munich

Roberts, D. H., F. M. Dunn and D. P. Fowler (eds) (1997). *Classical Closure: Reading the End in Greek and Latin Literature*. Princeton, NJ

Roberts, W. R. (ed. and trans.) (2010 [1902]). *Demetrius on Style*. Cambridge

Rohdich, H. (1990). 'Zwei Exkurse in die Vergangenheit'. *Antike und Abendland* 36(1): 35–46

Rose, G. P. (1967). 'The quest of Telemachus'. *Transactions and Proceedings of the American Philological Association* 98: 391–98

Rose, G. P. (1979). 'Odysseus' barking heart'. *Transactions and Proceedings of the American Philological Association* 109: 215–30

Rosen, R. M. (1990). 'Poetry and sailing in Hesiod's *Works and Days*'. *Classical Antiquity* 9(1): 99–113

Rosenbloom, D. (1993). 'Shouting "fire" in a crowded theatre: Phrynichos' *Capture of Miletos* and the politics of fear in early Attic tragedy'. *Philologus* 137: 159–96

Rösler, W. (1980). 'Die Entdeckung der Fiktionalität in der Antike'. *Poetica* 12(3/4): 283–319

Rougé, J. (1970). 'La colonisation grecque et les femmes'. *Cahiers d'histoire* 15: 307–17

Russo, J. (1982). 'Interview and Aftermath: Dream, Fantasy, and Intuition in *Odyssey* 19 and 20'. *American Journal of Philology* 103(1): 4–18

Russo, J., M. Fernandez-Galiano and A. Heubeck (1992). *A Commentary on Homer's Odyssey*, vol. 3: *Books XVII–XXIV*. Oxford

Russo, J. A. (1997) 'The formula', in *A New Companion to Homer* (*Mnemosyne* supplement 163), ed. by I. Morris. Leiden, 238–60

Rüter, K. (1969). *Odysseeinterpretationen: Untersuchungen zum ersten Buch und zur Phaiakis*. Göttingen

Rutherford, R. B. (1985) 'At home and abroad: Aspects of the structure of the *Odyssey*'. *Proceedings of the Cambridge Philological Society* 31: 133–50

Rutherford, R. B. (1986). 'The philosophy of the *Odyssey*'. *Journal of Hellenic Studies* 106: 145–62

Rutherford, R. B. (1992). *Homer, 'Odyssey' Books XIX and XX*. Cambridge

Said, E. W. (1978). *Orientalism*. London

Saïd, S. (1979). 'Les crimes des prétendants, la maison d'Ulysse et les festins de l'Odyssée', in *Études de littérature ancienne*, ed. by S. Saïd, F. Desbordes, J. Bouffartigue and A. Moreau. Paris, 9–49

Saïd, S. (2011). *Homer and the Odyssey*. Oxford

Sandy, G. N. (1982). *Heliodorus*. Boston, MA

Sbordone, F. (1976). *Ricerche sui papiri ercolanesi*, vol. 2: Φιλοδήμου Περὶ ποιημάτων *Tractatus tres*. Naples

Scaliger, J. C. (1964 [1561]). *Poetices libri septem*, ed. by A. Buck. Stuttgart

Schadewaldt, W. (1960). *Hellas und Hesperien: Gesammelte Schriften zur Antike und zur neueren Literatur*, ed. by E. Zinn. Zurich

Schapp, W. (1953). *In Geschichten verstrickt: Zum Sein von Mensch und Ding*. Hamburg

Schefold, K. (1993). *Götter- und Heldensagen der Griechen in der früh- und hocharchaischen Kunst*. Munich

Schein, S. L. (1970). 'Odysseus and Polyphemus in the *Odyssey*'. *Greek, Roman, and Byzantine Studies* 11(2): 73–83

Schein, S. L. (1999. 'Homeric Intertextuality: Two Examples', in *Euphrosyne: Studies in Ancient Epic and Its Legacy in Honor of Demetrios N. Maronitis*, ed. by J. N. Kazazis and A. Rengakos. Stuttgart, 349–56

Schmidt, J.-U. (1998). 'Ares und Aphrodite: Der göttliche Ehebruch und die theologischen Intentionen des Odysseedichters'. *Philologus* 142(2): 195–219

Schmidt, E. A. (2010). 'Die Gerechtigkeit Gottes als Axiom frühgriechischer Weltdeutung: Zum Recht in der frühgriechischen Dichtung von Homer bis Solon', in *Recht und Literatur: Interdisziplinäre Bezüge*, ed by B. Greiner, B. Thums and W. Graf Vitzthum. Heidelberg, 29–74

Schmidt, J.-U. (2003). 'Die Blendung des Kyklopen und der Zorn des Poseidon: Zum Problem der Rechtfertigung der Irrfahrten des Odysseus und ihrer Bedeutung für das Anliegen des Odysseedichters'. *Wiener Studien* 116: 5–42

Schmiel, R. (1972). 'Telemachus in Sparta'. *Transactions and Proceedings of the American Philological Association* 103: 463–72

Schmitt, A. (1990). *Selbständigkeit und Abhängigkeit menschlichen Handelns bei Homer: Hermeneutische Untersuchungen zur Psychologie Homers*. Stuttgart

Schnapp-Gourbeillon, A. (1981). *Lions, héros, masques: Les représentations animales chez Homère*. Paris

Scodel, R. (1998). 'Bardic performance and oral tradition in Homer'. *American Journal of Philology* 119(2): 171–94

Scully, S. (1987). 'Doubling in the tale of Odysseus'. *Classical World* 80(6): 401–17

Seaford, R. (1994). *Reciprocity and Ritual: Homer and Tragedy in the Developing City-State*. Oxford

Segal, C. (1994). *Singers, Heroes, and Gods in the 'Odyssey'*. Ithaca, NY

Sloterdijk, P. (2018). *What Happened in the Twentieth Century?*, trans. by C. Turner. Cambridge

Smith, A. D. (1999). *Myths and Memories of the Nation*. Oxford

Snell, B. (1953 [1946]). *Discovery of the Mind: The Greek Origins of European Thought*, trans. by T. G. Rosenmeyer. Oxford

Snodgrass, A. M. (1998). *Homer and the Artists: Text and Picture in Early Greek Art*. Cambridge

Squire, M. (2009). *Image and Text in Graeco-Roman Antiquity*. Cambridge

Squire, M. (2013). 'Apparitions apparent, ekphrasis and the parameters of vision in the elder Philostratus' *Imagines*'. *Helios* 40(1–2): 97–140

Stanford, W. B. (1963). 'Marginalia'. *Hermathena* 97(1): 107–9

Stanford, W. B. (1965). 'The ending of the *Odyssey*: An Ethical Approach'. *Hermathena* 100: 5–20

Starobinski, J. (1975). 'The inside and the outside'. *The Hudson Review* 28(3): 333–51

Steiner, D. T. (2010). *Homer: Odyssey, Books XVII and XVIII*. Cambridge

Steinhart, M. (1995). *Das Motiv des Auges in der griechischen Bildkunst*. Mainz

Stewart, A. (1993). *Faces of Power: Alexander's Image and Hellenistic Politics*. Berkeley, CA

Stier, H. E. (1970). *Die geschichtliche Bedeutung des Hellenennamens*. Cologne

Stoevesandt, M. (2004). *Feinde—Gegner—Opfer: Zur Darstellung der Troianer in den Kampf-szenen der Ilias*. Basel

Stössel, H.-A. (1975). *Der letzte Gesang der Odyssee: Eine unitarische Gesamtinterpretation* (inaugural dissertation, FAU Erlangen-Nürnberg). Erlangen

Strauss Clay, J. (1983). *The Wrath of Athene: Gods and Men in the Odyssey*. Princeton, NJ

Suerbaum, W. (1968). 'Die Ich-Erzählungen des Odysseus: Überlegungen zur epischen Technik der *Odyssee*'. *Poetica* 2: 150–77

Taplin, O. (1990). 'The earliest quotation of the *Iliad*?', in *'Owls to Athens': Essays on Classical Subjects Presented to Sir Kenneth Dover*, ed. by E. M. Craik. Oxford, 109–12

Tchekhov, A. (1974 [1927]) *Literary and Theatrical Reminiscences*, ed. by S. S. Koteliansky. New York

Thornton, A. (1970). *People and Themes in Homer's 'Odyssey'*. London

Todorov, T. (1977). *Théories du symbole*. Paris

Torelli, M. (1986). 'La religione', in *Rasenna: Storia e civiltà degli Etruschi*, ed. by M. Pallottino. Milan, 159–237

Torelli, M. (1996). 'The encounter with the Etruscans', in *The Western Greeks: Classical Civilization in the Western Mediterranean*, ed. by G. Pugliese Carratelli. London, 567–76

Touchefeu-Meynier, O. (1968). *Thèmes odysséens dans l'art antique*. Paris

Touchefeu-Meynier, O. (1992). 'Odysseus', in *Lexicon iconographicum mythologiae classicae*, 6.1, ed. by H. C. Ackermann. Zurich, 943–70

Tsagalis, C. (2007). 'The metaphor of sailing and the athlon of song: Reconsidering the 'Nautilia' in Hesiod's *Works and Days*', in *Contests and Rewards in the Homeric Epics: Proceedings of the 10th International Symposium on the 'Odyssey' (15–19 September 2004)*, ed. by M. Païzi-Apostolopoulou, A. Rengakos and C. Tsagalis. Ithaca, 269–95

Tsetskhladze, G. R. and F. De Angelis (eds) (1994). *The Archaeology of Greek Colonisation*. Oxford

Tuplin, C. (2003). 'Heroes in Xenophon's *Anabasis*', in *Modelli eroici dall'antichità alla cultura europea*, ed. by A. Barzanò, C. Bearzot and F. L. Gattinoni. Rome, 115–56

Ulf, C. (ed.) (2003). *Der neue Streit um Troja: Eine Bilanz*. Munich

Van Compernolle, R. (1983). 'Femmes indigenes et colonisateurs', in *Modes de contacts et processus de transformation dans les sociétés anciennes: Actes du colloque de Cortone (24–30 mai 1981)*. Pisa, 1033–49

Vernant, J.-P. (1979). 'À la table des hommes: Mythe de fondation du sacrifice chez Hésiode', in *La cuisine du sacrifice en pays grec*, ed. by M. Detienne and J.-P. Vernant. Paris, 37–132

Vidal-Naquet, P. (1986). *The Black Hunter: Forms of Thought and Forms of Society in the Greek World*. trans. by A. Szegedy-Maszak. Baltimore

Walcot, P. (1977). 'Odysseus and the art of lying'. *Ancient Society* 8: 1–19

Waldenfels, B. (2002). *Bruchlinien der Erfahrung: Phänomenologie, Psychoanalyse, Phänomeno-technik*. Frankfurt a. M.

Waldenfels, B. (2004). *Phänomenologie der Aufmerksamkeit*. Frankfurt a. M.

Walsh, G. B. (1984). *The Varieties of Enchantment: Early Greek Views of the Nature and Function of Poetry*. Chapel Hill, NC

Wender, D. (1978). *The Last Scenes of the Odyssey*. Leiden

West, M. L. (ed.) (1966). *Hesiod: 'Theogony'*. Oxford

West, M. L. (2011). *The Making of the 'Iliad': Disquisition and Analytical Commentary*. Oxford

West, M. L. (2014). *The Making of the 'Odyssey'*. Oxford

Whitman, C. H. (1958). *Homer and the Heroic Tradition*. Cambridge, MA

Wilamowitz-Moellendorff, U. von (1906). *Über die Ionische Wanderung*. Berlin

Wilamowitz-Moellendorff, U. von (1927). *Die Heimkehr des Odysseus: Neue homerische Untersuchungen*. Berlin

Winkler, J. J. (1990). *The Constraints of Desire: The Anthropology of Sex and Gender in Ancient Greece*. New York

Wöhrle, G. (1999). *Telemachs Reise: Väter und Söhne in Ilias und Odyssee oder ein Beitrag zur Erforschung der Männlichkeitsideologie in der homerischen Welt*. Göttingen

Wollheim, R. (1980). 'Seeing-as, seeing-in, and pictorial representation', in Wollheim, *Art and Its Objects*, 2nd edn. Cambridge, 205–26

Wollheim, R. (1987). *Painting as an Art*. London

Xian, R. (2017a). 'Der Chronotopos der Ziegeninsel (Hom. *Od.* 9.116–41)'. *Mnemosyne* 70(6): 899–919

Xian, R. (2017b) 'Die Ithakalandschaft in *Od.* 13'. *Mnemosyne* 70(4): 537–61

Zeitlin, F. (1996). 'Figuring fidelity in Homer's *Odyssey*', in *Playing the Other: Gender and Society in Classical Greek Literature*, ed. by F. Zeitlin. Chicago, 19–52

Zipfel, F. (2001). *Fiktion, Fiktivität, Fiktionalität: Analysen zur Fiktion in der Literatur und zum Fiktionsbegriff in der Literaturwissenschaft*. Berlin

INDEX

Achilles: Alexander the Great modelled himself on, 129; allegorical interpretation of, 57–58; anticipation of death in *Iliad*, 231–32; on arbitrariness of gods, 222; armouring scene in *Iliad* and, 19; bath scenes in *Iliad* and, 20–21; compared to lion, 215; emotional impact of shared lament and, 53; epithet 'swift-footed' for, 19–20; fate compared to those of Agamemnon and Odysseus, 241–43; *Iliad* emphasizes mortality of, 21, 231–32; met by Odysseus in underworld, 9; parallels between Odysseus and, 202, 205, 212, 215–16; in Pindar's seventh Nemean Ode, 96; represents *Iliad* in comparisons with Odysseus, 79–80, 242–43; in songs of Demodocus, 76, 78–80, 254

Achilles Tatius, 12, 71, 147–48

Adorno, Theodor, 5–6, 271

Aeaea, 9, 163, 201

Aegisthus: incurs divine retribution, 219–20, 225, 228; Orestes's revenge on, 49; parallels between Odysseus's companions and, 196, 228; parallels between suitors and, 39, 196–97, 205, 209, 216, 228; warned by gods, 219, 225

Aeneas, 22, 126

Aeolia, 89, 91, 103, 107

Aeolus: gives Odysseus bag of winds his companions open, 9, 89, 103, 155; refuses further help after Odysseus's companions open bag of winds, 89; in structure of Apologoi, 91–93, 103, 107; violates norms of Greek civilization, 93

Aeschylus, 34, 125, 245–46

Agamemnon: allegorical interpretation of, 57–58; armouring scene in *Iliad*, 19; as Bronze Age aristocrat, 121; compared to Odysseus, 39, 241–42; compares Achilles to Odysseus, 241–43; fate compared to those of Achilles and Odysseus, 241–42; later Spartan historical claim traced back to, 129; met by Odysseus in underworld, 9; on murder of suitors, 210–11; parallels between his homecoming and Odysseus's, 38–40, 155, 197, 205, 255; in songs of Demodocus, 78–79

Aigyptios, 65, 201, 204, 244

Ajax, 35, 38–39, 96, 210

Ajax the Lesser, 47, 49

Alcinous: parallel between promise of help to Odysseus and Telemachus's rebuke of Penelope, 64; possibility of association between Greek colonists and indigenous populations and, 125–26; reaction to Odysseus's Apologoi, 76, 84, 98, 190, 260; welcomes and assists Odysseus, 8, 76, 99–100

Alexander the Great, 129

Allan, William, 230

American Pie, 67

Amphimedon, 158, 166, 210–11, 240–41, 245

Amphinomus, 211–12, 221–22

anagnorisis. *See* recognition

Andromache, 20–21